A LITTLE PRIMITIVE

A LITTLE PRIMITIVE

KENNETH LYSONS

CHURCH IN THE MARKET PLACE
PUBLICATIONS
BUXTON
2001

British Library Cataloguing in Publication Data

A record for this book is available from the British Library

ISBN 1 899147 30 6

CHURCH IN THE MARKET PLACE
PUBLICATIONS
BUXTON

Typeset in Monotype Baskerville by
Strathmore Publishing Services, London N7

Printed in Great Britain by
Biddles of Guildford

Contents

List of Tables

To my friends

Dorothy Clayton MA, PhD

Bob Davies

John Newton CBE, MA, PhD, DLitt., DD

John Ridyard MA, MD, FRCP

who each helped to make this book a reality

Foreword

Dr Kenneth Lysons has combined his scholarly gifts and his personal experience to produce a most lively and readable portrait of Primitive Methodism and its people. He traces the complete life cycle of this vigorous denomination, from its beginnings in 1811 to its entry into Methodist Union in 1932.

One of the strengths of Dr Lysons' book is the skilful way in which he sets the Primitive Methodist Church into the wider social and political context, and shows its interaction with the larger British society.

The author has another string to his bow, in addition to the insights of the historian and sociologist. He can draw vividly on his own experience, in childhood and youth, of growing up within Primitive Methodism. Proverbially, 'If you want to make it real make it local.' Dr Lysons does precisely that, drawing on his rich store of memories of local people and events – at church, circuit, and district level – to put flesh on the bones of his historical account.

Given the lapse of time since 1932, there are inevitably few people still able to draw on personal experience of Primitive Methodism in the way that Dr Lysons has done. He gives a lively and memorable account of the Church which formed him, and whose story richly deserves to be told. Readers will find here a fascinating story, told with insight and humour, and I warmly recommend it.

JOHN A. NEWTON
Bristol, April 2001

Acknowledgements

The writer is indebted to many organisations and people.

Every writer is indebted to libraries and librarians and I would put on record the assistance received from Dr Dorothy Clayton, Dr Peter Nockles and Mr Gareth Lloyd of the John Rylands University Library of Manchester, Mrs Irene Marshall and the staff of the Prescot branch of Knowsley Library Services and the staffs of the British Library, the Liverpool University Library and the Picton Library, Liverpool and Dr Williams Library, London.

Among individuals to whom I owe a special debt are Gilbert Braithwaite, Colin Dews, Stephen Hatcher and Alan Rose. Dr John Newton kindly agreed to provide a short foreword, and Bob Davies and Pat Saunders piloted the book through the press. Jeanne Ashton again helped in the research and Judith Ray expertly text processed the manuscript.

I am particularly grateful to Mrs F. Spibey and Mr L. Worsley who provided the photographs of the Bridge Street and Lane Head churches for the cover. In a clockwise direction they show the first Lowton Primitive Methodist Chapel, built in 1842 at a cost of £130 and still standing; the second Lowton Primitive Methodist Chapel, built in 1880 at a cost of £900 and demolished in 1985; the first Golborne Bridge Street Chapel, built in 1853 at a cost of £254.13s.1d, which has now been converted into a house; and the second Golborne, Bridge Street Church, opened in 1895 at a cost of £1,800 and demolished in 1986.

There are two others sources to whom I owe a lifelong debt. My parents, Joseph and Beatrice Lysons encouraged me to love the things that are 'true, lovely and of good report'. The influence of home was, however, further nurtured by the chapel culture in which I grew up. When George Tomlinson, Minister of Education in the 1945 Labour Government, was asked for details of his education for entry in *Who's Who* he wrote simply 'Rishton Wesleyan School'. I have had the good fortune to be associated with several educational institutions but I am not ashamed to acknowledge the debt I owe to the informal education I received from the Lowton Road and Bridge Street Churches in the now defunct Lowton Primitive Methodist Circuit.

Introduction

This book attempts to study the life cycle of a denomination, Primitive Methodism, from both macro and micro perspectives.

The macro perspective was suggested by two writers, Moberg and John Munsey Turner. Moberg in describing a theoretical five-stage life cycle of religious bodies, stated: 'There yet remains to be either explained or described the life cycle of a particular church as an institution.'[1] The Methodist scholar, John Munsey Turner, however, has described Primitive Methodism as 'the perfect example of the development of an evangelistic sect into a full blown denomination.'[2] The first four chapters of this book are, therefore, devoted to the development of Primitive Methodism from its antecedents, its inception in 1811 as an offshoot of Wesleyan Methodism, its development from sect to denomination and, in 1932, its reintegration into a reunited Methodist Church.

The micro-study was suggested by Brian Wilson who points out that a standard technique for the study of sects is 'participant observation', in which the sociologist participates in the activities of the sect as a revealed outsider seeking by observation and association to understand its members who accept him into their midst and submit to being observed. Wilson further claims that participant observation 'opens the way for empathic understanding for acting with, feeling with and perhaps living within a sect, and that this adds a dimension of social knowledge from which the historian is precluded.'[3]

The five later chapters of the book are written not from the standpoint of an 'outsider' but an 'insider' and record something of the beliefs, ethics and moral theology, worship and Anglican Primitive Methodist relationship as the writer was taught about them or experienced them at first-hand in a typical Primitive

Methodist circuit when making the journey from childhood to adulthood between the years 1923–32.

This approach is open to two criticisms. First, as stated, Primitive Methodism ceased to exist in 1932. By 1939, however, in many circuits, including that to which this book relates, Methodist union had had little perceptible effect. Most members still considered themselves to be primarily Primitive Methodists. Nearly seventy years after its demise, the denomination still exercises an influence on the now rapidly diminishing numbers of those who, like the writer, were born into its culture.

Secondly, it may be questioned whether an insider, and especially at that time a fairly immature insider, could make observations with sufficient objectivity. Against this, the writer would claim that his subsequent academic training enables him to appraise both folklore and experiences objectively and also to relate them both to the history of the denomination and the wider Nonconformist and national environment in which Primitive Methodism existed. The second part of the book is, therefore, only incidentally autobiographical. Edmund Gosse in the preface to his book *Father and Son*, published in 1907, stated that this narrative was 'offered as a record of educational and religious conditions which having passed away will never return.'[4] Chapters 5 to 9 have a similar purpose.

The title derives from the lines by W. S. Gilbert:

> Every boy and every girl
> that's born into the world alive,
> is either a little Liberal
> or else a little Conservative.[5]

I was probably born a little Liberal. Most certainly I was born a little Primitive Methodist.

KENNETH LYSONS
St Helens, April 2001

Part One
Primitive Methodism

1

Precedents, Pioneers and Polity

In 1932 the Primitive Methodist, along with the United Methodist and Wesleyan Methodist Churches ceased to exist as separate denominations and joined together to form the Methodist Church. The aim of this and the following three chapters is to provide an outline of the life cycle of Primitive Methodism covering its origins and development from sect to denomination. The word 'outline' is used advisedly. The early history of Primitive Methodism has already been extensively covered by other writers[1] and the present chapter attempts to do no more than provide an introduction to Primitive Methodist precedents, pioneers, beginnings and early polity.

Precedents

Primitive Methodism can only be understood in the context of its Wesleyan Methodist antecedents, especially field preaching and early Wesleyan secessions and offshoots.

Field preaching

Davies rightly states that the originator of the Methodist revival was neither John nor Charles Wesley but George Whitefield (1714–70).[2] After ordination as deacon, Whitefield spent the years 1736–9 in the American State of Georgia. Early in 1739 he returned to England both to be ordained priest and obtain funds for the Orphan House he had founded in Savannah for destitute children. In Georgia, Whitefield often preached out-of-doors and, on Saturday, 17 February 1739, he preached to some 200 colliers of Kingswood Close, Bristol, who 'feared not God and regarded not man'. Subsequent out-door preaching attracted ever-increasing crowds and the initial 200 hearers rose to a vast congregation of 20,000 people. The problem was how to maintain the impetus of the revival in view of Whitefield's imminent return to America. Whitefield, therefore, asked his friend, John Wesley, to join him in Bristol and continue the revival by 'confirming those who have been awakened'. On Saturday, 31 March 1739, Wesley records:

> In the evening I reached Bristol and met Mr Whitefield there. I could scarce reconcile myself at first to this strange way of preaching in the fields of which he set me an example on Sunday; having been all my life (till very lately) so tenacious of every point relating to decency and order that I should have thought the saving of souls almost a sin if it had not been in church.

Two days later, however, Wesley put his scruples on one side and followed Whitefield's example:

> At four in the afternoon, I submitted to be more vile and proclaimed in the highways the glad tidings of salvation, speaking from a little eminence in a ground adjoining the city, to about three thousand souls. [3]

Wesley's text, Luke 4.18, was that expounded by Jesus in the synagogue of his native Nazareth:

> The Spirit of the Lord is upon me
> Because he has anointed me;
> He has sent me to preach good news to the poor;
> To proclaim release to the captives …

Thus began the field preaching by which Wesley and his followers carried the gospel through the length and breadth of Britain. On 7 October 1790, Wesley delivered his last open-air sermon at Winchelsea. Between 1732 and 1791, it is estimated that he travelled on his itinerant work over 250,000 miles at an average of 18–19 miles daily.

Wesley was actually averse to field preaching but he recognised its effectiveness in reaching the unchurched.

> The Devil does not like field preaching. Neither do I. I love a commodious room, a soft cushion, a handsome pulpit. But where is my zeal if I do not trample these underfoot in order to save one soul. [4]

John Wesley died on 2 March 1791. J. R. Green observes that: 'in the calm of old age', Wesley by his 'calm commonsense ... discouraged in his followers the enthusiastic outbursts which marked the opening of the revival. His powers were bent to the building up of a great religious society which might give to the new enthusiasm a lasting and practical form.' [5]

Wesleyan secessions and off-shoots

After Wesley's death, it was not surprising that there should be divergence of opinion regarding the direction Methodism should take. Eayrs identifies three viewpoints. The first was 'that the Conference preachers took the place of Wesley and should continue his special work.' The second deprecated 'anything that indicated independence of the Church of England.' The third 'desired to complete the work of separation begun by Wesley and made necessary by the condition and attitude of the Church of England.' [6] There were also those concerned to preserve the evangelical zeal of early Methodism. Conversely, others favoured a conventional form of worship and regarded 'enthusiasm' with suspicion. So many opinions carried the danger that without strong, central control, Methodism would fragment.

Centrally the required control was provided by the Conference which, by the Deed of Declaration of 1784, comprised the 'Legal Hundred' of preachers chosen by Wesley with power to fill vacancies in its ranks by invitation. Conference was, therefore, endowed with perpetuity as the governing body of Methodism with powers to appoint and station ministers, hold all chapels on trust and exercise authority over all societies.

The Deed of Declaration made no reference to laymen. It is

unlikely that the distinction would have occurred to Wesley since, apart from four ordained clergymen,[7] he probably regarded the other ninety-six preachers named in the Deed as laymen.

Effectively, the Deed vested the central government of the Connexion in a ministerial autocracy. Locally, the societies were grouped into circuits, each controlled by a Superintendent who derived his authority from the Conference.

Nevertheless, between 1796 and 1850, some fragmentation of Methodism took place, due to what Currie describes as 'off-shoots' and 'secessions'.[8]

'Secessions' from Wesleyan Methodism resulted from a concern for some kind of reform and included the Methodist New Connexion (1797), the Protestant Methodists (1829), the Wesleyan Methodist Association (1806) and the Wesleyan Reformers (1850).

'Off-shoots' were alliances of evangelistic lay people who reacted against the apathy and formalism of the contemporary Wesleyanism as they saw it. These were small groups such as the Quaker Methodists, Warrington (1796), the Bandroom Methodists, Manchester (1803), the Magic Methodists of Delamere Forest (*c.* 1805), the Independent Methodists (1806), the Primitive Methodists (1811), the Bible Christians (1815), the Tent Methodists (1820) and the Armenian Methodists (1832). Most of these bodies had a very short life. Thus, the Quaker Methodists were absorbed into the Independent Methodists, and the Bandroom Methodists and Magic Methodists into the Primitive Methodists. As shown below, two other small bodies, the Camp Meeting Methodists and Clowesites, united to form the Primitive Methodists. Survivors among the 'secessionists' were the Methodist New Connexion and the Wesleyan Reformers. Of the 'off-shoots' only the Independent and Primitive Methodists eventually became established denominations.

*

Pioneers

The Camp Meeting Methodists

By the time I was eight years old I had acquired from my father a fair grasp of Primitive Methodist history and folklore. If, at that age, I had been asked who were the two most important men in early-nineteenth-century history, the Iron Duke (1769–1852) and William Pitt (1759–1806) or Hugh Bourne (1772–1862) and William Clowes (1786–1851), respectively the leaders of small Wesleyan off-shoots known as the Camp Meeting Methodists and the Clowesites I would, without hesitation, have chosen the latter pair.

Bourne, the third son of Joseph and Ellen Bourne, was born at Ford Hey Farm, Stoke-on-Trent, on 3 April 1772. In addition to farming, his father worked as a wheelwright and trader in timber. Probably before the age of twelve, Bourne left school to work on his father's farm and learn the trade of a wheelwright. In 1788, the Bournes moved to a farm at Bemersley in the Parish of Norton-le-Moore. Later, he entered the employment of his uncle, William Sherratt, a noted engineer and millwright who had also successfully speculated in timber on his own account.

Bourne had a somewhat introspective personality. Aged seven, he was, by constant reading and studying, convinced of his sinfulness and continued in this state for some twenty years until the spring of 1799 when, in his own words:

> One Sunday morning I was reading and meditating and praying and endeavouring to believe. Suddenly, the Lord was manifested to me as filling the universe with his presence, and I heard an inward voice proclaiming twice, 'Thy iniquity is forgiven and thy sin is covered.' Light, life and liberty and happiness flowed into my soul, and such rapturous joy that I could scarce tell whether I was in the body or not. When I could articulate anything it was 'My Father, my loving Father! My God, my reconciled God! My hope, my heaven, my all!' I now felt that I was able to

> believe in Christ with all my heart unto righteousness and with my mouth make confession to salvation: the burden of my sin was quite gone … I now felt the love of God shed abroad in my heart by the Holy Ghost given unto me, enabling me to love every child of man, and ardently desired that all might come to the knowledge of salvation, and taste the happiness that I have experienced, and be everlastingly saved.[9]

In June 1799, Bourne accepted a ticket for admission to a love feast held in the Burslem Methodist chapel, little thinking that receiving the ticket constituted him a member. Afterwards, Bourne wrote:

> This love feast I shall ever remember. In it the Lord manifested to me that it was His will for me to be a Methodist; and notwithstanding my timidity. I was near rising up to speak, and at the close I was head and hand a Methodist.[10]

In 1802, Bourne read in the *Methodist Magazine* of the camp meetings held in Georgia. A camp meeting, an evangelistic gathering for preaching and praying, lasted for several days and was attended by people who, having travelled great distances, camped for the duration of the meeting in tents. Essentially, camp meetings were field preaching on a larger scale. The desire of Bourne and other revivalists to hold a camp meeting was given further impetus in 1805 by the arrival in England of an American evangelist, Lorenzo Dow.

'Crazy Dow' as he was known to his detractors, was as Dolan states, 'the necessary catalyst to bring together the small revivalist groups which he [Dow] named "The Third Division of Methodists",'[11] the first and second divisions being respectively the Wesleyans and the Methodist New Connexion. Dow records that in 1806 these groups held a conference 'to know each other's minds and see how near they come towards the outline of a general meeting.'[12] Dolan dates the origin of the Independent Methodist Connexion from this meeting.[13]

Dow's main objective, however, was 'to revive street and field meetings and introduce Camp Meetings'.[14] On the eve of Dow's return to America, Bourne heard him preach four times on two days, first at Harrisehead, then at Burslem and at 5 a.m. and 9 a.m. on the following day at Congleton. William Clowes was also present at the early morning service and noted that Bourne bought some books from Dow. These were Dow's book *An Account of the Origin and Progress of Camp Meetings and the Method of Conducting them* and *A Defence of Camp Meetings* by Revd G. K. Jennings MA. While the aphorism 'No Dow no Mow' is questionable, there is no doubt that Dow's descriptions of the result achieved in America caused Bourne and his friends to resolve to hold a camp meeting in their own locality.[15]

The first camp meeting was held on 31 May 1807 at Mow Cop, a hill 1000 feet above sea level on the boundary of Staffordshire. The meeting began at six in the morning. Initially, there was one preaching stand but, throughout the day, the attendance grew until, in Bourne's words 'the multitude was immense'. By the afternoon, five preachers – none of them itinerants – were simultaneously in action. Gradually the crowd diminished and, at about eight-thirty in the evening, the first camp meeting ended. A second camp meeting was held at Mow Cop on 19 July 1807 and a third, to counteract the drunkenness and depravity of the Norton Wakes, from Sunday 23 to Tuesday 25 August 1807.

Camp meetings and the presence in England of American evangelists, were discussed at the 1807 Wesleyan Conference meeting at Liverpool, before the Norton Camp Meeting stated:

> It is our judgement that even supposing such meetings to be allowable in America, they are highly improper in England and likely to be productive of considerable mischief; and we disclaim all connection with them.

Conference also directed that no local preacher from America or elsewhere should be allowed to preach unless fully accredited with a note of recommendation from his superintendent.[16]

The Conference pronouncement was conveyed by the

Superintendent to the local preachers of the Burslem Circuit who were warned against attending the Norton or other camp meetings. Bourne, however, disregarded the Conference ruling and organised further camp meetings at the Wrekin (1 May 1808), Bug Lawton (15 May 1808) and Mow Cop (29 May 1808).

On 27 June 1808, Bourne, in his absence, was expelled from Methodist membership by the Burslem Quarterly Meeting. Clowes, who was present, states that the charge was that, for some time, Bourne had not attended his class meeting. Expulsion for such a reason could have been dealt with at a meeting of Trustees and Leaders, since Bourne was a Trustee. The fact of expulsion at a Quarterly Meeting leads Bowmer to suggest an alternative to the commonly accepted view that the real reason for expulsion was Bourne's flouting of the Conference disclaimer of camp meetings.[17] In July 1803, Conference ruled that anyone who applied for a preacher's licence, as required by the Toleration Act (1689), without the consent of his quarterly meeting, would be expelled from membership.[18] Prior to the Norton Camp Meeting, and after an unsuccessful application at Lichfield, Bourne had obtained such a licence by a personal appearance at the Stafford Quarterly Sessions.

In any event, Bourne was a maverick member. He rarely met in class; he preached in his own circuit without the authority of the Superintendent minister and visited other circuits without the necessary invitation and authorisation. Bowmer concludes that the Burslem Quarterly Meeting condemned Bourne for violating the rule on licences. At a later date, the Burslem Superintendent stated that the true reason was Bourne's tendency 'to set up other than ordinary worship'.

Bourne accepted the expulsion without rancour and continued his evangelical activities, believing that

> the camp meeting movement was raised up by the hand of the Lord for the salvation of sinners and the renewal of believers.[19]

Between September 1809 and 1810, five further camp meetings

were held at Ramsor, Derbyshire. Most converts were formed into 'societies' which, for pastoral oversight, were handed over to the Burslem Circuit. Thus, a 'society' was formed at Ramsor which, from 1808–10, was supplied with preachers from the Burslem Circuit and Bourne and his associates on alternative weeks.

This *modus vivendi* ended in March 1810 when the Superintendent of Burslem Circuit, Johnathan Edmundson, refused to extend the Ramsor arrangement to a small society of ten members formed, in 1810, at Standley, four miles north of Bemersley. Standley, which had a short life and had ceased to be a society by 1814, is notable for three reasons. First, the first sermon was preached at Standley on 14 March 1810 by Mary Dunnell. Wilkinson notes that Mary Dunnell, a local preacher at Tunstall, had manifested an interest in camp meetings in 1807. It was believed that, to prevent her participation in the Norton Camp meeting on 23 August 1807, the Burslem Circuit Superintendent asked her to take his appointment at Tunstall on that day. In January, probably because of the opinion expressed by the 1803 Wesleyan Conference that 'in general, women might not be permitted to preach among us', the Tunstall pulpit was closed to her. Later that year, she was employed by James Bourne and James Alcock (with some reservations by Hugh Bourne in whose absence the appointment was made) to work for the Camp Meeting Methodists in Cheshire. She thus became their first female itinerant. After 1811, due to some 'impropriety of conduct' in urging societies to separate from the general movement and an ill-advised marriage, she disappears into oblivion.

Secondly, it was the refusal of the Burslem Superintendent to agree to any joint direction of Standley that precipitated the final break with the Wesleyans. As Bourne wrote:

> It was not my intention to have anything to do with raising separate societies, but to have raised up as many people into the service of the Lord as I was able to do, and then to have encouraged them to join other societies. This view I had from the vehement attachment to the Old

> Methodists, and a peculiar aversion to having any ruling part. But Mr Edmondson's conduct has quite put a different turn upon things. Hence, necessity is laid upon us and we are obliged to go on in the work without them.[20]

Thirdly, the words 'First Class Formed March 1810' which appeared on Primitive Methodist class tickets from 1829 onwards, was later a subject of some controversy and even hostility between Bourne and Clowes.

The Clowesites

The name 'Clowesites' was applied to the followers of William Clowes (1780–1861). Born at Burslem, Clowes was a skilled potter, lived a profligate life and narrowly escaped apprehension by a press gang in Hull where he had gone to work. After this experience, he returned to Tunstall. On 20 January 1805, Clowes was soundly converted at a Methodist prayer meeting. He broke with his former companions, paid outstanding debts both in Hull and Staffordshire, joined a class meeting at the Tunstall Wesleyan Chapel and made his house available for prayer and class meetings. Later, Clowes himself became the leader of two classes at Tunstall and Kidsgrove. A strong bond was quickly established with Hugh Bourne. As Wilkinson observes, 'Clowes was deeply impressed by the quality of Bourne's spiritual experience: none rejoiced more than Bourne at the conversion of Clowes.'[21] On 20 April 1805, Bourne wrote:

> William Clowes has become a labourer, and the Lord owns his work.
>
> He is one raised up immediately by God – a man of uncommonly deep experience, of an unusual growth in grace, deep humility, steady zeal, and flaming love: such a man scarcely ever met with.[22]

He was also closely associated with James Crawfoot, the leader of the Magic Methodists of Delamere Forest. Crawfoot's home became 'the college' in which Clowes received instruction.

Clowes was present at the two Mow Cop meetings held in May and June 1807. After the first, Clowes wrote:

> At the termination of this memorable day, I felt excessively exhausted as I had laboured from the commencement of the meeting in the morning until about eight o'clock in the evening with very little cessation, but the Glory of God that filled my soul on that day far exceeds my power of description to explain. Much of the good wrought at this great meeting remains; but the full amount of that good, eternity alone will develop to the myriads of the angelic and sainted inhabitants who will everlastingly laud the Eternal Majesty on account of the day's praying on Mow Hill.[23]

Probably due to the Conference ruling of 1807, Clowes attended no further camp meetings for fifteen months. He did, however, attend all the Ramsor Camp meetings. At the second of these, on 9 October 1809, he preached for the first time, his text being John 5:12. Soon after, he was asked to preach a trial sermon at Tunstall, after which the Superintendent Minister said: 'You have done very well; but you will kill yourself.' In late 1808 his name appeared on the preachers' plan with appointments. Whether Clowes ever became a fully accredited local preacher in the Wesleyan Connexion is doubtful.

In September 1810 Clowes' name was omitted from the list of preachers and his class ticket withheld. When Clowes enquired the reason for this omission, he was informed that he had attended camp meetings contrary to Methodist discipline and could not continue as a preacher or class leader without undertaking not to do so in future.

Clowes records:

> •I told the members of the meeting that I would promise to attend every appointment in the plan which should be put down for me, and to attend all the means of grace and ordinances of the church; but to promise not to attend any

> more camp meetings, that I could not conscientiously do, for God had greatly blessed me in these meetings which were calculated for great usefulness and my motive for assisting in them was simply to glorify God and bring sinners to a knowledge of the truth as it is in Jesus. I was then told I was no longer with them, that the matter was settled. I, therefore, immediately delivered up my class papers to the meeting and became unchurched.
>
> Of my Eden dispossessed
> The World was all before me where to choose
> My place of rest, and Providence my guide. [24]

Clowes did not depart alone. Nor was he bereft of a meeting place. Members of his two classes, comprising some thirty to forty members, wished him to continue as their leader. Almost three years earlier, Bourne records that at the close of 1807 he had visited the house of John Smith who, together with James Steel, was 'in trial of mind' because 'the female preacher (Mary Dunnell) being again at Tunstall, was shut out of the local chapel under a plea of Conference.' Smith and Steel were for a secession, but Bourne persuaded them against forming a separate society and to use the kitchen only for preaching. Bourne, therefore, arranged for the kitchen to be licenced for preaching on Friday evenings. [25] On Clowes' expulsion, Smith, who previously had refused permission for Clowes to preach on his premises, invited him so to do.

Before long the worshippers in Smith's kitchen became known as the Clowesites. From this kitchen, Clowes, sometimes accompanied by Bourne, made further forays into Derbyshire and Lancashire.

In January and April 1811 respectively, James Nixon and James Steele also suffered expulsion. James Nixon was alleged to have been too outspoken at a love feast held in the Burslem chapel. Nixon is important since, in December 1810, he, together with Thomas Woodnorth, the brother-in-law of Clowes, had proposed that the latter should become a full-time evangelist and that they would each contribute five shillings weekly to his support. Clowes accepted the offer, even though it involved both his wife and himself in considerable financial and domestic sacrifice.

James Steele, Trustee, chapel steward, local preacher and Sunday School superintendent and leader of two classes at Tunstall, was expelled because he was alleged to have attended a love feast in John Smith's kitchen on Good Friday, 12 April. His departure was also accompanied by class members and Sunday School scholars who attached themselves to the Clowesites. Smith's kitchen was inadequate for the enlarged congregation, which found temporary accommodation in a warehouse offered by James Boden, a master potter. Here, on 28 April 1811, Clowes records that 'he … opened Sunday preaching in Tunstall'. [26] The incident strengthened the already close relationship between Bourne and Clowes. The Clowesites needed a permanent preaching place. Bourne was approached for advice. On 10 May, he had 'much conversation about a chapel'. Three days later, a site was chosen. On 11 June, the land was purchased by Hugh and James Bourne. Six days later, plans were approved for a building sixteen feet wide and eight yards long to be constructed in house rather than chapel form so that, if required it could easily be converted into three cottages. This precaution was taken because 'it could not be known whether the Connexion would be of long continuance.' [27] The chapel was opened by James Crawfoot on 13 October and remained the property of the Bournes until its transfer to the Connexion in 1834.

Beginnings

'Union and concentration' between Camp Meeting Methodists and the Clowesites, as Clowes records, 'gradually took place in carrying on the work of the Lord … which none of us ever supposed would become a distinct denomination.' [28] May 1811 marks the beginning of Primitive Methodism as a distinct body. Probably because of his better education, financial resources and business knowledge, the leadership was assumed by Hugh Bourne. The immediate tasks were to print class tickets, make a plan, adopt a name and consider issues of finance and polity.

Class tickets

For some time the Ramsor Society had urged that class tickets similar to Wesleyan usage should be issued. The objection of cost was met when a Ramsor member, Francis Horobin, offered to meet the expense of printing. Accordingly, Bourne records: 'Thursday 30 May 1811, I ordered Tickets to be printed for the first time.' [29] As shown below the first ticket carried no name, but only the date, initials H.B. and the text:

MAY 1811

But we desire to hear of thee what thou thinkest : for as concerning this sect, we know that every where it is spoken against.

Acts xxviii, 22

A

H. B.

As Kendall observes, 'these class tickets were the sign and seal of the union of the Camp Meeting Methodists and the Clowesites.'[30]

The plan

The illustration opposite shows that the first 'plan' covering the June to September Quarter 1811, comprised eight societies. [31] Only two of these, Stanley and Ramsor, had been associated with the Camp Meeting Methodists. In 1810, however, the Camp

	June					July				Aug.				Sept.			
1811	2	9	16	23	30	7	14	21	28	4	11	18	25	1	8	15	1. J. Crowfoot
																	2. J. Steele
Tunstall 2 & 6	3	1	2	4	7	5	6	2	4	3	5	1	6	7	2	4	3. J. Bourne
																	4. H. Bourne
Bagnell 10																	5. W. Clowes
Badley Ridge 6	13	15	7	11	5	9	11	12	5	14	15	6	13	14	7	9	6. R. Bayley
																	7. W. Alcock
Stanly Bridge 2																	8. T. Woodnorth
Brown Edge 6	10	5	8	14	15	6	11	4	12	7	3	9	10	8	15	6	9. E. Macery
																	10. W. Turner
Ramsor		3		8		12		9		4		7		3		8	11. W. Nixon
																	12. Mattison
Lax Edge 2																	13. T. Alcock
Gratton 4		14		9		8		7		6		13		12		15	14. T. Hulme
																	15. J. Marsh

When it happens a preacher does not attend, an endeavour must be made to supply.
If any other person be present whom the congregation wishes to speak, the wish of the congregation must be complied with.

TABLE I: COPY OF THE FIRST WRITTEN PLAN AFTER THE AMALGAMATION OF THE SOCIETIES, JUNE – SEPTEMBER, 1811

From *Primitive Methodism: A Sketch of the History, Doctrines, etc., of the Primitive Methodist Connexion*, by Revd James Peet, 1867
(The spelling of the original as given by Peet has been preserved)

Meeting Methodists had five preaching places in Cheshire and Lancashire – Macclesfield, Warrington, Stockton Heath, Risley and Runcorn – and six in Staffordshire and Derbyshire – Ramsor, Whootton, Tean, Caldon Lowe, Lask Edge and Standley. The reason for the reduced number of places is that several, founded by Bourne, had been entrusted to the Wesleyans; others had joined the Independent Methodists.

The eleven societies named above had been served by eleven preachers. Only five of these – J. Crowfoot, J. Bourne, H. Bourne, W. Alcock and W. Turner appear on the plan for June to September 1811.

The second quarter's plan, from September to December, lists seventeen societies and seventeen preachers.[32] At this time, the membership in society numbered two hundred.

The name

By February 1812, the new organisation had thirty-four preaching places and twenty-three preachers, but no name. This deficiency was remedied when, in Bourne's words:

> Thursday, 13 Feb, 1812, we called a meeting and made plans for the next quarter and made some other regulations; in particular we took the name of the Society of Primitive Methodists.[33]

The word 'primitive' was used as the opposite of 'modern'. Brief mention has already been made of John Crawfoot.[34] In 1809 Hugh and James Bourne had agreed to pay Crawfoot, a farm labourer then facing destitution, ten shillings weekly until Lady Day to 'labour in the vineyard'.[35] Two years earlier, Crawfoot's name had been removed from the Northwich Circuit plan for preaching to the Warrington Quaker Methodists. In his defence, Crawfoot related that, in 1790, he had heard Wesley preach at Chester exhorting his itinerants 'to go out … into the streets and lanes to preach the gospel wherever there is an open door'. 'This', said Wesley 'is the way the Primitive Methodists did.'[36] 'Mr Chairman,' declared Crawfoot, 'if you have deviated from the old usages, I have not; I still remain a Primitive Methodist.' Bourne also declared:

> I never knew a Burslem Circuit travelling preacher perform what Mr Wesley calls 'field preaching' all the time I was a member ... this then, was and is modern, not Primitive Methodism and I think there is a broad difference between the two. [37]

Rack casts doubt on the authenticity of the Crawfoot story and points out that Hugh Bourne claimed to have been asleep when the matter was discussed and that it is uncertain whether Crawfoot was actually present at the meeting. [38]

Rack provides evidence that:

> In fact the term Primitive Methodist was not an invention of the new connexion but a slogan widely used in Wesleyanism before the formal emergence of the Primitives in 1812 ... So it seems probable that the new Primitives simply chose a label already familiar, to assert their claim to be reviving the original Methodist character.

Finance

'Other regulations', agreed at the meeting on 12 February 1812, related to the appointment of paid itinerants and finance. James Crawfoot and William Clowes were already receiving payment for their services and it was confirmed that they should continue 'to be given up to the work'. [39] A later meeting, held in October, fixed the weekly remuneration of Crawfoot and Clowes at 10s 6d and 14s respectively. The higher rate was because Clowes' house 'was a kind of pilgrims' inn' and was subject to higher rent.

Crawfoot's association with the new Connexion was short; in February 1813, he was 'suspended till the quarter day' for having declined, without notice, to take his appointments. He also failed to attend a meeting convened in April to discuss the charges laid against him and thus placed himself outside the Connexion. Crawfoot died, aged eighty-one, on 16 January 1839.

The Tunstall meeting also discussed 'the best method of conducting money matters'. Wilkinson notes that there had been some hesitancy about asking class members for contributions.[40] This was, in part, influenced by the doctrine of an unpaid ministry held by the Independent and Quaker Methodists at Macclesfield and Warrington. The somewhat vague decision was made 'that the circumstances be mentioned to the people, and what they voluntarily gave to be collected by proper persons and to be paid into the hands of a Steward; and what fell short to be made up out of private subscriptions.' James Steel was appointed and thus became the first Primitive Methodist Circuit Steward.

Polity

Organisationally, Primitive Methodism followed the Wesleyan pattern of a number of societies grouped into a Circuit.

The first Primitive Methodist Conference was held at Hull in 1820 and, in 1824, the then seventy-two circuits were grouped into four Districts – Tunstall, Nottingham, Hull and Sunderland. Although, from 1820, Conference was the ultimate legislative authority, there were, as stated in Chapter 4, a number of reasons why, between 1843 and 1876, the District Meetings grew in power and popularity at the expense of the Conference.

From 1814–19 Hugh Bourne acted as the Superintendent of three far-flung circuits, Tunstall, Nottingham and Loughborough. In 1819 he also became the Editor of the *Primitive Methodist Magazine* published at Bemersley Farm, the home of the Bournes, which became the Book Room and Connexional headquarters until 1843. The growing Connexion could not remain under the superintendency of one man. A preparatory meeting of representatives held in Nottingham in August 1819 made arrangements for a 'regular annual meeting or yearly Conference of the whole Connexion.'[41] This meeting laid down the principle that Conference should comprise 'three delegates from each circuit, only one of whom shall be a travelling preacher.[42] This principle was clearly designed to obviate any possibility of Wesleyan-style ministerial autocracy.

It also went further than the Methodist New Connexion where Conference comprised equal numbers of ministers and laymen. Effectively, it marked out Primitive Methodism as a democratic, egalitarian body in which no office or function from President of Conference downwards was denied to a layman. The respective relationships between minister and laymen in the Wesleyan, New Connexion and Primitive branches of Methodism are humorously depicted below.[43]

Between 1811 and 1820 Bourne, Clowes and their helpers had established the rudiments of an organisation. Aspects of the subsequent development of Primitive Methodism from sect to denomination are considered in the next three chapters.

EMBLEMS OF THE POLITY OF METHODISM

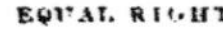

2
Expansion 1810–60

Influenced by their superintendent, from 1811–13, Joseph Sutcliffe, who 'laboured and struggled to effect a reconciliation', the Burslem Circuit invited the 'Primitives' to rejoin the Wesleyan fold. Sutcliffe observed that 'he could not wholly requit his predecessors of haste or inexperience' The invitation was discussed by all the Primitive Methodist societies which, in 1812, numbered thirty-four. Clowes records that none were willing to rejoin:

> The resolution was unanimously carried that we should remain as we were. A letter was then sent to our old friends ... stating that as soon as ever we saw that to incorporate ourselves with them would promote the glory of the Most High and enlarge the Redeemer's Kingdom ... we would immediately do so.[1]

The expansion of Primitive Methodism in the fifty years 1810–60 may be considered under several headings: geographical, numerical, social, pioneers and methods. The growing movement was also not without its tensions.

Geographical expansion

Having agreed to remain separate, the new Connexion had to decide whether to consolidate locally or expand nationally. From 1811–19 a majority of Tunstall members, led by James Steele, favoured the former course. This policy, termed the 'Tunstall Non-Mission Law', was anathema to Bourne, Clowes and others, notably John Benton, who maintained that 'Primitive Methodism should be allowed to go through the nation as it was intended to do'. Benton, a man of private means, had a thousand copies printed of Lorenzo Dow's *Collection of Spiritual Songs used at Camp Meetings in America* and, in 1813, successfully missioned several Staffordshire villages before advancing into Derbyshire, where, in 1814 at Belper, the Primitive Methodists were first termed 'Ranters'. Petty observes:

> Though this uncouth name (Ranter) has a bad meaning and a nickname which no well-bred person or courteous Christian will apply to the Primitive Methodists unless through ignorance of their proper name, we are not sure whether in some localities it has not been rendered subservient to the interest of the Connexion, by awakening curiosity and inducing numbers to attend to the preaching of the missionaries, who could not otherwise have been brought under the Ministry of the Word.[2]

In 1815 a society was formed in Derbyshire by Sarah Kirkland who, in February 1816, became the first Primitive Methodist female travelling preacher. The year 1816 was notable because Derby became the head of a second circuit and for the holding of a great Camp Meeting in Nottingham Forest attended by over 12,000 people.

From Nottingham, which superseded Derby as head of the second Primitive Methodist circuit, the work extended into Lincolnshire, Rutland and Leicester and in 1818, Loughborough, missioned by Benton, became head of a third circuit.

By 1818, an invitation from a group of revivalists led the Nottingham Circuit to plan a mission in Hull and requested the help of Tunstall. William Clowes, who, apart from occasional forays into Nottinghamshire and Leicestershire, had been employed at Tunstall since 1811, was nominated. On 15 January 1819 he arrived in Hull from where, some fifteen years earlier, he had ignominiously departed. Six months later, Hull became the fourth circuit with about three hundred members. Under Clowes, Hull became, geographically and numerically, the most progressive circuit. From Hull, Primitive Methodism spread along the north-east coast of Yorkshire to Durham, Northumberland and across northern England to Cumberland and Westmorland. At one period, the Hull Circuit extended for more than 200 miles from Carlisle in Cumberland to Spurn Point in Holderness. Within seven years, Hull created twenty-one independent circuits with a combined membership of 8,455. In 1824 and 1825 respectively, the Hull Circuit sent Clowes to mission London and Cornwall.

Meanwhile, missionaries from Nottingham had entered Norfolk from where Primitive Methodism spread into Cambridge and Suffolk.

In 1819, the Tunstall 'non-mission' rule was rescinded. A camp meeting held by John Wedgewood led to a great revival which increased the Tunstall Circuit membership by 1,013 in fifteen months. Tunstall now became a centre of missionary activity in Manchester, South Staffordshire and South Shropshire. From Tunstall, the Darlaston, Oakengates, Burland and Manchester Circuits were formed. These circuits became bases for further advances. Darlaston extended the work to Birmingham, Worcester, Presteigne and Radnorshire. From Oakengates, circuits were formed in Shrewsbury, Bishops Castle and other South Shropshire areas. Oakengates also missioned Wiltshire, and in 1827, established the Brinkworth Circuit. Burland was the mother of the Chester, Liverpool, Prees Green, Wem, Ellesmere and Oswestry Circuits and, later, missioned Northampton.

Manchester propagated the Bolton, Oldham, Stockport, Bury, Rochdale and Stalybridge Circuits. In turn, the Bolton Circuit introduced Primitive Methodism into the Isle of Man. Through the efforts of pioneers including John Ride, Thomas Russell, John Petty, Richard Jukes and George Warner, astonishing progress was made in the agricultural areas of the southern counties.

There was also, due to emigration to the Dominions, some expansion overseas. In 1829, the Tunstall and Hull Circuits each sent two missionaries, one a woman, Ruth Watkins, to the United States where societies were established which, in 1840 were designated the American Primitive Methodist Church. In 1829, a missionary was sent to Canada, and, three years later, the Canadian Mission was placed under the care of the Hull Circuit. Primitive

Methodist missionaries to New Zealand and Australia departed in 1843 and 1844.

When the first Primitive Methodist Conference met at Hull in May 1820, eight circuits were represented. By 1824, the number of circuits had increased to seventy-two, now grouped into four districts – Tunstall, Nottingham, Hull and Sunderland. Henceforth, district replaced circuit representation at the Annual Conference. By 1860, the number of circuits had increased to 264 (313 if overseas stations are included) and the districts to ten by the addition of Norwich (1825), Manchester (1827), Brinksworth (1833), Leeds (1845), Bristol (1848) and London (1853).

Numerical expansion

By 1820, the initial 200 Primitive Methodist members had increased to 7,842. The subsequent rapid growth of the Connexion in its first fifty years is best appreciated by comparing the percentage membership increase at the end of each decade with that ten years earlier.

Year	Membership	Increase over previous decade	Per centage increase
1820	7,842	–	–
1830	35,733	27,257	357%
1840	73,900	38,257	107%
1850	104,762	30,772	42%
1860	132,114	27,352	26%

Currie [3] observes that churches tend to recruit most successfully in their early days when, given relatively large constituencies and small memberships, they are able to achieve their highest growth rates. In 1821–2, for example, Primitive Methodism grew from 16,394 to 25,218 members, a 54 per cent increase in one year. Currie also notes another fact exemplified by early Primitive Methodism: that in this high growth phase churches 'recruit whole communities or whole families rather than isolated individuals and adults rather than children'. Kendall states that between 1819 and 1824, the membership rose from 7,842 to 33,507 'so that in the short space of four years the Connexion had more than quadrupled its numbers. Such progress greatly exceeded that of early Methodism.'[4]

Obelkevitch reminds us that, particularly in its early years, Primitive Methodist membership tended to fluctuate violently at every level: Connexion, circuit and society.[5] It is also necessary to reflect that the figures refer to *members*. In 1851, the Census of Religious Worship estimated that in Methodism generally, adherents outnumbered members by three to one.[6] On this basis, the numbers influenced by Primitive Methodism were much in excess of those returned by the societies.

Primitive Methodist membership also needs to be related to the wider aspect of religious affiliation. The 1851 Census, referred to above, based on a count of attendances at each service on 30 March 1851 provided the following figures:[7]

Church of England	3,773,474
Roman Catholics	305,393
Wesleyan Methodists	907,313
Independents (Congregationalists)	793,142
Baptists	587,978
Primitive Methodist	266,555

Based on the above returns, on Census date Primitive Methodism was the fourth best attended Nonconformist body. The attenders at Primitive Methodist chapels on Census Sunday exceeded the combined totals of the Methodist New Connexion (61,319), Bible Christians (38,612), Wesleyan Association (56,430), Independent Methodists (1,659) and Wesleyan Reformers (53,494).

Social aspects of early Primitive Methodism

In its first fifty years, and for some time afterwards, Primitive Methodism was the Nonconformist body that had the greater attraction for the poorer and working classes. This was largely due to historical, geographical and social factors. The latter are considered later in this chapter and in the section on Finance.

Historically, Primitive Methodism began in the later years of the Napoleonic War and developed in the period of economic distress that followed 1815.

Geographically, Primitive Methodism flourished in agricultural, mining and some other industrial areas. In agricultural areas, legislation such as the 1836 and 1845 Enclosure Acts, the 1815 Corn Law and the 1834 Poor Law Amendment Act, together with the Law of Settlement and the Game Laws, reduced farm labourers to virtual serfs. In 1842, the *First Report of the Children's Employment Commission relating to Mines* revealed the extensive use of women and children below ground. Although, in general, miners were better paid and therefore better clothed and housed than other workpeople, there were anomalies such as the 'tommy shop' and 'truck' systems. The work was dangerous, with high accident and mortality rates, factors which made mining villages tight-knit communities. Miners were noted for recklessness, hard living and degradation. In other industries such as cotton and silk, handworkers were fighting a losing battle against the machine. Luddism, which in 1812 became a capital offence, was rampant.

Field has provided the most useful study of the social structure of English Methodism in the eighteenth to twentieth centuries based on a modified version of the Registrar General's 1951 schema of five social class gradings: [8]

1 Major employers, merchants, bankers, property owners, professional people.
2 Intermediate non-manual workers including minor employers, retailers, local government officers, teachers, and, prior to the 1930s, clerks, commercial travellers and insurance agents.
3 Routine non-manual occupations, artisan crafts, skilled manual tasks chiefly in construction and manufacture.
4 Semi-skilled employees mainly in transport, agriculture, mining, wood, textiles, domestic and municipal service.
5 Labourers and other unskilled persons.

TABLE 2 provides a comparison of the social structures of Primitive Methodism in the period 1800–1837:

	England	Wesleyan Methodism	Primitive Methodism
		4,385	2,407
	%	%	%
Merchants/manufacturers	2.2	1.7	0.5
Shopkeepers	6.2	5.8	3.9
Farmers	14.0	5.5	5.6
Artisans	23.5	62.7	47.7
Colliers/miners	2.5	7.6	12.5
Labourers	17.0	9.5	16.1
Others	34.6	7.2	13.7

TABLE 2: SOCIAL STRUCTURE OF ENGLISH METHODISM, 1800–1837 (NON-PAROCHIAL REGISTERS)

Field points out that, up to 1837, Primitive Methodism achieved its greatest successes within ranks 3–5. In TABLE 2, the combined totals of categories 1–2 only reached half the expected level in the total population, 48 per cent of supporters being artisans, 16 per cent labourers and 13 per cent miners. He also refers to local studies that confirm Primitive Methodism's early identification with the lower strata of society. About a third of 511 names appearing on the Norwich baptismal register before 1850 were those of skilled workers, and three-fifths were semi- or unskilled. The three to four thousand persons present at a Caistor camp meeting in August 1819 were chiefly 'farmers' servants, day labourers and village mechanics'. In the Ilkeston Circuit, 98 per cent of 622 fathers were engaged in manual pursuits, 51 per cent being miners and 19 per cent framework knitters. Primitive Methodists in the Potteries were said to be 'yeomen, butchers, shopmen, tailors, shoemakers, smiths, carpenters, potters and colliers'. The conclusion reached by Field is that 'whilst 80–100 per cent of nineteenth-century Methodists were certainly engaged in the manual sector, by no means all of them belonged to the poorest grade' and that they were often far less likely to be labourers than semi-skilled persons or craftsmen.

Field's comparisons in TABLE 2 show that colliers/miners and labourers had a significantly higher Primitive than Wesleyan affiliation. The proportion of farmers in the two bodies was almost identical. Artisans were more likely to be Wesleyans than Primitives.

Field's statistics relate to males. In 1818, however, one in five Primitive preachers were women. Of a sample of 100 obituary notices taken from early issues of the *Primitive Methodist Magazine* by Werner 55 per cent related to females.[9] It is likely therefore that women must have constituted a large proportion of Primitive Methodist membership. Bebbington indicates that in eighteenth-century Methodism, women members outnumbered men and quotes a statement of 'a rather jaundiced ex-Methodist':[10]

> I have heard Mr Wesley remark that more women are converted than men; and I believe that by far the greatest part of his people are females; and not a few of them sour, disappointed old maids.

In 1851, *The Report of the Census of Religious Worship* stated categorically:

> The community whose operations penetrate most deeply through the lower sections of the people is the body called Primitive Methodists, whose trespasses against what may be thought a proper order will most likely be forgiven when it is remembered that perhaps their rough informal energy is best adapted to the class to which it is addressed, and that, at all events, for every convert added to their ranks, society retains one criminal, one drunkard, one improvident the less.[11]

Yet it is important to get both the general expansion of Primitive Methodism and its impact on 'the lower sections of the people' into perspective. Inglis rightly states that in 1850 the total membership of Primitive Methodism was only a little over 100,000 and 'even making a generous guess about the ratio of members to adherents, it is clear that the proportion of working class people reached by Primitive Methodists was small.'[12] Conversely, while Primitive Methodism only reached a small proportion of the poor, it was probably more successful in doing so than any other Christian body then extant.

The high proportion of members in agricultural occupations reflects the fact that in its early days and for much of its later history Primitive Methodism prospered in rural villages and small towns rather than large urban centres. Petty in his *History of the Primitive Methodist Connexion*, commissioned by the 1857 Conference as a Jubilee record of the Connexion's first fifty years, states that at the time of writing, Primitive Methodist societies in many large towns were:

> few and feeble, its Sabbath Schools far from numerous, and its chapels small and uninviting compared with the population.[13]

'Something worth naming' had been effected in Leicester, Nottingham, Sheffield, Hull, Yarmouth and Sunderland but the Connexion had 'done little' in London, Plymouth, Bristol, Liverpool, Manchester, Birmingham, Leeds, Bradford and Newcastle-on-Tyne. Some of these places had given their names to circuits and even districts but the real strength of the Connexion was in the surrounding villages and small towns. Political factors were partly responsible. Werner mentions that in towns with Liberal and Nonconformist traditions, the Ranters were well received.[14] The opposite applied in urban centres of Tory influence such as York, Newark and Lincoln. In agricultural areas where Wesleyan Methodism was already entrenched, Primitive Methodist itinerants encountered 'attitudes ranging from indifference to moderate interest'. As late as 1896, the

Primitive Methodist Conference was informed that a survey taken two years earlier showed that 'to a much larger extent than was generally thought, we are a village church. Nearly seventy-five per cent of our chapels and a large proportion of our preaching places are in the villages.'[15] The Ranters often penetrated tiny hamlets untouched either by other dissenting denominations or the established church. In rural areas, as Obelkevich observes, Primitive Methodism provided a religious counter to the parish church and the old village culture.[16] It could also, as shown later, easily provide a training ground for both political and collective activity aimed at bettering the economic conditions of those regarded as 'the lower orders'.

Pioneer preachers

Ritson states that the travelling preacher was the 'nucleus' round which the early Primitive Methodist societies gathered.[17] It was on these pioneer preachers that the expansion of the Connexion depended. The essential attributes of an early travelling preacher were strong legs, a powerful preaching and singing voice, 'a passion for souls' and great physical courage.

Strong legs

The need for strong legs is evidenced by the examples of Hugh Bourne and William Garner. Kendall declares that Bourne:

> used frequently to walk forty or fifty miles a day and that under circumstances of self-denial, little practised or even known by most. He used to put into his pocket two or three hard-boiled eggs and a little dry bread in the morning and during his journey he would sit down by a well of water and take his humble fare and then travel on in pursuit of his great object of winning souls.[18]

William Garner records in his diary that between 8 January 1823 and 27 July 1830 the distance covered by forty-eight of his principal journeys was 1,068 miles at an average of rather more than twenty-two miles daily.[19]

A powerful speaking and singing voice

This was needed not only for preaching outdoors but often to be heard above the noisy crowd that gathered to hear 'the Ranter'. It was also important that the travelling preacher could speak to his hearers in their own vernacular and be able to sing. Ambler relates that, as late as 1848, the sort of education that made a man unfit to speak to the most illiterate congregation was unsuitable for a Primitive Methodist itinerant and instances John Oxtoby nick-named 'Praying Johnny'.[20] Oxtoby's sermons were described as 'often crude'. 'In his pronunciation and attitude, he was uncouth.' Oxtoby had 'no wish to add to his strong faith, ceaseless prayer and deep piety those mental stores which embellish the man, expand and refine the mind of the Christian and give increasing qualification and sweetness to the zealous and powerful preacher.' Yet, under Oxtoby's preaching in both Driffield and Filey 'a great many were awakened and stirred up to seek the Lord.' In 1808 a female candidate for the itinerancy was rejected 'because her language was "not well adapted to the common people".'[21]

Open-air preachers often began by striking up a hymn and instances abound of Primitive Methodist mission bands gathering a crowd by singing some stirring tune as they marched into a town or village. 'Ranter hymns', as Werner states, 'belonged to the world of ballads and street songs, colliers' ranks and coster-mongers' cries' in contrast to the 'more staid hymns sung in Wesleyan chapels and the drone of Anglican chants'. She also quotes the comment of an early Primitive Methodist:

> Children stand and listen to us, and thus get hold of a few lines or so of the chorus, and with the tune, or as much of it as they can think of, they run home, and for days, they sing it in their homes, and their mothers and sisters get hold of it.[22]

Two examples of the use of song to promote Primitive Methodist evangelism can be cited. The first, an adaptation by William Jefferson of the words set to a stirring tune sung by the Chartists as they processed through Leicester:

The Lion of Freedom is come from his den;
We'll rally around him, again and again:
We'll crown him with laurel, our champion to be:
O'Connor the patriot for sweet liberty!

In turn, the Primitives marched through the streets to the same tune but different words:

For the Lion of Judah shall break every chain,
and give us the victory again and again.

The second, the hymn 'Hark the Gospel News is Sounding', became known as the Primitive Methodist 'Grand March'. It first appeared in the *Large Hymn Book for the use of Primitive Methodists* published by Hugh Bourne in 1824. The authorship, along with that of 137 others in a collection of 536 hymns, is jointly ascribed to 'W. S. and H. B.' (William Sanders and Hugh Bourne). William Sanders began his work as an itinerant in the Tunstall Circuit in 1820 and the following year contracted to supply Bourne with twenty-five hymns for one shilling each. Open air services and camp meetings often began with the hymn and its challenging chorus:

Turn to the Lord and seek salvation
Sound the praise of His Dear Name.
Glory, honour and salvation,
Christ the Lord has come to reign.

A passion for souls

Salvation and conversion were the fundamental elements in Primitive Methodist pioneer preaching. The message of salvation was an appeal to both fear and love and had both future and present implications. As evidenced by a typical Bourne hymn, he, Clowes and their followers believed literally in hell and Satan:

His vengeance will my soul pursue
If I refuse His grace.

And ah! – alas what must I do
If banished from His face.
Eternal darkness I must see
And hope will never come.
But fiends will my companions be
And Hell will be my home.[23]

Heaven, however, was just as real as hell. This is evidenced by an extract from a sermon preached by Bourne to children:

> Now, my dear childer, when you get to heaven, you'll all be clothed with fine robes; (you know what robes are my childer – they are long garments, trailing on the ground, which kings and queens wear). And you'll have a crown on your head, finer and grander than Queen Victoria's; and when your daddies and mammies see you they'll scarcely know you. They'll say – 'Hay! is yon our Mary or our Tommy? Why, they look as nice as nice and as grand as grand'. And there's tree o'life in heaven and nicer tasted fruit than it grows never was – it's nicer and sweeter than sugar: and there's t'river of water of life, too, clear as crystal: nicer and better tasted water never was. And you'll have no more sore eyes nor aches and pains, nor sickness of any sort there – so you must all strive to get there. When you get to heaven, my childer, you will, after a while, see this old world burning up ... and you'll say – 'There goes t'old world on which we sinned so much and suffered so much and in which old Satin tempted us so much'; but after all, you'll say ' it sarved our purpose very well', for we heard of Jesus on it, said our prayers on it, and lived to God on it, and got to Heaven from off it, so we have no fault to find with it.[24]

What a prospect for poor children in the Potteries!

The message of salvation evoked a response because it met the needs of many hearers. Maslow classified human needs into a hierarchy sub-divided into lower and higher order needs.[25] The former, physiological and security needs, must be satisfied to ensure an individual's very existence. The latter, comprising social esteem and self-actualisation, are concerned with personal development and the realisation of individual potential. Apart from such physiological needs as food, clothing and sex, the message of salvation satisfied all the needs identified by Maslow. The message of salvation offered security. Death was an ever present feature of life. Infant mortality was high and average life expectancy low. Bebbington shows that crises, political, economic and, 'most insistent of all', death, provide favourable conditions for evangelism and instances the cholera epidemic of 1832. 'The twelve months to 1833 saw the largest membership ever recorded in Wesleyan history and other denominations also reaped a harvest.'[26] Werner also notes that 'this awful visitation of the cholera swelled the Leeds Primitive Methodist Circuit and added 250 members in a single quarter in both Hull and South Shields.'[27] In 1832–3, Primitive Methodist membership grew by 7,120. Werner also suggests that one reason why Primitive Methodism flourished in mining communities was that 'colliers lived quite literally in the valley of the shadow of death.' The high risk of death at sea might also be a factor in the growth of Primitive Methodism in such fishing communities as Hull and Grimsby.

'Social' needs were also met. 'The New Testament', as John Wesley observed, 'knows nothing of a solitary religion.' 'Saved' persons were welcomed into the fellowship of a society which nurtured the delicate shoot of newly acquired faith and prescribed mores for Christian living. Soon, such persons became aware of having also entered into a wider connexional fellowship which was a kind of extended family.

In the chapel fellowships, many converts found salvation not only from sin and hell, but also from low esteem and low self-worth.

Primitive Methodist preachers, like their Wesleyan antecedents, preached to the scum of society. The appeal of both was epitomised in Charles Wesley's hymn, 'Where shall my wondering soul begin' described as 'the birth song of the Evangelical Revival':[28]

> Outcasts of men, to you I call
> Harlots and publicans and thieves
> He spreads His arms to embrace you all
> Sinners alone His Grace receives.[29]

The lives of such people were usually 'nasty, brutish and short'. Even the 'respectable poor' were downtrodden, often living below subsistence level. In many agricultural and mining districts, they were only slowly emerging from serfdom. But when such people entered into salvation, they acquired new significance as the objects of God's love. In their chapels, all sense of inferiority vanished. Agricultural labourers living on a pittance with no prospect of earthly betterment claimed to be high born because they were new born; no longer serfs, but sons and daughters of the King of Kings, heirs of an eternal heritage and an everlasting kingdom.

Such awareness of significance led to self-actualisation. Converted persons are commonly concerned to convert others. Hobsbawm describes Primitive Methodists as a 'sect of activists' and mentions that up to 1853 it never contained much less than 10 per cent of members who were either travelling or local preachers.[30] As with other branches of Methodism, this activism could also find expression in chapel, circuit or district offices that members might undertake irrespective of social standing or sex, although Hempton notes that from the 1840s Primitive Methodism shuffled women to the margins in the same way as happened in Wesleyanism half a century earlier.[31] As shown later, such activism often extended beyond chapel walls into political and trade union activity.

Evangelicalism, of course, was not peculiar to Methodism. Four ingredients of Methodist conversion which were the prerequisites of salvation have been identified by Scotland:[32]

1 A feeling of despair related to an acknowledgement of sin;
2 A realisation of peace and forgiveness through a contractual relationship with Christ;
3 A continual full assurance associated with feelings of love;

4 A maintenance of the foregoing experience by means of a 'methodical' lifestyle. When Ranter preachers exhorted their hearers to 'Turn to the Lord and seek salvation' they were issuing an invitation to undergo the sense of liberation and changed outlook that they themselves had experienced.

What distinguished Methodist conversion from that of other groups was the note of assurance, the knowledge of release from sin's guilt and power accompanied by a sense of wholeness, the certainty of the love of God being shed abroad in the heart and the desire to press on to Christian perfection.

Physical courage

John and Charles Wesley and their helpers were often in great physical danger from the mob and Primitive Methodist pioneers often received the same treatment. A Primitive Methodist preacher required great courage to enter a strange locality, often unaccompanied, and preach in the open, vulnerable to the rougher elements of the populace. Such elements were often encouraged by local clergy to ridicule or assault the preachers. The law was also invoked to interrupt or prevent an itinerant from preaching. Typical of many examples from what is termed 'The Ranter and Rotten Egg' period of Primitive Methodist history were the experiences of Thomas Russell, William Lockwood and George Wallis.

In May 1830, Thomas Russell was sentenced to three months hard labour nominally for selling connexional magazines without a licence but actually for preaching in the streets of Chaddleworth, Berkshire. On one day in April 1832, Russell preached at Wantage, Faringdon and Shrivenham. At Wantage, he was pelted with slime, mud and rotten eggs; his clothes were torn and flesh bruised. When alone, he washed his stained garments in the canal and, putting them on wet, proceeded to Faringdon. Here the persecution was repeated and he washed his clothes again in a pool outside the town. At Shrivenham, another violent reception and he had to cleanse himself a third time. Russell then went on to another village where he preached in peace, except that someone threw a stone, cutting his lip.[33]

William Lockwood, drenched with water from the Newark town fire engine, gurgled to his persecutors: 'You can't quench the fire within.'

George Wallis, attempting to preach at Andover in 1833, was knocked down, pelted with rotten eggs and attacked by a mob shouting: 'Kill him! Kill him!' Not withstanding this experience, Wallis preached there the following Sunday. Again he was subjected to rough usage. Despite the opposition, a society was established and a chapel erected in 1838.

Not all the pioneers were men. The Wesleyan Conference of 1803 considered whether women 'should be permitted to preach among us' and decided 'that they ought not'. Even where 'a woman believed she had an extraordinary call from God to speak in public', Conference was of the opinion that she 'should address only her own sex'.[34] Primitive Methodism had no such reservations. Mention has been made of Sarah Kirkland, who in 1814 was employed by Hugh Bourne as the first female Primitive Methodist travelling preacher at two guineas a quarter. By 1834, the Connexion had twenty-six female itinerants.[35]

Thereafter, the number declined. The last woman itinerant, Elizabeth Bultitude, retired in 1862 after travelling 29 years.[36] Bourne's acceptance of women preachers was, as Werner recognises, not influenced by 'advanced ideas concerning the place of women in society'.[37] If, by their employment, Bourne contributed in any way to the emancipation of nineteenth-century women, this was fortuitous. Bourne's single concern was to save souls. If women contributed to this end, that, in his view, was sufficient justification for their employment.

Methods

Organisationally, the process of expansion has been well described by Ritson:

> A number of places having been missioned, and regular preaching services arranged, they were placed upon the

> Plan, and supplied with preachers to conduct the services. The whole might consist of a dozen or twenty places, or more, scattered over a considerable area of country and taking its name from some town or village. It might be a Mission, or Branch or a Circuit.
>
> Only in the latter case would it possess complete autonomy. As a Mission or a Branch, it would be under the control of, and receive perhaps some financial assistance from, the parent circuit. As soon as it was strong enough financially, and in regard to its official life, it would be made an independent circuit with its own superintendent preacher, its local preachers, its circuit steward, society stewards, Sunday School superintendents, and its class leaders.[38]

This 'domino' process, by which, directly a circuit found itself in possession of sufficient financial resources, it turned its attention to the work of missioning new areas in which to form new societies and circuits, is exemplified in the geographical expansion described earlier in this chapter.

3
Tensions

Expanding organisations concerned with larger numbers of people and a wider external environment experience tensions as they meet problems, situations and inter-personal conflicts not encountered at earlier stages of their development. Three such tensions associated with Primitive Methodism's first fifty years relate to finance, politics and founder rivalry.

Finance

The expense associated with the building and maintenance of even small chapels and the support of the travelling preachers could make heavy demands on society members, which, as shown, tended to be poor. Like other religious bodies, Primitive Methodism was affected by economic factors. Slump conditions were generally detrimental to both membership growth and stability. Kendall ascribes the loss of 2,055 members in 1854–55 to the attraction of the Californian and Australian goldfields and mentions that in one year, 672 members were lost to the Connexion from this single cause.[1] Storms, floods, strikes, the abnormal price of food and depression also led to decline, possibly because of the inability of members to pay their society and circuit contributions. The previous year, 1853–54 had witnessed the even greater loss of 1,020 members, explained as follows:

> Provisions have risen, to the humbler classes of society, to almost a starving price. The result is that thousands who were recently cheerful supporters of the Connexional funds and creditable members of society, have fainted beneath the pressure of poverty, and withdrawn from

> church fellowship, notwithstanding all earnest endeavour to retain them on terms which could not, in the slightest degree, diminish their pecuniary resources. In dear times there is an essential difference between the circumstances of the rich and the conditions of the poor. The former *know* that the means of subsistence are unwontedly expensive – the latter *feel* it difficult to subsist at all. [2]

On occasions, penury led to demands for 'cheaper' religion. Not surprisingly to a poor community, an unpaid ministry such as that provided by the Independent Methodists was attractive.

In 1828, the societies at Bingham, Nottinghamshire and its immediate vicinity seceded from Primitive Methodism and added the word 'Independent' to their title, thus becoming 'Independent Primitive Methodists'. The new body rejected connexionalism, adopted a voluntary, unpaid ministry and continued to exist separately until they joined the Independent Methodists at the end of the century.[3]

Ten years later, another Nottinghamshire society, Selston, left the Belper Primitive Methodist Circuit when it was proposed to increase the superintendent ministers' weekly stipend from 14 to 16 shillings. The 'Selstonities' persuaded other disaffected Primitive Methodist societies to join them and adopted the title of 'Protestant' and, later, 'Original' Methodists. Unlike the Independent Primitive Methodists, they were not opposed to connexionalism or a paid ministry but differed from the parent body regarding the amount of stipend. By 1851 the Original Methodists had sufficient societies to constitute two circuits. In 1870, however, the Original Methodists ceased to exist and no fewer than eleven of their societies joined or rejoined the Primitive Methodist Connexion. Not only Primitive but also Wesleyan Methodists sometimes seceded to the Independent Methodists for financial reasons. Vickers states that in the 1830s, Barnoldswick, a small Yorkshire village, experienced a period of depression. The Circuit officials expressed the view that the contributions of the Barnoldswick society to Circuit finance was inadequate. 'The

Society at Barnoldswick expected sympathy instead of reproach but their remonstrance was treated with contumely. Five class leaders therefore resigned and met those who rallied round at the house of one, George Pickup.' [4] Here a congregation was gathered. In 1840, a chapel was erected costing £400. The society met as a self-contained community for over ten years before joining the Independent Methodists.

The demand for 'cheaper religion' could, occasionally, benefit the Primitive Methodists. Watts mentions that in 1818 the Wesleyan Conference asked the societies to contribute to discharging the Connexional debt. Contributions were to be in proportion to society memberships. This basis encouraged superintendents to prune their membership lists and possibly led to defections to the Primitive Methodists since it was claimed that 'the Ranters in comparison with the Methodists offered a "cheaper" religion.' [5]

Politics

Primitive Methodism began and developed in a climate of political ferment. The American Declaration of Independence (1776) with its assertion that 'all men are created equal', the French Revolution (1789–99) and Tom Paine's *The Rights of Man* (1791) had opened vistas of hope to radicals and the threat of sedition and revolution to rulers. Radicalism was often associated with religious dissent. A Bill prepared by the then Home Secretary, Lord Sidmouth, in 1811, sought as Semmel says to restrain the rapid spread of Methodism 'by such irregular means as lay-preaching and itinerancy – methods which the Dissenters were now adopting – as subversive to the Church and the State, a foretokening of what had already come to pass on the other side of the Channel.' [6] The Toleration Acts required dissenting preachers to be licensed by the local Justices. Sidmouth's Bill ostensibly sought to limit the issue of such licences which he held had given rise to 'abuses'. Applicants for preaching licences included those 'who were cobblers, tailors, pig-drovers and chimney sweepers' – 'situations' which 'disqualified them from being teachers and instructors of their fellow subjects'. England's security depended upon the firmness of the Establishment. Unless action was taken to defend the Church, there would be the danger of having a nominal Established Church and a sectarian people. After heavy opposition outside and within Parliament, Sidmouth's Bill was defeated. The attack on 'radicalism' reached its climax with the 'Peterloo' massacre and the 'Six Acts' of 1819. Such revolutionary violence as existed diminished after the Cato Street conspiracy of February 1820 when extremists plotting to murder the Cabinet were caught red-handed.

The development of Britain as a modern bourgeois society immune from the revolutions prevalent in Western Europe between 1789 and 1848 was attributed by the French historian Elie Halévy to the imbuing of the working and middle classes by the evangelical movement 'with a spirit from which the established order had nothing to fear.'[7]

This view of Methodism as a restraining force had previously been suggested by other historians including Taine in France and Macauley, Lecky and Green in England and is quoted approvingly by Townsend in the *New History of Methodism.*[8] The thesis is also supported by later writers including Semmel and Gilbert.[9] The writers probably exaggerate the influence of Methodism in restraining and redirecting revolutionary fervour. Conversely, the Marxist historians, Hobsbawm and Edward Thompson, underestimate the Methodist contribution to maintaining English political stability.

Between 1800 and 1820, when attempts to suppress radicalism were strongest, it was understandable that Wesleyan and, later, Primitive Methodism should seek to rebut Anglican attempts to associate Methodists of all varieties with sedition. The consequence of Wesleyan neutrality and Toryism was that as Hempton states, 'the era which ended with Peterloo also saw the end of Wesleyan Methodism as a force within working class culture.'[10] Even in Primitive Methodism, the most politically radical of all Nonconformist bodies, a neutralist policy was adopted. On both scriptural and pragmatic grounds, Hugh Bourne supported obedience to the Government and acceptance of the political status quo. At the Annual Meeting held at Tunstall in 1821,

Bourne interrupted the proceedings by demanding the expulsion of a speech-making radical, 'a man who is employed in speaking against the government.' This demand was opposed and other speakers attacked the King, Government and Bourne himself. The latter, owner of the Tunstall chapel, eventually prevailed:

> I told them that scripture required us to be subject to the Government under which we lived … that … as the Government had its eye upon us, measures might be taken to stop our camp meetings, and the Connexion might receive an injury from which it would never recover … After a time, the speeches against the government slackened and the more thoughtful began to intervene. [11]

Wearmouth holds that Bourne's intervention saved the Connexion from an official alliance with political radicalism. [12]

In 1835, the Primitive Methodist Conference, asked to rule on 'public speechifying on politics', declared:

> That none of our travelling preachers be allowed to make speeches at political meetings, nor at Parliamentary Elections, and it is strongly recommended to our local preachers to avoid such things. [13]

A supplementary rule laid down:

> that none of our chapels or preaching rooms be lent on any account, for either political or religious controversy.

These rules were passed in the period preceding the decade 1838–48 when Chartism was at its zenith. These rules are sometimes cited as evidence of Tory leadership within a radical movement. The more likely explanation is that Bourne was anxious that the new Connexion should not be diverted from its primary objective of evangelism, should avoid giving offence to the Government and should prevent political factions which might give rise to divisions within the membership.

Wearmouth shows how Chartist leaders adopted Primitive Methodist practices including camp and class meetings for political purposes.[14] Camp meetings were easily organised and publicised, inexpensive, avoided the hire of buildings and attracted large crowds. Wearmouth states that the first mention of political class meetings is a resolution of the National Union of Working Classes held in the Rotunda, Blackfriars Road on 24 October 1831 that class leaders be appointed for the different districts of the metropolis … 'With an average of twenty-five members to each class and forty class leaders to one thousand members.'[15]

Rules passed by a somewhat remote Conference are difficult to implement when at variance with local inclinations. For many Primitive Methodist preachers, itinerant and lay, politics and religion were synthetical rather than antithetical, and many combined impassioned evangelism with progressive politics influenced by the thought and behaviour of Old Testament prophets and prophecies. Some travelling preachers interpreted the Conference rule on 'public speechifying on politics' as only applying to Tory meetings. In 1836 Conference was informed of 'two or three instances' in which the use of chapels or preaching rooms for 'political agitation' had been disregarded so that 'piety had suffered'. How many cases were not reported will never be known.

James Skevington, John Markham and William Thornton are examples of prominent Primitive Methodist Chartists.

Skevington, leader of the Loughborough Chartists and a local preacher at the age of sixteen, declared towards the end of his life, 'though a man may be a Chartist and not a Christian, a man cannot be a Christian and not a Chartist.'[16]

Markham, first leader of the Leicester Chartists and also a local preacher, was expelled from the Connexion for his political activities.

Thornton, one of several local preachers present, opened the proceedings at one of the first great Chartist camp meetings with prayer 'that the wickedness of the wicked may come to an end' and won a tribute from Feargus O'Connor: 'Well done, Thornton, when we get the People's Charter, we will see that you are made Archbishop of York.'[17] Hobsbawm observed that 'for a remarkably large number of leaders' political consciousness and activity began with or shortly after a conversion experience.[18] Conversion can result in an enhanced sensitivity to the needs of the whole world which expands the traditional evangelical concept to relate not only to matters spiritual, futuristic and individual but also temporal, present and social. This fact partly explains the appeal of Chartism to many members in the earlier days of Primitive Methodist history and of the later appeal of Liberalism and Socialism. It was also a factor in the contribution of Primitive Methodism to trade unionism.

Repeal of the Combination Laws in 1824 opened the door to trade unionism. Apart from the social consequences of conversion mentioned earlier, Hobsbawm identifies four reasons why Primitive Methodism was predominantly a labour sect. First, 'the general suitability of evangelistic technique and doctrine to their kind of working class.' Secondly, 'nothing in Primitive Methodist teaching discouraged organisation for working class defence and much encouraged it.'

Thirdly, 'Chapel and particularly the small self-contained village chapel, provided a school of organisation for all purposes. Among both coal miners and farm labourers it is possible to see their unions borrowing from Primitive Methodist polity and practice.' Finally, the anti-sacerdotal nature of Primitive Methodism 'provided a first-rate mechanism for selecting and training leaders and cadres. Without education and without any social sanction against "making himself prominent" the lay preacher could come forward among his fellows; and the practice of preaching gave him self-confidence and facility.'[19]

The last of the above reasons is important. Thompson observes that Methodist working men and local preachers who were active in politics and trade unionism, were (with the exception of trade unionism in the pits and, later, agriculture) rarely initiators, a role more often filled by Owenites and free-thinkers.[20] The doctrines of the latter were likely to be derived from political theorists including the Levellers, the Diggers, Locke, Montesquieu, Voltaire and, of course, Tom Paine. The Methodists looked to the Old and New Testaments. Old Testament prophets fearlessly preaching righteousness and justice provided role models for Methodist Chartists and trade unionists. New Testament teaching on spiritual equality, the church as a society in which there was neither 'bond nor free' and the worth of every person in God's sight provided the doctrinal basis for the struggle against exploitation and oppression. Thompson's exception in respect of trade unionism in the pits is well exemplified by Tommy Hepburn. Hepburn, Primitive Methodist and leader of the Pitmans' Union of Tyne and Wear, is regarded by Webb as 'the first effective leader of the miners'.[21] Under Hepburn's guidance, a strike in 1830 occasioned little violence and obtained most of the miners' demands. The victory was short-lived. Within a year, the coal owners revoked the agreement. Hepburn encouraged the miners to stand by the union. The owners retaliated by using police to break up union meetings. Cavalry and London police were used to evict hundreds of mining families from their homes. Blacklegs were imported from Wales, Staffordshire and Yorkshire. Gradually, the miners surrendered, Hepburn being the last to do so. Thereafter he wandered homeless, workless and alone, trying to earn a pittance by selling tea. Destitute, he was driven to ask for work. He got it at Felling Colliery but only after undertaking never again to take part in union activity. He kept his word. Understandably embittered by the events of 1832, Hepburn for a time abandoned his Primitive Methodism but later rejoined.

Three conclusions can be drawn from the involvement of Primitive Methodism in politics and trade unionism up to 1860.

First, as Scotland says, 'Methodist social theology found its first expressions on the lips of those men who were in the front line of social action.'[22] In both Wesleyan and Primitive Methodism official support for such social action was for political reasons initially absent or hesitant. Only later was social theology more carefully formulated by the professional leadership of each church.

Secondly, while some Methodists, driven by economic necessity or revulsion against injustice, sought to achieve change by political or trade union activity, they were a minority. The mass following of evangelical nonconformity was, as Watts states:

> drawn from people who were poor, uneducated, prone to superstition, young and disproportionately female ... For the majority, the brevity of life, the certainty of death and the sense of hopelessness in a frightening world, all of which had predisposed them to accept the evangelical message in the first place, militated against either political involvement or revolutionary action.[23]

Thirdly, Primitive Methodist polity, along with, but more strongly than, other non-Wesleyan Methodist sects, emphasised lay democracy, and at first, for utilitarian rather than democratic reasons, gave equal opportunities to women. In repudiating an hierarchical despotism, Primitive Methodism was a microcosm of the radical movements prevalent in the national politics of the early nineteenth century.

Founder rivalry

At the Newcastle Conference of 1842, Bourne and Clowes, then aged 70 and 62 respectively, became supernumeraries. Both received an annuity of £25 and Conference recorded:

> thanks to Almighty God for the very great service rendered by Bros. Hugh Bourne and William Clowes to the Primitive Methodist Connexion, which under God they have been the chief agents in raising or founding, and whose services are still blest by the Lord: and furthermore, we unite in fervent prayer for their future welfare.[24]

In the early years of their retirement, Bourne and Clowes had differing fortunes. Bourne waned; Clowes waxed. Bourne's retirement was overshadowed by the disgrace of his brother James arising from the irregularities at the Bemersley Book Room.[25] Hugh Bourne himself, by his carelessness in authorising payments requested by his brother, was not free from implication in the scandal. Probably because of this event, Hugh Bourne, with the blessing of the Connexion, sailed from Liverpool on 2 July 1844 to visit the Primitive Methodist societies in Canada and the USA.

This self-imposed exile lasted until he landed at Liverpool on 26 March 1846. Apart from the 1847 Halifax Conference referred to later, his involvement in Connexional affairs gradually diminished until his death, aged 80 years, on 11 October 1852.

In contrast, Clowes, although superannuated, was President of the Conferences held in 1844, 1845 and 1846. Afterwards, failing health led to a reduced Connexional commitment, although he continued to preach and hold class meetings in the Hull Circuit. He died, ten days short of his seventy-first birthday, on 2 March 1851.

From the first, relationships between Bourne and Clowes appear to have oscillated. In 1805, Bourne rejoiced at Clowes' conversion. Although Clowes participated in the Mow Cop Camp Meetings on 31 May and 19 July 1807, some difference apparently took place between the two since Bourne regarded Clowes as 'no friend' of the new venture and his attitude to camp meetings as unprimitive. Clowes absented himself from subsequent camp meetings until he accompanied Bourne to that held at Ramsor on 4 September 1808. Again, there was some difference. Wilkinson records that 'whilst walking together along the canal side, Clowes seems to have spoken somewhat critically and Bourne reacted strongly: "My natural timidity was suspended … I broke in upon him firmly and said: 'If you cannot approve of it, you may find your way home again.'" It was a harsh rebuke. Clowes was silenced, and they proceeded without further words.'[26] Relations between the two seemed to have quickly improved. Bourne was concerned at Clowes' expulsion from the Burslem Society in September 1810. Thereafter, Bourne and Clowes, as leaders of the Camp Meeting Methodists and the Clowesities respectively, enjoyed an increasingly closer co-operation which culminated in the making of a joint preaching plan in May 1811.

For some years relationships between Bourne and Clowes appear to have been reasonably cordial. From 1819 onwards, however, several factors led to renewed tension.

These factors included debate regarding the respective contributions made by each of the two men to the founding of the Connexion, the success of the Hull Circuit and teetotalism.

There is no doubt that Bourne used the Bemersley Book Room with its printing press to propagate the primary place of himself and his brother James as the founders of the Connexion. In 1819, the Preparatory Meeting held at Nottingham had resolved that a brief history of the Connexion should be published with a portrait of Hugh Bourne. Clowes noted that 'it became a disputed question whether Hugh Bourne or William Clowes was to be considered the actual founder ... It was, however, agreed ... to waive the decision on the question, but to submit it to the opinion of the Tunstall friends, as amongst them, the work had its origin; they must, therefore, be best able to settle the matter.' [27]

The history of the Connexion, written by Bourne, was first serialised in the *Primitive Methodist Magazine* beginning with the issue for January 1821. Bourne states that in addition to his personal journals the Committee of the Tunstall Circuit had 'bestowed much time and trouble in duly ascertaining the facts and examining the circumstances.' The history was subsequently published by the Bemersley Book Room under the title: *History of the Primitive Methodists giving an account of their Rise and Progress up to the Year 1823*.

Bourne's account relegated Clowes to the background. Clowes records that when the history was read to the Book Committee appointed to approve matters 'to be inserted in the magazines' James Steele asked whether it was a history of Hugh and James Bourne or whether a history of the Connexion? [28] When read at the 1820 Hull Conference, one member suggested that Clowes should 'look it over before it was passed'. Clowes did so. Although he 'did not approve of it being drawn up in the way it was but thought the shortest way to get shut of it and be at peace was to say nothing about it.'

Kent mentions that Bourne also tended to play down the contribution of Lorenzo Dow, effectively obscuring that when Bourne's efforts to reform the English Camp meeting system had become ineffective, it was largely Lorenzo Dow's return which had set the Connexion moving again. [29] As Sheard points out, however, it is unlikely that a glaring error, such as an attempt to assign credit rightly belonging to Lorenzo Dow to Hugh Bourne and others including Peter Phillips, Joshua Marsden and William Ride, would have gone unchallenged by those who read Bourne's *History* in draft form. [30]

Although the Tunstall Committee had apparently agreed that Bourne was the Connexion's founder, Clowes was hurt when the published *History* carried a portrait of Bourne as a frontispiece and also by a condescending reference to the appointment by Bourne of Clowes as a travelling preacher:

> He had the prospect of entering into the field of labour occupied by H. and J. Bourne, so that his way appeared fully open and his prospects of usefulness was large and extensive. [31]

Bourne's preface to the *Primitive Methodist Consolidated Minutes of 1832* also implies that he and his brother James were the Connexion's architects:

> In [God's] Providence the Primitive Methodist Connexion rose undesigned by man.
>
> It was long composed of two members, Hugh and James Bourne who continued to expend their property and labours in promoting religion.
>
> They visited new places; and in one of these, Standley in Staffordshire, they, in March 1810, raised up a class of ten members. These they attempted to join to the Wesleyans. But their design being frustrated, they, contrary to their inclinations, were necessitated to take upon them the care of a religious connexion ... and towards the latter end of the same year a class at Tunstall joined them. [32]

Baker observes that the phrase relating to 'the class at Tunstall' is a half-hearted reference to the fact that the leader of a parallel movement, William Clowes, had joined them. Baker also quotes from a note by John Flescher who succeeded Bourne as Connexional Editor:

> If the facts of the case be as the people speak of them the history of Primitive Methodism, as published by H. Bourne must be defective, in as much as Clowes is there comparatively hidden, whereas he ought to be brought before the public as one of the founders, if not the founder. To say the least, the affair is deserving of enquiry and I think a history of the Connexion ought to be written which will place the rise of the Connexion on a legitimate basis.[33]

The truth is probably that Bourne and Clowes looked at the matter from different perspectives. Bourne regarded the Connexion as originating with the Camp Meeting movement. Clowes emphasised the class at Tunstall. As Wilkinson says, 'He [Clowes] did not view the matter in this light. He asked, "Did this class [at Tunstall] join them or did they join it?" To Clowes everything was moving towards Tunstall as the centre of what was to become a combined movement. Bourne regarded the expansion of the work in Tunstall as an advancement of the cause established by himself and his brother.'[34]

Clowes arrived in Hull on 15 January 1819. Certainly between 1819 and 1827 Hull was more successful as a centre of growth and expansion than its Tunstall counterpart. Seven years after commencing work at Hull, Clowes had created twenty-one new northern circuits with a total membership of about 12,000. Hatcher notes certain differences between the two centres. Hull had a stronger economic base. It is possible that the people of the adjacent agricultural community of the East Riding, whose territory had endured recent hardship from the enclosure movement would be more receptive to Primitive Methodist preachers. Hull Primitive Methodists 'appear to be less often in conflict with the law in the open air and in less conflict politically.' They were also resistant to what they saw as 'the aggressive encroachment of the teetotal movement'. In terms of worship and church order, Hull appears to have been more traditional. As Hatcher says:

> A picture emerges of a Hull Primitive Methodism that was a little less angular and a little more comfortable, but no less zealous than that of Tunstall. At a lower level on the social scale, there was in Hull Primitive Methodism a hint of Wesleyan Methodism, or for that matter, even of Wilberforce. Leading participants from Hull Circuit were also well enough educated and organised to have gained connexional control by 1843.[35]

On 5 May 1830, Clowes wrote: 'H. B.'s prejudices run heavy against Hull.'[36] The Leicester and Sunderland Conferences of 1831 and 1834 were marked by sharp interchanges between Bourne and Clowes. Particularly in 1833, Bourne 'spoke harshly and at length in criticism of Clowes and the Hull Circuit and the wounds went deep.'[37] The immediate issues appear to have been Bourne's criticism that the low book sales achieved by some Hull preachers were detrimental to the Book Room. There was also contention regarding the fitness of a preacher sent to America from the Tunstall Circuit on Bourne's recommendation but about whom Clowes had reservations. Brown notes a further factor relating to both the success of Hull and the friction between Bourne and Clowes. This was that the Hull Circuit with Clowes as Superintendent had a pool of full-time preachers available for deployment anywhere in the north of England. 'The highest number remunerated in any one quarter was 36 and the total for the five years (1822–7) was 139.'[38] In contrast, Bourne was content to set forward the work from Tunstall without any large-scale employment of paid preachers. As Brown states:

> It is understandable that Hugh Bourne was reluctant to expend the Book Room resources and policy for Northern Primitive Methodism which he himself did not employ in the Potteries. The strained relations between Bourne and Clowes at this period may have had some origin in the more cautious policy of Bourne and the demands made upon the Bemersley Book Room by the more enterprising policy of Clowes.[39]

Relations were further exacerbated by the appearance in 1833 of a pamphlet published by the Book Room under the title of: *A Few Plain Facts; Faith and Industry Superior to High Popularity as Manifested in the Primitive Methodist Connexion between the Conference of the year 1824 and that of 1833 – Nine Years.*

Somewhat illogically, the pamphlet claimed that the districts of 'high popularity' in Nottingham, Hull and Sunderland had only added few members to the Connexion while those of 'low popularity' – Tunstall, Norwich and Manchester – had, 'through faith and industry' contributed many thousands. Although published anonymously, the author was almost certainly Bourne and aimed at Clowes, who 'expressed his astonishment at the unprovoked and needless attack; but … did not allow it to do much harm.'[40]

The assertion made by the pamphlet was easily rebutted by an examination of Circuit records undertaken by the Hull preachers. This showed that between 1819 and 1835 the Circuit had raised 14,116 members.

Teetotalism was a further contentious issue. Hugh Bourne was a life-long opponent of what he termed 'strong drink'. This opposition probably derived from his childhood experience. The craving of his father, John Bourne, for alcohol resulted in some family impoverishment and occasionally violence to his wife and children. After his superannuation in 1842, however, Bourne appears to have developed an almost fanatical zeal for teetotalism. In September 1843, through the medium of a dream, Bourne received guidance on 'the manner in which to preach on alcohol.' On 23 September, he joined the Rechabites in his first 'teetotal procession at Broad Town and when he was called on to preach, it was his first teetotal sermon.'[41]

Although the Connexion recommended temperance societies in 1832, and recommended the use of unfermented wine at the Lord's Supper in 1841, the early attitude of Primitive Methodism was that intoxicants, in moderation, were permissible. Bourne declared that it was not he that had joined the teetotallers, but the teetotallers that had joined him. The Hull Circuit, however, as Hatcher states, displayed real resistance to what they saw as the aggressive encroachment of the teetotal movement. [42] This, together with Clowes' more relaxed attitude to alcohol, provided Bourne with ammunition for further attacks on both Clowes and Hull. He described Clowes as

> ... a drunkard mightily converted – reformed but not wholly so as he kept to strong drink. William Clowes said he could drink to the glory of God. [Bourne says he should have rebuked Clowes but was too timid.] If you swallow strong drink down the devil will swallow you down ... strong drink is not only the way of the devil, but the devil's way into you.[43]

The Hull District also appears in a poor light in tables prepared by Bourne showing the relationship between teetotalism and increases in membership.

Districts: majority not teetotal			**Districts: majority reckoned teetotal**		
	Travelling Preachers	*Increase in Members*		*Travelling Preachers*	*Increase in Members*
Tunstall	63	381	Sunderland	64	1964
Nottingham	45	174	Norwich	58	1007
Hull	99	198	Manchester	48	992
Toronto	6	242	Brinkworth	105	1214
	213	995		275	5107

These figures are reminiscent of the assertions made by Bourne against Hull in his pamphlet published in 1833.

Shortly before Bourne's departure for America in 1844, Clowes had published his own *Journals*. Wilkinson states that Bourne made no reference to these until September 1845 when, in his American Journal, he regarded a Connexional decrease of 800 members as a consequence of Clowes' *Journals*.[44] Possibly because the *Journals* underplayed his contribution to the founding of the Connexion, Bourne described them as 'misrepresentation and deceit mixed with some truths'. After returning to England,

Bourne's strictures on Clowes continued, to the dismay of many members. Eventually, matters came to a head at the 1847 Halifax Conference when Bourne made a public and written apology for his conduct: [45]

> I hereby give this Conference held at Halifax, 1847, a Pledge in the sight of God and my brethren that I will, from this time, cease from the course I have persued (sic) on speaking disrespectfully of Mr William Clowes, whether publicly or privately, throughout the Primitive Methodist Connexion or elsewhere.
>
> Signed by me in the presence of my brethren in open Conference this eleventh day of June, one thousand eight hundred and forty-seven.
>
> HUGH BOURNE

Whether the apology was made 'freely and frankly' as Wilkinson suggests or was demanded from Bourne is not clear. Notwithstanding this pledge, Bourne, on a visit to the Isle of Man, appears to have criticised the *Journals* and also written a hurtful letter to Clowes. These facts were the basis of charges against Bourne made by Clowes and James Nixon at the 1849 York Conference. Conference did not, however, regard these lapses as a breach of Bourne's pledge.

It is not easy to adjudicate on this founder rivalry. Bourne, as Kent says, was undoubtedly the 'institutional founder' of Primitive Methodism. [46] He instigated camp meetings. With his brother James he built the first Primitive Methodist chapel and provided the Connexional headquarters at Bemersley Farm. He was 'the chief architect of Primitive Methodist polity.' [47] He provided Primitive Methodism with its first magazine and hymn books. Together with John Benton and some of the country preachers, he opposed the Tunstall 'non-mission' rule which advocated 'consolidation' rather than a policy of aggressive evangelism. Bourne's influence prevented a fusion with the Independent Methodists and the adoption of an unpaid ministry. He also saved the Connexion from a political alignment with Chartism. In the early years of Connexional growth, he was both administrator and leader.

Conversely, it is difficult to rebut Kent's verdict that Bourne was a 'a jealous man ... uneasy about William Clowes' and that he also played down the contribution of Lorenzo Dow.[48] Probably Bourne regarded Clowes, Dow and others such as Benton as leading the assault in the field while he provided generalship back at base. Although, as shown earlier, he himself tramped many miles on evangelising missions, Bourne's resentment that, in later years, his contributions to the founding and development of early Primitive Methodism were insufficiently recognised is understandable. His weakness appears to have been an unwillingness to recognise, as Sheard observes, that:

> Primitive Methodism was the product of several elements which coalesced in 1810 and 1811 ... To consider it simply as the product of a union between two groups of Staffordshire revivalists is to read into the situation some of the tensions which emerged later; and to talk of Bourne and Clowes as 'joint-founders', much as Wesley was the 'founder' of eighteenth-century Methodism, is an oversimplification which misrepresents the nature of early nineteenth-century revivalism.[49]

Wilkinson attempts to mitigate Bourne's hostility to Clowes on the grounds that their rivalry was due to the 'particularism' of early Primitive Methodism and 'the gathering weakness of old age'.[50] It is true that, as evidenced by Bourne's 1833 pamphlet and attempt to relate district membership increases to teetotalism, 'particularism' set one district against another. While, however, increasing age seems to have caused Bourne's strictures on Clowes to increase in vehemence, relationships between the two oscillated between affection and animosity. In all probability, the root cause of their rivalry derived from differences in personality. Bourne, as Hatcher states, 'lived a lonely anxious youth' and was 'converted through reading'.[51] Clowes in his youth was 'wild and profligate' and was converted in a noisy prayer meeting. Bourne was a self-employed moorlander. Clowes had been employed in urban areas including Warrington and Hull, as well as Burslem. Bourne was a bachelor; Clowes married. 'Bourne's was an inner strength springing from his complex mind and dominant will. Clowes' strengths were revealed in his relationships with others, where warmth and spiritual discernment often evoked a positive response.' Clowes was unquestionably the more charismatic individual and, on occasion, Bourne must have resented being overshadowed by Clowes' more dominant personality. Clowes' successes in Hull and claim to be co-founder of the Connexion would exacerbate Bourne's over-reaction to the perceived threat that his contributions to the Connexion would be insufficiently recognised.

In attempting to adjudicate on the issue, it is probably impossible to improve on the balanced statement of Petty:

> Their talents and acquirements materially differed and so did the sphere of their labours. Mr Bourne had more strength of mind; Mr Clowes more fire of the imagination. The former had more learning; the latter had a richer command of language and a more fluent utterance. Mr Bourne took a much larger share in the management of the Connexion than Mr Clowes; the latter did incomparably more than he in active labours to extend its borders. While Mr Bourne was efficiently serving the denomination as Editor of its magazine and as the ruling mind of its General Committee and annual assemblies, Mr Clowes was pursuing evangelical labours or Home Mission operations with apostolic ardour and success. [52]

Thus Petty concludes:

> Mr Bourne could not have accomplished what Mr Clowes effected; Mr Clowes could not have performed what Mr Bourne achieved.

4
From Sect to Denomination

Kendall states that by 1843, the year following the superannuation of Bourne and Clowes, the 'heroic' period of Primitive Methodism had ended.[1] By the Jubilee year of 1857 Primitive Methodism was nationally recognised and increasingly respectable. Within the confines of a single chapter it is impossible to do more than identify and discuss eight trends that may be discerned in the development of the Connexion from a sect into a denomination and its re-integration along with the Wesleyan and United Methodist Connexions to form the Methodist Church. These eight trends indicate movements from (1) penury to prosperity; (2) emotion to education; (3) revivalism to recreation; (4) self-centredness to social concern; (5) political neutrality to political activism; (6) confederation to centralisation; (7) Connexion to Church and (8) independence to integration.

Penury to prosperity

While not entirely rejecting the view that temperance, thrift and self-help cause the members of a sect to become more wealthy, Liston Pope advanced the hypothesis that in any sect a few members are likely to prosper, sometimes as a result of personal qualities but more often by chance.[2] 'As such members became more "responsible" they would either desert their sect or re-shape it in keeping with their new position', not a difficult thing to do if a sect is in need of the funds which these members can provide.[3] In Primitive Methodism this is best exemplified by the influence and munificence of Sir W. P. Hartley, which is described later. As early as 1849 the Conference Address reported that the

Connexion was rising in wealth and numbers.[4] By 1860 there was an increasingly prosperous element in Primitive Methodist membership. This prosperity is evidenced by the establishment of fee-paying schools and an era of chapel building.

Fee-paying schools

In 1860, when advocating the establishment of 'a school for preachers' children and the children of members', Dr Samuel Antliff pointed out that:

> when families prospered they wanted intellectual as well as religious culture for their children, and not being able to find what they wanted in their own community they sought elsewhere.[5]

The Primitive Methodist Jubilee School (afterwards Elmfield College, York) opened as a boys' school in 1864. Sometime later the *Primitive Methodist World* observed that:

> The College was the outcome of the strong conviction that if the Connexion did not provide thorough and liberal education for the sons of our ministers and prosperous laymen, we should not retain them in communion with us. The blessing of God upon the industry and economy of our people has raised many of them into comfortable circumstances, and enabled them to provide somewhat liberally for the education of their sons. So long as these sons had to receive their scholastic training in the schools provided by other denominations, they would be influenced by the doctrines and ecclesiastical principles of such denominations and would most likely be alienated from us.[6]

The opening of Elmfield was followed in 1876 by the opening of a further boys' school, Bourne College, Birmingham, 'with a curriculum and scale of charges similar to those adopted in the York school.' Probably in the same year a Primitive Methodist Ladies' College was opened to provide secondary or middle class education for girls. This appears to have been a short-lived venture since no report on the College appears in the Primitive Methodist Minutes after 1881 and as Graham says 'thereafter all real trace of the Ladies' College is lost.' [7] Bourne College closed in 1928. Following Methodist Union, Elmfield College closed in 1932 and the pupils' scholarships and memorials were transferred to Ashville and New College, Harrogate.

Chapel building

Watts quotes the comment of Kitson Clark that the building of churches and chapels 'commanded more of a disinterested enthusiasm of Victorian Englishmen in all districts than any other achievements of the reign' and calculates that between 1801 and 1851 some 13,201 Nonconformist chapels were built.[8] This was five times the number of Anglican churches erected in the same period.

The era of Primitive Methodist chapel building came later. Kendall reports that in 1847 Connexional returns showed 1421 chapels and 3,340 rented chapels and rooms.[9] By 1864 the respective numbers had become 3,340 and 3,235. The era of Primitive Methodist chapel building reached its height during 1863–1872 when 1,191 chapels were reported to have been built giving an average of two chapels weekly in the decade. This chapel building had several facets.

In the early days of Primitive Methodism most chapels were village societies and, due to penury, tended to be smaller and cheaper than those of other Nonconformist bodies. Watts reports that the median cost of a sample of seventy-two Primitive Methodist chapels built prior to 1850 was £200. [10] Many such chapels required subsequent extension so that the trustees and members were involved in what must have seemed an unending struggle with chapel debt. In many societies there was an identifiable pattern of continuous fund raising, first for a chapel, then a Sunday school, followed by subsequent extensions and the installation of an organ.

The period of chapel building also saw the growth of Primitive

Methodism in towns and cities. Wickham shows that until 1855 the Primitive Methodists had only one chapel in Sheffield: a 1,900-seater building. Between 1855 and 1897 a further thirty-one chapels were erected in the City, 'some of them very small and some of them large, and mostly in the more working class centres of the Parish, where new artisan terraced streets were being built.'[11]

Hull, however, was the centre where the era of Primitive Methodist chapel building began. By 1881 the number of Primitive Methodist chapels in Hull had increased from three in 1847 to eleven. The new buildings were large. Jarrett Street had 1,400 sittings; Anlady Road, a Gothic building, 1,420; Williamson Street, 1,400; Lincoln Street, 950; Fountain Road, 800; Ebenezer, 1,200; Hassel Road, 1,000; St. George's, 850. The costs varied between £3,000 and £9,000. Elsewhere in the Connexion imposing chapels were erected such as the Central Church, Newcastle-on-Tyne which opened in 1899 at a cost of £15,563. Sometimes schemes for the erection or purchase of a chapel were ill-advised. Travelling preachers moved frequently and occasionally an itinerant's excess of enthusiasm over discretion could leave both members and his successor with a burden of debt.

Milburn states that of fourteen chapels built in Hull between 1851 and 1894 all but one was in debt, in most cases substantially so. The total Hull debt in 1890 was over £27,000, 'two to three million in modern [1990] values.'[12]

As early as 1770 when Wesley banned all new buildings 'unless the proposers thereof can and will defray the whole expense' the Wesleyans had taken steps to control indiscriminate chapel building and in 1770 established a Building Committee with powers to veto the erection of any new chapel. Three years later the powers of this Committee were delegated to District Meetings.

Primitive Methodism took similar action. District Building Committees were established in 1835 followed by District Chapel Committees in 1847. In 1836 Conference laid down that any preacher who encouraged the building of a chapel 'without reasonable prospect of its being supported should forfeit one fourth of his salary.'[13] In 1843 Conference decreed that no building project should be sanctioned unless the promoters could show that one-third of the cost would be raised within one year of the chapel opening. This time was reduced to six months in 1882 when promoters were required to have raised one fourth of the estimated cost of a building.[14] The year 1847 also saw the creation of a General Chapel Fund similar to that established by the Wesleyans in 1818 to help chapels pay off their debts. The title of the General Chapel Fund was changed in 1898 to the General Missionary and Sustentation Fund.

Despite such innovations the overall Connexional building debt in 1890 was over one million pounds. The need to put the cost of chapel building on a more business-like footing was met by the incorporation in 1890 of the Primitive Methodist Chapel Aid Association. The Association was the brainchild of W. P. Hartley who recognised the need of chapel builders for low cost finance. In 1870 Hartley suggested the formation of a company to operate on the banking principles of accepting and paying interest on deposits. The money deposited would be loaned for Primitive Methodist building schemes. The proposal was accepted by the Conference of 1887 and the Primitive Methodist Chapel Aid Association Ltd. incorporated on 1 January 1890. Hartley, who by 1894 had deposited £15,000 of his own money in Chapel Aid, was the first Treasurer of the Association. Milburn points out that, 'In essence, Chapel Aid was both the Primitive Methodist Savings Bank and the source of loans to the trustees of Primitive Methodist property.'[15] The initial interest rate for depositors was 3.5 per cent which contrasted favourably with the 2.5 per cent offered by the Post Office Savings Bank. The interest charged on loans was 3.75 per cent. Concern was expressed regarding the adequacy of the tiny margin of one-quarter per cent out of which administrative expenses had to be met. As Milburn states, however, Hartley conceived of the Association as 'not primarily or simply a commercial venture but rather as a business-like way of raising money which would be made immediately serviceable as loans to debt-ridden chapels on the easiest feasible terms.'[16] Hartley's financial acumen was amply justified. Between 1890 and

Methodist Union in 1932 it was calculated that Chapel Aid had loaned £2.75 million to Primitive Methodist trustees of which almost £2 million had been repaid.[17]

From 1900 the Chapel Aid Association occupied the same premises in York as the Primitive Methodist Insurance Company which had been founded in 1866 to insure chapels, school, manses and ministers' personal belongings. The Company had the distinction of being the oldest denominational insurance company in the UK. In 1933 the Primitive Methodist Insurance Company merged with the Methodist Insurance Company in Manchester. The Chapel Aid Association located in York is still extant and serves the wider Methodist Church.

The era of chapel building was one in which Primitive Methodism began the transition from what Liston Pope termed 'economic poverty to economic wealth'[18] and also moved towards parity with other Nonconformist denominations. The transition to relative prosperity was not accompanied by corresponding spiritual growth but rather as Obelkevich states from 1860 by 'a declining interest in revivalism'.[19]

Chapel building contributed to this decline in several ways. Chapels caused societies to turn inwards with a consequent waning of revivalist enthusiasm. Even where camp meetings survived they were more associated with nostalgia than revivalism. Much effort was also diverted into fund raising involving the organisation of bazaars and entertainments which, while raising essential money, tended to stifle the spiritual life of the society. Primitive Methodists began to adopt the practice of Wesleyans and other Nonconformist bodies of levying pew rents to meet the erection and maintenance costs of buildings. Pew rents were opposed by Wesley and in Primitive Methodism tended to be charged in urban rather than rural areas. Such rents were a deterrent to attendance by the poor and a negation of early Primitive Methodist openness and democracy. In some areas pew rents lingered on until the 1940s. In 1942 the writer recalls a visiting relative returning from morning worship at the Lane Head Chapel in the Lowton Circuit and reporting that she had been asked to move from the (unoccupied) seat in which she was ensconced because 'someone has paid for this pew'. In 1932 Primitive Methodism had over 4,356 chapels and other property valued at £7,769,500.[20] The upward mobility of the denomination is, however, reflected in other ways as shown in the next sections.

Emotion to education

Primitive Methodism began as a fundamentalist sect with a theology based on the literal interpretation of the Bible. Initially it was also a charismatic movement. Conversion was often accompanied by an intense conviction of sin, horrific dreams or visions and crying out for mercy followed by a strong emotion of release or deliverance accompanied by an overwhelming sense of peace and joy. A further frequent characteristic was the hearing of 'voices' which gave directions or assurance. 'Noisy times' when the power of the Spirit fell were a common feature of early Primitive Methodist worship. Preachers such as William Clowes were often able to achieve a dynamic rapport with their congregations in which their hearers were moved to become participants by such ejaculations as 'Glory!' or 'Praise the Lord!' The chorus of an evangelistic hymn would be sung again and again. Individuals would be moved to fervent prayer. As Hatcher states there were 'occasions when the "spirit of burning" came upon the believer resulting in terminal exhaustion.'[21] Morrell has shown that charismatic manifestations such as falling down, groaning, uncontrollable laughter and speaking in tongues were often present in the early camp meetings and especially the cottage prayer meetings attended by the followers of Bourne and Clowes.[22] The noise and emotion of such prayer meetings, where conversions often occurred, contrasted sharply with the growing rigidity of the conventional class meeting. Morrell further points out that as Primitive Methodism grew and consolidated, the intensity of the charismatic phenomena seems to have lessened and ceased. Nevertheless, until the late nineteenth century noise and emotionalism was often a characteristic of Primitive Methodist worship in many areas. Obelkevich quotes 'an unsympathetic outsider' who, writing in the *Retford News* on 29 August 1868, complained of:

> The vain, foolish, noisy and disgraceful ebullitions of excitement in which pleasure seekers love to indulge …
>
> The thudding and thumping of hundreds of boots and shoes till every fibre in the floor shivers as with an electric shock – and of such comments from the congregation as 'Isn't that a cutter' … 'First class' … 'Well done old—!' [23]

Eventually, however, as Obelkevich states, 'the vulgarity once a virtue at length became an embarrassment and spontaneity yielded to decorum in the chapels as in the wider society.' [24] By 1902 the Primitive Methodist could assert that 'people may no longer be got at through their emotions but by reason.'[25] This statement is psychologically and sociologically flawed but it reflects how far Primitive Methodism in general had moved from the noisy, charismatic worship particularly of its 'heroic period' when as shown earlier education on the part of its pioneer preachers was regarded as disadvantageous rather than the converse.

The movement from emotion to education is exemplified by the development of ministerial training and attempts to improve the standards of local preachers and Sunday school teachers.

Ministerial Training

Training 1820–65

Until 1865 a new entrant to the Primitive Methodist ministry received no formal training. The first Annual Meeting held at Hull in 1820 distinguished between 'local', 'hired local' and 'travelling' preachers. The first two were removable only by agreement of the circuits or districts. Travelling preachers could not be removed, except by the Connexional Annual Meeting. The minute was careful to point out that this was 'all the difference between them, in all other respects they are alike.' [26]

The Hull Annual Meeting also laid down the procedures for the admission of travelling preachers. Local preachers of either sex who were aspirants to the itinerancy were first interviewed by a circuit committee regarding their conversion and experience, doctrines held and which they intended to inculcate, views of the ministry and call to the work. Minutes of this interview were laid down before the 'quarter-day' board which might further examine each individual and recommend the candidate, in writing, to the district meeting. The recommendation would be accompanied by details of the candidates' personal circumstances and a 'description of his talents; how long he has been a local or hired local preacher; with an account of his usefulness, Christian experience, and conduct in the Society and a statement of the doctrines he holds.'[27]

The district meeting had the power either to set aside the circuit recommendation or to forward it to the Annual Meeting, which alone had the power to accept aspirants as travelling preachers. No candidate above the age of forty-five was acceptable.

An accepted candidate would then embark on a probation normally of four years after which, if approved, they would be placed on the 'Annual List'. Candidates not approved were either continued on probation or if there was no prospect of them being able to 'make their way' their probation would be discontinued and they would honour a pledge to return quietly, peaceably and at their own expense to their recommending circuits.[28]

Various modifications were made to the above procedure. In 1855 circuits were required to examine candidates not only on their doctrines but also on their ability to read and write and knowledge of the English language. In 1869 the ten District Examining Committees were replaced by only two, one called the Northern, the other, the Southern for the whole of the Home Stations.[29]

Although left to their own devices, this did not mean that probationers were not expected to study. The Consolidated Minutes of 1849 recognised that no rule could be made prescribing exactly what time a traveller should spend in sleep, study and ministerial labours but recommended that 'when health and circumstances allow not more that seven hours should be spent in sleep and not less than four hours in study and the rest of his time in family visiting and other active ministerial labours allowing necessary deduction for the time occupied in taking his meals.' [30] Probationers were also required to furnish their Examining Committees with a list of books read in each year. In 1862 probationers' examinations based on recommended set books were also prescribed for candidates for the ministry. [31] By 1869 probationers were required to pass written examinations based on papers furnished to their superintendent by the General Committee. [32]

The need to help probationers both with their studies and practical problems was recognised by Colin Campbell M'Kechnie who in 1854 founded the Sunderland Preachers' Association 'to associate the preachers more closely for purposes of mutual improvement with a view especially to aid and encourage probationers in qualifying themselves for their important work.'[33] The Association met for three days each year during which papers were read relating to ministerial work. Some of these papers were published in the *Christian Ambassador* which made its appearance in 1854 'to guide the younger brethren in their work.' From 1879 the title for the *Christian Ambassador* changed to the *Primitive Methodist Quarterly Review*, the *Holborn Review* (1910) and, after Union, the *London Quarterly and Holborn Review* until it ceased publication in 1968.

Kendall records that the establishment of the Preachers' Association was 'eyed askance' since it was feared that it 'might become a hot bed of revolutionary ideas and disturb Connexional peace.' [34] Nevertheless it led to the setting up of a similar Association by James Macpherson for the Manchester District. A scheme whereby young ministers were put under the care of senior ministers responsible for directing the studies of their junior colleagues and otherwise promoting their efficiency was adopted by the Connexion in 1860.

The need for the training of entrants to the ministry was increasingly recognised even though a proposal by John Gordon

Black in 1844 to establish a ministerial training college similar to the Wesleyan Colleges at Hoxton (1835), Richmond (1843) and Didsbury (1844) was soundly defeated. Writing of a Theological Institution John Petty stated in 1860 that:

> unquestionably the great body of our people would look upon such an institution with disapproval if not with jealousy and alarm, and whatever advantages might result from an institution of this character they would be dearly bought if they should be secured at the expense of Connexional peace and harmony and thereby hinder the activity and general co-operation of our societies to spread spiritual holiness throughout the land.[35]

Several factors contributed to this opposition. One was finance. The *Primitive Methodist Magazine* for 1855 recognised 'the fact that our community has not the means of affording us those facilities for mental culture which most older denominations have.'[36] There was a widespread fear that college training would adversely effect the Primitive Methodist emphasis on evangelism. The above article also warned junior preachers against:

> attaching too high an importance to merely intellectual acquirements or becoming aspirants after literary fame instead of aiming to win souls for Christ.[37]

In some quarters there was apprehension that college-trained men might become too professional and lose the ability to appeal to uneducated people. Milburn mentions a Mr E. Brick who in a debate on probationers' examinations at the Conference of 1871 contended that 'young men who were so gentlemanly that they could not blend with colliers, puddlers and tinkers were not the men for our ministry.'[38] Poor pay, arduous work and frequent changes of station also resulted in a high turnover of itinerants. Brown notes that over 40 per cent of Primitive Methodist itinerants who began between 1831 and 1871 did not last for more than four years.[39]

Yet by 1854 there were also several factors that highlighted the need to provide training for ministerial candidates. Several cases of ministerial inefficiency reported to the 1854 Conference led James Macpherson to move a resolution 'to prepare some legislation for testing the efficiency of candidates for the ministry either on entering or closing their probation.' [40] The result was the introduction in 1855 of standardised procedures both for the selection of candidates and the testing of probationers.[41] At first such tests were oral but later written examinations were also instituted. Gradually the process of candidature resolved into the involved process described in Chapter 5.

Circuits were also becoming smaller and retaining their ministers longer. In consequence ministers preached more frequently to the same people. The spread of secular education had caused many congregations to demand edification and literary culture rather than sermons which were variations on the themes of 'Ruin, Repentence and Redemption'. Although as Brown[42] says it was doubtful if the majority of them would have gone so far as the Editor of the *Primitive Methodist* who declared:

> The rustic dwellers in our villages, as well as the inhabitants of the large towns and cities, are better able to appreciate the truths of the gospel when they are presented decently and in order, and accompanied with the gifts and graces of a cultivated mind, than when they are flung pell-mell from the voluble mouths of ignorant and totally unlettered men.[43]

Ministers themselves must often have recognised the gulf between their own efforts at self-improvement and the education of their college-trained Baptist, Congregational and Wesleyan counterparts.

In 1865 Conference recognised the importance of ensuring that:

> Our young preachers should know how to prepare their own sermons and how to go through all the duties exacted of them in an efficient and successful manner.

and also that without such training:

> our Connexional status will be compromised and lowered. Sound scriptural theology and an acquaintance with the elements of a good English education are now, perhaps, more that ever necessary.[44]

Accordingly it was resolved to provide accommodation in the Elmfield House School for twenty students intended for the ministry.[45] Thus began the provision of full-time training for Primitive Methodist candidates, first at Elmfield, York, then at Sunderland and finally Manchester.

Elmfield (1865–8)

The first students were admitted to Elmfield with John Petty as their tutor on 25 July 1865. Petty had therefore not only responsibility for providing 'religious, commercial and classical' education for a school of boys aged between nine and fourteen but also ministerial training for up to twenty young men. In addition his wife acted as Matron of the school. The responsibilities were clearly an impossible burden and may have precipitated Petty's death at the age of sixty in April 1868.

Training at Elmfield seems to have been voluntary rather than compulsory since an accepted candidate could elect either to train or go straight into a circuit appointment. It was hoped that at least one candidate from each district would go to Elmfield.[46]

The fees for ministerial students were fixed at £30 of which the student was expected to pay at least half, the balance being met by the Connexion which set up a committee 'to devise means to raise funds for the purpose of affording instruction to young men intended for the ministry.'[47]

No details of the one-year ministerial curriculum provided at Elmfield appear to have survived. In any event Elmfield was only a temporary expedient. In 1866 Conference appointed a Committee 'to look out for suitable premises should they be required for a Ministerial Candidates' Institution and to report to the next Conference.'[48] In 1867 the former Infirmary in Chester Road, Sunderland, was acquired for this purpose.

Sunderland (1868–82)

The Sunderland Institute opened on 23 July 1868 with an initial intake of fifteen students. The Principal was Dr William Antliff (1813–84) who had begun his ministry 'ere he was seventeen, with little more learning than the proverbial "Three Rs".'[49] He applied himself to self-improvement and was awarded an honorary DD by an American university for his writings.

The curriculum of the Sunderland Institute is shown opposite. Students must have risen shortly after 5 a.m. to be ready for their first two-hour lecture from 6 to 8 a.m. and must have been ready for their breakfasts. The morning period of study was long. There was little time for relaxation and Saturday afternoons, when lectures finished for the day at 1 p.m., must have been the highlight of the week. On Sundays the students preached in the Sunderland District.[50]

The curriculum shows that of the forty-four hours spent in study, twelve (27 per cent) were devoted to such subjects of general education as arithmetic, geography and English grammar and history. This emphasis was essential since according to examiners' reports at least four-fifths of the students were on admission of 'very meagre academic attainments',[51] a fact which led to the institution of an entrance examination. Some six hours (13 per cent) were devoted to homiletics and other aspects of preaching.

Dr Antliff was described by a former student as 'a tall and stately person ... kindly and considerate to the men (such as were prepared to work) with a pawky kind of humour, which he doled out for our edification.' He did not, however, 'succeed as a tutor'.[52] It was almost impossible for one tutor to cope with all the subjects of the wide curriculum even at an elementary level and in 1877 Thomas Greenfield (1813–97) became Assistant Theological tutor. Kendall observes that Greenfield 'was a born teacher and would rather sit at the feet of a child and learn something than go to Conference.'[53] When Antliff retired in 1881 Greenfield was appointed Principal. His tenure only lasted one year because, not withstanding the enthusiasm of the Sunderland District for ministerial training, there was a desire for a more centrally located

MONDAY	*6 am–8 am* Biblical Literature & Hermeneutics	*9 am–11 am* Theology	*11 am–1 pm* Grammar	*3 pm–5 pm* Geography	*6 pm–8 pm* Arithmetic & Penmanship	
TUESDAY	*6 am–8 am* Logic	*9 am–11 am* English History	*11 am–1 pm* Examination & Instruction by Principal	*3 pm–5 pm* Elocution	*6 pm–8 pm* Primitive Methodist History	
WEDNESDAY	*6 am–8 am* Ecclesiastical History	*9 am–11 am* Sermonising	*11 am–12 pm* Lecture on Homiletics or some other subject by the Principal	*12 pm–1 pm* Sermonising	*3 pm–5 pm* Geography	*6 pm–7 pm* Biblical Literature & Hermeneutics
THURSDAY	*6 am–8 am* Logic	*9 am–11 am* Theology	*11 am–12 pm* Lecture on Theology or Ecclesiastical History by the Principal	*12 pm–1 pm* Theology	*3 pm–5 pm* Ecclesiastical History	*6 pm–7 pm* PM Methodist Rules & Usage
FRIDAY	*6 am–8 am* Biblical Literature	*9 am–11 am* Theology	*11 am–12 pm* Criticism of Thursday evening sermon	*12 pm–1 pm* Grammar	*6 pm–8 pm* English History	
SATURDAY	*6 am–8 am* Rhetoric	*9 am–11 am* Mental Science	*11 am–1 pm* Moral Science			

An hour is allowed for breakfast and family worship	8 am–9 am
Two hours are allowed for dinner and relaxation	1 pm–3 pm
An hour is allowed for tea	5 pm–6 pm
An hour is allowed for relaxation in the evening	8 pm–9 pm
Supper and family worship	9 pm–10 pm
Retire at 10.30 pm	

The students meet in class on Wednesday evening at 7 pm led by the Principal.
They preach in turns on Thursday evenings at 7 pm led by the Principal
The half holiday on Saturdays is at the discretion of the Principal
Sundays are spent in preaching in Primitive Methodist and other chapels

TABLE 3: PROGRAMME OF STUDIES, PRIMITIVE METHODIST THEOLOGICAL INSTITUTE, SUNDERLAND

college. In 1875 a Conference Committee recommended the establishment of a college in Manchester to accommodate thirty students.[54] The original intention was to supplement rather than supplant Sunderland but after 1882 the Sunderland Institute virtually ceased to operate. Over the fourteen years of its existence the Sunderland Institute provided training for some three hundred men, some of whom had distinguished ministries. By 1880 it was reported that 'the necessity for a well trained ministry is generally acknowledged. The growing intelligence of the people demand it and it is not now possible to regard the matter with indifference.'[55] Financial support was, however, meagre as evidenced by a plaintive note in the 1871 minutes 'surely with more than 160,000 members in the Connexion more than £147 a year might be expected.'[56]

Manchester (1881–1932)

Manchester was chosen not only because of its centrality to the body of the Connexion but because an association with Owens' College, founded in 1851, might enable some students to acquire an even wider training than their own Church could provide.[57] A site in the Alexandra Park area of Manchester was acquired in 1876 but it was not until 24 June 1878 that the stone-laying of the new College took place and 22 August 1881 before the new building, costing £8,203, was inaugurated with James Macpherson as Principal.[58]

The beginnings of the new College were not auspicious. In 1880 the Connexion had over-estimated the demand for probationers and had difficulty in funding places for all those becoming available. It was therefore decided to temporarily close both the Sunderland and Manchester Colleges for a year and it was not until July 1882 that Manchester received its first intake of ten students although the College had accommodation for thirty. Sunderland never re-opened. The new College was also burdened by debt on the building and the expenses of maintenance. In 1886 an appeal to the districts was disappointing. Nine districts failed to respond, eight others promised or contributed £21.10. The

Liverpool and Manchester Districts gave £14.10s and £60 respectively. Private donations from eight persons, including W. P. Hartley who gave £200, amounted to £580. The rest of the Connexion promised £77.[59]

By 1889, however, when Revd Joseph Wood DD succeeded Macpherson as Principal, the debt had been paid and the Connexional finances put in order by a system of annual levy on the circuits for the 'Connexional Fund' out of which the expenses of the College were met by a yearly grant.[60]

The two great names in the history of what initially was known as the Manchester Theological Institute are Hartley and Peake who together revolutionised Primitive Methodist ministerial training.

W. P. Hartley (1846–1922)

In 1891 Hartley promised to donate £200 annually for five years, conditional on the extension of training from one to two years and the appointment to the College staff of a university graduate who 'would have a free hand in tuition without interference from the Principal.'[61] This latter requirement was met in 1892 by the appointment of Peake. In 1895 Conference resolved that some extension of the College was essential to meet the increased need of the Connexion for probationers. Hartley assumed the entire £12,500 cost of the extensions, which included a new dining hall, a lecture room, common room, clock-tower and increased accommodation to cater for sixty students. This gift was conditional on the course of training being ultimately extended to three years and help given to students who because of straitened circumstances found difficulty in meeting their college expenses.[62] The latter point was important. In 1894 four students asked to be recommended for stationing because of their inability to maintain themselves for a second year of training.[63] These extensions were completed in 1898. In 1903 Conference regarded it as eminently desirable to extend the course of training to three years. This involved providing accommodation at the College for an additional forty students or a total complement of 100. Again

Hartley promised to provide the additional buildings and furniture costing £20,000 and also to fund certain other expenses in relation to the third-year fees of students and additional tutorial assistance.[64] The new buildings included a large dining hall, study block, library and College chapel. The new buildings were opened at the Conference of 1906. The following year Conference resolved that the Institution should be renamed Hartley College.[65] By 1905 the College staff comprised the Principal, William Johnson FLS, A. S. Peake MA, A. L. Humphries MA and W. Lansdell Wardle MA, BD. In addition to Peake, Hartley had agreed to finance the salaries of the other two members of staff for a limited period. The same arrangement was made on the appointment of a fourth tutor, Atkinson Lee, in 1908.[66] When, in 1905, the College affiliated with the Divinity Faculty of Manchester University, Hartley agreed to pay the fees not only of third-year students but of those taking a College course of five years to obtain BA and BD degrees. This arrangement was continued up to Hartley's death in 1922. On the twenty-first anniversary of Peake's appointment Hartley marked the occasion by donating three stained-glass windows to the College chapel and also a number of scholarships and half-scholarships for needy students.[67] For many years Hartley also made an annual book allowance of five guineas to ministers[68] and in 1896 founded the Hartley Lectureship. Other ways in which Hartley moulded the Connexion, such as Chapel Aid, the provision of orphan homes and Connexional headquarters at Holborn Hall, are all examples of the point made by Liston Pope that affluent members are 'the more easily able to influence the life of an institution after they have attained comparative economic wealth because a struggling sectarian group stands in need of many things money can buy.'[69]

A. S. Peake (1865–1929)

In May 1891, Arthur Samuel Peake, MA, Fellow of Merton College and tutor at Mansfield College, Oxford, was introduced to Hartley by Mr J. Harryman Taylor, then preparing for the Primitive Methodist ministry at Mansfield College. The fact of a

Primitive Methodist candidate studying at a Congregational college is itself of interest. Peake, like Taylor, the son of a Primitive Methodist minister, was disturbed at the gulf between the three-to-four-year course provided at Mansfield and the one year of training with a curriculum that was 'antiquated and reactionary'[70] available at the Primitive Methodist College in Manchester. Peake's views were conveyed by Hartley to the Committee of the Manchester institution along with the suggestion that they should adopt a new approach to training and endeavour to induce Peake to leave Oxford for Manchester. Peake initially found the proposal in nearly every way unattractive. On the other hand he recognised that the opportunity of serving his church was a great one and his mind gradually moved in the direction of acceptance.[71] Peake's appointment was ratified at the 1892 Conference. When outlining his proposed curriculum to Conference, Peake explained that its purpose was 'not to produce showy men but plain, practical, hard working men and good Primitive Methodist ministers.' His aim was to make 'cultured evangelists'.[72]

Immediately on his appointment as tutor Peake instituted six distinct biblical courses, three on the Old and three on the New Testament.[73] Thus, as Peake stated, 'for the first time, the official training of the ministry in the Primitive Methodist Church was in contact with the modern spirit and outlook.'[74] As shown in Chapter 6 there were always those who viewed Peake's critical approach to biblical study with suspicion and hostility. Such opposition was, however, largely dissipated by Peake's humour and Christian character. As a contemporary testified 'he was Christ-like, just as you imagined Christ was and desired men to be.' His students were proud to be 'Peake's men'. Far from being destroyed, faith was strengthened and their understanding of the Bible enriched.

In 1904, the first interdenominational Faculty of Divinity in a British university was founded at Manchester and Peake was appointed John Rylands Professor of Biblical Exegesis. He thus became the first non-Anglican to become a professor of divinity in an English university.

Peake's industry was phenomenal. In addition to his work at Hartley and the University he lectured at the Lancashire Independent and United Methodist Colleges. On vacations he often worked for fifteen hours daily. He wrote or edited over thirty books including the famous *Commentary on the Bible* and numerous authoritative articles. This scholarship was recognised by honorary DD degrees from Aberdeen and Oxford.

He advocated Methodist Union not least because he believed it to be the harbinger of the reunion of Christendom. From 1922 he attended the Lambeth Conferences and in 1928 'The Reunion of the Christian Churches' was the title of his presidential address to the National Church Council. Shortly after his death in 1928 'one who knew him well' wrote:

> Perhaps it was Peake's greatest service, not merely to his own communion but to the whole religious life of England that he helped to save us from a fundamentalist controversy such as that which has devastated large sections of the Church in America.[75]

With the unfailing support of W. P. Hartley he transformed Primitive Methodism by imparting to his students a sense of vision, vocation and in the best sense of the term 'professionalism', which as ministers they transmitted to the whole church.

In 1922 the staff and students of Hartley united with those of the United Methodist, Victoria Park College.[76] This arrangement continued until 1934 when Victoria Park closed and Hartley was renamed Hartley-Victoria College.

Local preachers and Sunday school training

Developments in secular education and the increased expectations of members also compelled the Connexion to recognise the importance of improving the standards of local preachers and Sunday school teachers. A Local Preachers' Training Committee with District Training Secretaries and Tutors was established in 1904. Examinations for aspirant local preachers were also introduced for which correspondence training was provided. These examinations, however, were voluntary and in 1928 it was reported the number of examinees was 'hardly a third of the full strength of our recruits for this year.' [77]

Although a directive for the formation of a Primitive Methodist Sunday School Union was issued in 1832 this was not implemented until 1874. Unions at district level were, however, set up in Leeds and Manchester in 1857 and 1874 respectively. The Sunday School Union established Catechumen Classes (1877). Between them the Book Room and the Sunday School Union produced a mass of teaching aids and magazines for Sunday school teachers. The latter included *The Teacher's Assistant*, first issued in 1873, which became the *Sunday School Journal and Teacher's Magazine* and, as the *Primitive Methodist Sunday School Magazine*, last appeared in 1932. Teacher's examinations were also introduced which, from certificates in my possession, my father appears to have taken annually over a period of some thirty-two years. In 1900 the subject was 'Our Lord's Teaching'; in 1902, 'The Church of Christ'; in 1908, 'What has God wrought?' The latest certificates I have are for 1932 and 1933 when the subjects were respectively 'Nonconformity, Its Origin and Its Progress' and 'The ABC of Psychology'. In both years father obtained a First Class Advanced Division Certificate.

Revivalism to recreation

Random statements in the Annual Conference 'Address to the Stations' printed in the Minutes of the Primitive Methodist Conference suggest that at the Connexional level the revivalist ethos was never completely lost. 'We have been evangelistic through all our history and this gift and practice more than anything else explains our past and present. While our churches should be "societies of the saved" they should also be "societies of saviours". ' [78] In 1907 hope was expressed that the Connexional Centenary celebrations would harbinger 'the revival of a healthy evangelism and a return to orderly open air mission work.' [79]

At the local level, however, revivalism had a low priority

compared with concerns for the society to which members belonged. Such concerns related to the payment of chapel debts, extension or improvements of buildings, the provision of a social life centred in the society and internal chapel politics. Missions, conducted by visiting evangelists, might be held to 'revive a declining cause' but such missions were often to the converted rather than outsiders and had little permanent effect. What Obelkevich asserts of Primitive Methodism in rural Lincolnshire seems to have been broadly true of the whole Connexion. After 1860 'evangelism shifted its aim from outsiders to insiders, from adults to children, from the ungodly to the immature.'[80] Moreover, as Stark observes: 'dissenting bodies do lose their sectarian souls but they do retain their sectarian bodies.'[81] With both Wesley and early Primitive Methodism evangelism had been a life-or-death matter of saving souls from hell and, through such agencies as class and prayer meetings, developing a spirituality that would prepare them for heaven. By the end of the nineteenth and in the early decades of the twentieth centuries religion had for many people become one of several possible leisure or recreational activities.

While, as shown in Chapter 6, Puritan-derived Primitive Methodist attitudes to Sabbatarianism, temperance, gambling, dancing and novel reading persisted at the local level up to the 1930s, these were sometimes modified by local considerations. In 1866, for example, 'Annual Address to the Stations' protested against the introduction of an element of entertainment into Sunday school anniversary services.

> Is there not too much of the worldly element in the singing, reciting and other matters pertaining to anniversaries …? How often we feel that the devotions and moral influences of our special services are damaged and even destroyed by the excitement, singing, reciting etc. attendant in them. To put a sermon or a prayer into the midst of a concert or a dramatic exhibition would often seem sorely incongruous, and not less so does it seem frequently to mix the worship of God with the performance of

> worldly and profane musicians and singers and the amateur theatricals of Sunday School children ... We hope all who have the management of our schools will seriously ponder the necessity for honouring God in his house, and guarding against anything that tends to mental and religious dissipation, or to encourage among the young a love for display, for carnal amusements or for theatrical performances. We may pander too much to carnal appetites and be too anxious to attract crowds of mere onlookers or to secure large collections. There are higher considerations for Christian men and churches than merely winning applause, pleasing worldly people, or publishing large collections.[82]

'Higher considerations' there may have been but the principal consideration was usually to augment chapel and Sunday school funds by attracting the support of those whose connection with the society, apart from sending their children to Sunday school, was only nominal. Singing and recitations involving their children were inducements to such parents to attend and financially support the Sunday School Anniversary services.

In any event, especially in town chapels, the noisy, exuberant uninhibited worship of early Ranterism was gradually being replaced by services which emphasised respectability and decorum involving trained choirs who contributed anthems and solos. Congregations also required preaching to be edifying, with an intellectual content rather than the emotional appeal to 'turn to the Lord and seek salvation' of earlier years.

The consequence of the strict Primitive Methodist ethic of 'very strict Sabbath observance and abstinence from what were styled as "vain and worldly amusements" in which dancing, the theatre and card-playing were excluded' meant, as Peake recognised, that 'the social life of members was concentrated on a small scale in their homes, while on a larger scale it had its centre in their chapel.'[83]

Hours of work might be long and labour hard but:

> the week night preaching service, the class meeting, the tea meeting followed by the public meeting, the sewing meeting for the sale of work or bazaar, the choir practice, the occasional entertainment or lecture, the anniversary of the chapel or the school provided very rich opportunities for the cultivation of the spiritual life and the satisfaction of the religious instincts.

They also fostered a spirit of fellowship and camaraderie.

Indoor and outdoor recreational activities aimed to attract and retain members both young and old. Indoor activities for the young included Bands of Hope, the Christian Endeavour and later, uniformed organisations. Football and cricket teams attempted to retain the allegiance of young men. These developments were not universally welcomed.

As late as 1921 a correspondent in the *Primitive Methodist Leader* hoped that Primitive Methodist Societies 'would not respond to the "bribery of providing a football team".'[84] He was fighting a battle already lost. In 1890 the *Primitive Methodist Magazine* had daringly suggested that 'an occasional dance in the privacy of the home' was a matter that could safely be left to the individual conscience.[85]

It had to be conceded, however, that these attempts to attract adherents through recreation were unsuccessful. In 1924 another writer stated that many Primitive Methodist societies had become 'semi-institutional, finding room for tennis, cricket, football and billiards'. Sadly, he concluded 'we have experimented with every invention of which the novelty has gone and the failure remains.'[86] But at the local level revivalism had long given way to respectability as the Annual Address to the Stations for 1913 referred to 'the disconcerting fact that half the candidates [for the ministry] were unable to report any conversions, and that there was a lack of definiteness and the evangelical note in their sermons.' After considering some extenuating reasons it concluded with the revealing statement: 'It is probably true that these young men are reflections of the spirit of the churches from which they come.'[87]

Self-centredness to social and missionary concern

The movement from 'self-centred (or personal) religion to a culture-centred religion or from "experience" to a social institution' is one of the twenty-one facets of the movement from a sect to a denomination identified by Liston Pope. [88] With the decline in revivalism Primitive Methodism as a Connexion became inward-looking, obsessed by such issues as chapel building and ministerial training and not until the 1870s was attention given to such areas of social concern as the establishment of London and Provincial Missions and chaplains to Armed Forces. Connexional orphanages were an even later development. Outreach also encompassed overseas missions.

London and provincial missions

On 18 January 1895 a sub-committee appointed to consider the relationship of social work to the mission work of Primitive Methodism resolved 'that we recognise social work as a part of Christian endeavour and service.' [89] This resolution was only a recognition of social outreach in the slum areas pioneered by Thomas Jackson in Walthamstow almost twenty years earlier.

The condition of the inner-city poor was highlighted by the Congregational Union's pamphlet, *The Bitter Cry of Outcast London* (1883) and the enquiry of Charles Booth, *Life and Labour in London* (1886). The former referred to

> pestilential human rookeries … where tens of thousands are crowded together amidst horrors which call to mind what we have heard of the middle passage of a slave ship. [90]

The latter likened the life of inhabitants of the tenements courts and back-to-back houses of London's slums to that of 'savages, with viccisitudes of extreme hardship and occasional excess.' [91]

The churches, both Anglican and Nonconformist, were

already aware of such conditions and in 1864 William Booth had begun the Christian Mission (later the Salvation Army) in one of the worst London districts. In due course William Booth's *In Darkest England and the Way Out* (1890) again described the desperate economic, social and moral conditions in the slums. Slum inhabitants were, at best, indifferent and, at worst, hostile to the churches. The situation was as Munson says simply: 'if the poor will not go to the chapel on the chapel's terms, the chapels must go to the people on their terms.'[92] An attempt to do this was the Wesleyan Forward Movement initiated by Hugh Price Hughes, which, beginning with the West London Mission opened in 1887, endeavoured to wed evangelical zeal to Christian responsibility for the weak and destitute.

Munson points out that Primitive Methodism 'came relatively late in the race, partly because most, if not all, of their work in the largest cities was already with working people.'[93] The Primitive Methodist pioneers in this social outreach were Thomas Jackson and William Flanagan. In 1884 Jackson began home missionary work in Lower Clapton in a dilapidated former theatre known as the Old Dust Hole. The outreach provided by Jackson included dinners for the poor and breakfast in winter for school pupils. In 1892 it is recorded that in one week Jackson had given 1300 free meals to destitute children, distributed 570 quarts of soup and 100lbs of bread.[94] Other philanthropic activities were a clothes and boots store, the services of a doctor and the opening of a dispensary. Later a convalescent home was acquired at Southend-On-Sea and a holiday home for women and children in the same resort. In 1896 Jackson persuaded the Connexion to purchase the Working Lads' Institute in Whitechapel which *inter alia* became a Home for Friendless and Orphan Lads. The work of the Mission was later extended to homeless men, discharged prisoners and first offenders.

In 1891 James Flanagan began home mission work in the Old Kent Road in a former public house known as The Old Kent Road Tap. This building was demolished and in 1900 a new suite of buildings known as St George's Hall became the headquarters of the South-East London Mission which, like its Whitechapel counterpart, provided a wide range of social and philanthropic activities.

A Central Hall on the Wesleyan pattern was opened in Birmingham. By 1932, the Connexion had seventeen provincial missions in addition to five in London.

The Armed Forces

Outreach to the Armed Forces began in 1885 when a 'special agent' was appointed 'for work among the soldiers of Aldershot'. [95]

Although at the time there were only twenty-eight declared Primitive Methodists in the Army, George Standing was appointed in 1909 as officiating chaplain to Primitive Methodists under the Aldershot Command. On the outbreak of the First World War the United Army Board was formed to supply chaplains to Baptist, Congregational and Primitive and United Methodist members of the Forces. Between 1915 and 1918 forty-seven Primitive Methodist chaplains served under the United Board of whom one received the DSO, four MCs and three OBEs. [96]

After the 1914–18 war, Standing was commissioned as a Regular Chaplain, first class and, by 1932 had become deputy Chaplain General. By 1932 twenty-one Primitive Methodist ministers were serving the Forces (one Navy, seventeen Army and three Royal Air Force). It is not clear how many of these were full-time, regular appointments.

Connexional orphanages

Due to the initiative of the Revd Joseph Peck (1836–1900) the Conference of 1887 sanctioned the establishment of an orphanage 'for the fatherless children of Primitive Methodists and others who may be in needy circumstances.' [97] This was opened at Alresford, Hampshire in May 1889 and initially provided accommodation for fifty children of both sexes 'not under 5 or above the age of 10 years', who were not 'diseased, deformed or infirm'. [98]

Funding from Sir W. P. Hartley enabled a further two pairs of orphan homes to be built at Harrogate in 1907. These were later extended through the generosity of Sir Thomas Robinson. By 1932 the orphanages accommodated 132 children. After Methodist Union the Primitive Methodist homes became an auxiliary of the National Childrens' Home and Orphanage.

Overseas missions

In the late eighteenth and throughout the nineteenth century Christ's command to 'go out into all the world and preach the gospel to every creature' was the basis of missionary enterprise both at home and overseas. Evangelical concern for the redemption of every soul led to the establishment of a whole range of overseas missionary societies. The Baptist Missionary Society (1792) was quickly followed by the London Missionary Society (1795), the Church Missionary Society (1799), the British and Foreign Bible Society (1804) and the Methodist Missionary Society (1813).

Primitive Methodism spread to the USA and the Dominions through emigration and missionaries from the home country were sent to work among the white settlers in New York (1829), Canada (1830) and New Zealand and Australia (1844). In 1846 Robert Ward began to mission the Maori natives but was hindered by the Maori war of 1843–69. Ward's efforts represent the first Primitive Methodist attempts to evangelise a non-Christian overseas people.

Africa, however, was the focus of most missionary activity directed at the conversion of 'the heathen in his blindness'.[99] The Primitive Methodist Conference held at Norwich in 1837 considered whether the Connexion ought to prepare a mission to Africa. Financial stringency prevented any action as evidenced by a statement in 1857 that 'the Conference cannot at present, commence a mission at Port Natal.'[100] Three years later the Jubilee Conference held at Tunstall authorised the sending of 'two men to this interesting field of missionary labour as soon as suitable men could be found.'[101]

Ten years elapsed, however, before three missionaries landed at their respective destinations. On 21 February 1879 R.W. Burnett and Henry Roe arrived at Santa Isabel on the Spanish island of Fernando Po to minister to a small community of Protestant Christians left behind when, due to Catholic persecution, the Baptist Missionary Society had withdrawn from the island. This community had been discovered by two Liverpool Primitive Methodist sailors when their ship had anchored off the island. The dispatch of Burnett and Roe was the outcome of a petition to send missionaries to Fernando Po forwarded to Conference by the Liverpool Second Circuit to which the two sailors, W. Robinson and J. Hands, belonged.

The third missionary, Henry Buckenham, landed at Port Elizabeth, South Africa on 20 November 1870 and travelled some 300 miles before arriving at Aliwal North on the Orange River. In 1905 Kendall described Aliwal North, which then had 1,608 members in a circuit 150 miles long and 30 miles wide with eight sub-centres, as 'our widest and most prosperous mission station.'[102] Henry Buckenham was also in charge of a small team, which sailed from Dartmouth on 26 April 1889 to establish a mission in Central Africa. From leaving England it took the team four years and eight months to reach Mashukulmbwe-land, which became the base for the Primitive Methodist South Central African Mission in what was then Northern Rhodesia.[103]

Four days before the Buckenham party reached their destination, two other missionaries, Robert Farley and J. Marcus Brown, held their first service at Archibongville in Southern Nigeria on 17 December 1893.

As with most missionary work, evangelism went hand in hand with education and healing. Schools and training colleges were established at all centres. In 1915 Herbert Gerrard MB, ChB went to Northern Rhodesia as the Connexion's first medical missionary. At the time of the Union in 1932 the Connexion had three medical missionaries, two of whom were ministers, and four missionaries in Fernando Po, twenty-six in Nigeria and six in Central Africa.

Political neutrality to political activity

As shown in Chapter 3 from 1835 Primitive Methodism was, officially, politically neutral. The abandonment of this neutrality and the emergence of active Connexional support for the Liberal party is described in Chapter 9. The neutrality, however, applied only to the travelling preachers and the use of the chapels for the propagation of party politics. It could not apply to the laity and chapels, in fact, were often hot beds of political and trade union activity.

Davies correctly points out that when a former Secretary of the Labour Party, Morgan Phillips, declared that 'British Socialism owed more to Methodism than to Marx', [104] he was referring not to Wesleyan, but Primitive Methodism, for it was among the latter that the first leaders of the Labour movement were to be found.

Thompson states that to read the biography of the Wesleyan, Jabez Bunting besides that of Hugh Bourne who founded the Primitive Methodists 'is to pass between two different worlds':

> Bunting looked down upon the workers from the heights of Connexional intrigue: Bourne and Clowes were of the working people. Bunting was intent upon ushering Methodism to a seat on the right hand of the Establishment; the Primitives still lived in the world of hardship and persecution of Wesleyanism's origin. We can scarcely discuss the two churches in the same terms. [105]

Although, as Davies states, 'Primitive Methodists were active in the Trades Unions almost from the moment in 1825 at which it became legal for working people to "combine" for the purpose of redressing their grievances',[106] their influence was mainly confined to mining and agriculture. In these industries Primitive Methodist influence was immense. Wearmouth provides a mass of evidence to show the important contribution of Methodists and particularly Primitive Methodists to the development of trade unionism in the

Northumberland, Durham, Yorkshire and North Western coalfields, in agriculture and in textiles.[107] Sidney Webb also paid tribute to the Methodist influence in the Durham coalfields:

> It is the men who are Methodists, and in the Durham County especially, the local preachers of the Primitive Methodists, whom we find taking the lead and filling posts of influence. From their ranks have come an astonishingly large proportion of the Trade Union leaders from check weighers and lodge chairmen up to county officials and committee men.[108]

In agriculture, although the Tolpuddle Martyrs were Wesleyans, there was later the influence of such Primitive Methodist trade union leaders as Joseph Arch who were able to exploit a situation described by Scotland:

> For generations many labourers felt that they had been held down by the parson's oppressive, futuristic salvation, which argued them to be content with their present poverty stricken conditions in the hope of heavenly riches to come. By the early 1870s, many agricultural workers were no longer willing to tolerate such a doctrine. To have appealed to the mass of farm labourers therefore, the delegates needed to offer salvation 'Now'. It was because Methodist salvation was a 'present' salvation based on an inward assurance with its associated outworking of altruistic love that it contributed the necessary basis thus in the words of Professor J. H. S. Kent: 'The tiny Methodist chapels functioned as citadels from which attacks were mounted on the social and economic enemies.'[109]

As Hempton observes, however, 'the chief problem lies not in explaining why a high percentage of trade union leaders were Methodists, but in understanding what kind of trade unionism they led.'[110] This point is developed by Moore, who shows that while Methodism did produce political leaders among working men 'it did not produce leaders who would articulate class interests as such'.[111] This was a consequence of a perspective which divided society not along class lines but into the saved and the unsaved, the good and the bad. In Durham, where most mining companies were paternalistic and the owners in varying degrees Nonconformist, 'Methodists identified themselves as much with employers who shared their religious and moral outlook as with the wider working class community, which exhibited a mixture of respect and disdain for the Methodist religion and morality.'[112]

The emphasis of Methodist trade union leaders was therefore on conciliation rather than confrontation and with fairer shares and greater equality within the existing social framework rather than class conflict and revolution.

As shown in Chapter 9 Primitive Methodists, along with the other evangelical Nonconformists particularly the Baptists, hoped that a strong Nonconformist representation in a Liberal Government would achieve such aims as the disestablishment of the Church of England and the abolition of sectarian education, although Wesleyans and Congregationalists were less in sympathy with such objectives. Because of these denominational differences Liberal leaders tended to be wary of being too closely associated with Nonconformity. Opposition to Balfour's 1902 Education Act finally forced the Primitive Methodists to abandon what had become only a nominal political neutrality and become political activists. In 1903 and again in 1906 the Conference gave its official support to securing the return of a Liberal Government and the encouragement of a campaign of passive resistance to the payment of that part of the local rate applicable to education. In 1903 the Primitive Methodist Leader unequivocally asserted:

> Labour and Liberalism are one in spirit and aim and must act as one. Toryism is the historical and persistent foe of the labouring classes. For the sake of the million toilers of Britain we must defeat it. Every voter and non-voter is wanted in this fight. Cancel all engagements that interfere with election work. Give your nights and days to

the task. Seek first and seek only the Kingdom of God in and through the General Election.[113]

The emasculation of Birrell's 1906 Education Bill by the House of Lords and the repeated failures between 1906 and 1910 to reverse the 1902 Act led to Primitive Methodist disillusionment with Liberalism. In any event disputes between Asquith and Lloyd George during the First World War weakened Liberalism and its radical traditions were inherited by Labour. The decline in Primitive Methodist Liberal and increase in Primitive Methodist Labour parliamentary representation between 1906 and 1929 is shown below.[114]

Election	Primitive Methodist Liberal candidates	Primitive Methodist Liberal members	Primitive Methodist Labour candidates	Primitive Methodist Labour members	Total Members
1906	5	4	3	3	7
1910 (Jan)	2	2	7	5	7
1910 (Dec)	3	2	5	5	7
1918	–	–	6	6	6
1922	7	2	10	5	7
1923	10	4	8	6	10
1924	9	2	6	4	6
1929	16	1	11	9	10

Political activism enhanced the national standing of Primitive Methodism in at least two ways. Members who were active in local and national politics raised public esteem for the Church. In 1907 the Connexion could boast that representatives to the Annual Conference included 'two members of Parliament, two Mayors, a host of Aldermen, Justices of the Peace, Councillors and Guardians of the Poor.'[115]

The abandonment of political neutrality over the education issue strengthened relationships with other Nonconformist denominations through the National Free Church Council. Common cause over education was one important factor in the Connexion moving 'from non co-operation … towards co-operation with the established (Nonconformist) churches of the community.' Thus in 1904 the Annual Address to the Stations declared:

> We do not joy supremely in our denominationalism but rather in the fact that we are privileged to form part of the holy and catholic Church of the Lord Jesus Christ; and to take our place in the great task of the evangelisation of the world.[116]

Confederation to centralisation

Up to 1876 Primitive Methodism tended to be decentralised rather than centralised. Until 1843, the Book Room was located at Bemersley Farm, the home of the Bournes, which was also the Connexional headquarters or 'office'. Possession of the headquarters and the control of publications had the disadvantage of concentrating too much power in the hands of the Bournes. The remoteness of Bemersley and difficulties of transport and communication meant that there was only tenuous control of the circuits, and later, districts, some of which, as in the case of Hull were geographically extensive. Both circuits and districts had therefore considerable opportunities to take local initiatives. It was, in fact, local rather than central initiative that led the Connexion to expand.

Although from 1820 Conference was the ultimate legislative authority, in practice Primitive Methodism was, as Kendall states, a confederation, first of circuits and, from 1824, of districts. In this situation the publications of the Book Room, especially the *Primitive Methodist Magazine*, the *Children's Magazine* and the 'small' and 'large' hymn books which appeared in 1821 and 1824 respectively were not only a major source of revenue but also a means of unifying a somewhat loosely knit confederation.

Kendall identifies a number of reasons why, between 1853 and 1878 District Meetings 'gained in power, popularity and prestige at the expense of the Conference.'[117]

One factor was Conference itself. Until 1876 the Primitive Methodist Conference only comprised some eighty members. These were the twelve permanent members required by the Deed Poll, four persons appointed by the preceding Conference and six representatives from each of the districts in the proportion of four laymen to two ministers. By legislation passed in 1845 and only partly rescinded in 1865, lay delegates were required to have been officials for twelve years. Ministerial delegates had to have travelled for eighteen successive years, twelve as superintendents. These rules, as Kendall noted, tended to make the Conference 'a court of elders, cautious and conservative both in temper and legislative action.' Moreover, the Conference was 'seclusive as well as somewhat exclusive.'[118]

In contrast to the remoteness of Conference the District Meeting was, so far as the circuits were concerned, the gathering of the year particularly because at them ministers were stationed for the coming year. While 'Districtism' had its dangers, especially inter-district rivalry and the tendency to view issues from a district rather than a Connexional perspective, it also made for originality and variety. Some initiatives pioneered at district level were later adopted as Connexional policy. These included overseas missions, ministerial training, and the Sunday School Union associated respectively with the Norwich, Sunderland and Leeds Districts.

The removal in 1878 of the restriction by which ministers were required to 'travel' within the area of a particular district and the division in 1885 of the wide Sunderland District into three marked the end of 'Districtism'. The former, by allowing ministers to accept invitations from any part of the Connexion, led to the demise of the 'District Man' and the end of decentralised district stationing. The latter led to an era of partition, which removed the disproportionate influence due to their numerical representation of the larger districts.

OVERSIGHT OF THE CONNEXION

1 General Committee
2 General Secretary to the Church and Secretary to the General Holborn Hall Committee

Home and Overseas Missions

3 General Missionary Committee

5 Secretary to the Home Mission Committee
6 Temperance and Social Welfare Committee
7 Committee of the Temperance Society and Band of Hope Union
8 London Forward Movement Committee
9 White Chapel Institute and Homes Committee
10 Navy, Army and Air Force Committee

11 Orphan Homes General Committee
12 Orphan Homes Management Committee
13 Orphan Homes Executive Committee
14 Orphanage Gifts and Settlements Trustees
15 Secretary of the Foreign Missionary Committee
16 Women's Missionary Federation
17 Young People's Missionary Department

Publishing

Connexional Editor
General Book Steward and Secretary to Book Committee

4 General Book Committee

Control of Miscellaneous Funds

18 Connexional Fund
19 Connexional Equalisation Fund
20 Sustentation Fund
21 General Chapel Fund Committee
22 Ministers' Benevolent Fund
23 Chapel Loan Fund
24 Superannuated Ministers, Widows and Orphans Fund

Local Preache

25 Local Preachers Central Trainin
26 Local Preachers Central Trainin Council

isterial Matters	Sunday School and Youth Matters	Committees regarding Methodist Union	Miscellaneous
:andidates ieneral :xaminations :ommittee	31 General Sunday School Union Committee	36 Methodist Union Committee	40 Peake Members Committee
Iartley College :ommittee	32 Christian Endeavour Council	37 Consultation Committee	
itudents' :xaminations :ommittee	33 Executive Committee of Sunday School Union	38 Hymn Book Preparation Committee	
'robationers ieneral Examining :ommittee	34 Central Council of Christian Endeavour	39 Tune Book Committee	
	35 Education Committee		

TABLE 4:
PRIMITIVE METHODIST CENTRALISED COMMITTEES AND THEIR CONCERNS, 1932

Conference also became a larger and more representative body. The President of Conference also ceased to be simply the chairman of its proceedings and like his Wesleyan counterpart became the representative of the Connexion visiting all parts of the country during his year of office.

Many other developments also evidenced that the Connexion had ceased to be a confederacy and become an organic unity. These included the reorganisation of finance, such as the establishment in 1898 of the Sustentation Fund which ensured a minimum spend for each minister. Church building was controlled and assisted by the Chapel Aid Association and a Church Extension Fund established in 1889 and 1900 respectively.

By the end of the nineteenth century, Primitive Methodism like most denominations had begun to group its major activities such as ministerial training, welfare and oversight, home and overseas missions, Sunday school work and property, in addition to publishing, into centralised departments under the control of a designated head who reported to an appropriate committee. The growth of Primitive Methodist bureaucratisation is evidenced by the increase of such committees. In 1875 with 169,720 members with significant numbers in Australia, Canada and New Zealand there appear to have been two ministers in full-time Connexional appointments (Book Steward and Editor) and seven Connexional Committees namely the General Committee, General Missionary Committee, Book Committee, Superannuated Ministers, Widows and Orphans Fund, Conference Fund and Sunday School General Committee. By 1932 when the membership stood at 222,978 there were six ministerial committees the concerns of which are broadly grouped as shown in TABLE 4. Reporting to these centralised bodies were formidable layers of District and Circuit Committees.

Centralised departments and committees required accommodation. In 1843 the Book Room was moved from the Bemersley Farm to premises in Sutton Street, London. New premises at the Junction of Jewin and Aldersgate Street were acquired in 1895. In 1908 Sir William Hartley acquired the former Holborn Town Hall for use as Connexional headquarters. This enabled those in charge of departments including the General Secretary of the Connexion, the Missionary Secretaries, the Editor and the Book Steward, to have easy access to each other. The adaptation of the hall required extensive alterations and the Book Room was moved to the new premises in 1910. Hartley also proposed that the main building should be raised two stories thus providing more than fifty offices. The letting of the surplus office space would pay the working expenses and ground rent of the premises.[119] The total cost of the Holborn Hall as it was re-designated was bought from Hartley at cost price by the Primitive Methodist Church and in 1912 conveyed to the Bourne Trust Corporation. Sir William Hartley contributed £17,500 to the purchase price.

Connexion to Church

In 1871 the Wesleyan Conference decided to adopt the term 'Church' in place of 'Society'. Between 1870 and 1900 Primitive Methodism had also completed the transition from sect to denomination. In the Connexional address for 1898, Conference stated 'our credentials as a church are before the world' and recommended that the word 'Church' should be used instead of 'Connexion'.[120] This recommendation was implemented in 1901 when 'Church' superseded 'Connexion' on class tickets and other Primitive Methodist publications.

Independence to integration

Primitive Methodism always denied any deliberate intention to separate from the parent Wesleyan Connexion. As stated in Chapter 1 Hugh Bourne specifically declared that it was not his intention to raise separate societies. It was the refusal of the then Superintendent of the Burslem Wesleyan Circuit to take over the small class at Standley, except on the unacceptable terms that it would relinquish all contact with the Bournes, that convinced Hugh Bourne that he would have to take responsibility for societies not accepted by the Wesleyans.

The Primitive Methodist Deed Poll stated that the Connexion 'rose undesigned of man' and that

> This Connexion not having arisen from a split or division from any other Connexion, but being truly an original, it has had to follow the openings of Divine Providence, form its own movements and make arrangements to meet its own necessities.[121]

Time tends to heal wounds and, as the causes of discord and division receded into history, the secessions and 'offshoots' from Wesleyan Methodism began to consider the possibility of union either between themselves or with the parent Wesleyan body. As early as 1866, Samuel Hulme, then President of the Methodist New Connexion, authorised by his Conference, wrote to his Wesleyan counterpart urging that there was a strong disposition among the various sections of Methodism to make concessions for Union and that:

> under those hopeful conditions we [the Methodist and New Connexion] press upon the Wesleyan Conference both the honour and the duty of taking the first practical steps towards the grand consummation.[122]

W. Arthur, the Wesleyan President replied cordially but stated:

> We apprehend that the legal and practical difficulties in the way of an organic union are such as cannot be overcome by any action it is possible to take.[123]

The issue was raised again in 1881 and received a warmer response from some leading Wesleyans including Hugh Price Hughes. The Wesleyan Conference appointed a Committee 'to consider … as to the ways in which the waste and friction in the actual working of the various sections of the Methodist Church may be lessened and prevented and brotherly love promoted.'[124]

It is not known whether the Committee ever met.[125]

The softening of Wesleyan attitudes between 1866 and 1881 was possibly due to the admission in 1878 of lay representatives to the Wesleyan Conference. As Kent states, 'this step removed the biggest single constitutional difference between the English Methodist denominations and involved a definite break with the traditional Wesleyan view of the Ministry.'[126]

Meanwhile, the so-called 'junior' branches of Methodism began to explore the possibilities of more limited unions among themselves. In 1894 the Primitive Methodist Conference passed a resolution in favour of union with the Bible Christians 'as a first step towards at least a union of minor Methodist bodies.'[127] Discussions between the two Connexions went favourably and it was suggested that the name of the united denomination should be 'The Primitive Methodist and Bible Christian Church'. In 1899, however, a Primitive Methodist opposition movement appeared. On the eve of the Quarterly Meetings which were asked to vote on the proposed union an appeal was made that the principle of two laymen to one minister at Conference, District and other meetings should not be surrendered. The Quarterly Meetings decisively rejected the proposals by 9,583 to 2,402 with 988 neutral votes.[128]

In 1902 the Methodist New Connexion, United Methodist Free Churches and Bible Christians began conversations which led in 1907 to their amalgamation into the United Methodist Free Church. Both the Wesleyan and Primitive Conferences were kept informed of the progress of these deliberations. At the 1904 Wesleyan Conference a resolution moved by R. W. Perks and seconded by Scott Lidgett was unanimously adopted. This expressed:

> the hope that the negotiations now proceeding between the New Connexion, the United Free Methodist and Bible Christian Churches may prove a valuable contribution to the ultimate complete unity of British Methodism.[129]

Meanwhile, other factors combined to give impetus to all branches of Methodism to recognise the importance of moving towards organic union. At the first Ecumencial Conference of World Methodism held in Wesley's Chapel, London in 1881 papers were read on 'How Christian unity may be maintained and increased among ourselves and made manifest to the world' and also 'The catholicity of Methodism'. These themes were continued at similar gatherings in 1891, 1901 and 1911. Methodist union had been successfully achieved in Canada (1884) and in Australia and Ireland (1902). At the instigation of R. W. Perks the Wesleyan Conference of 1913 appointed a Committee to explore the possibility of union between the various branches of Methodism and report to the next Conference.[130] Although the 1914–1918 war prevented further action this committee continued to meet. Eventually on 9 January 1918 representatives of all three branches of Methodism met for the first time to discuss reunion and a 'Tentative Scheme' was put before the three Conferences in 1920.[131]

The obstacles to organic union were formidable and can be grouped under sociological, political, theological and administrative factors.

Sociologically, by 1920 there was little social distinction between the three denominations although Wesleyans were widely regarded as being one rung higher on the social ladder. The popular Primitive Methodist and United Methodist views were that Wesleyans were 'snobbish'. Bowmer also points out that:

> In a way little known today lay folk were closely identified with their own brand of Methodism … let a Wesleyan go on holiday on a Saturday his first act would be to reconnoitre for a Wesleyan chapel in which he could worship next day – but it must be Wesleyan! – and the same applied *mutatis mutandis* for a Primitive and United Methodist.[132]

To most lay persons of pre-union days the disappearance of their own denominations meant the end of the deepest loyalty of their lives.

Politically, the Primitive Methodists were much further to the left than the Wesleyans. Especially in agricultural and mining areas they were often identified with the trade unions. As shown in Chapter 9 they were in the van of the passive resistance movements against the 1902 Education Act and Tithes. When passive resistance failed there was a widespread transfer of Primitive Methodist allegiance from the Liberal to the Labour Party.

Theologically, the three churches had much in common. Until 1921 the Primitive Methodist Deed Poll declared that Connexional doctrines were 'to be interpreted agreeably to the teaching of John Wesley as set out in his first four volumes of sermons (the *Fifty-three Sermons*) and his *Notes on the New Testament.*'

The removal of this provision was not due to anti-Wesleyanism but rather the recognition that in the light of biblical criticism the exegesis of Wesley's *Notes on the New Testament* published in 1754 was unsound.

Yet there were radical differences between the Wesleyan and non-Wesleyan doctrines of the Church, the ministry and the sacraments. Kent states that 'for the Wesleyan minority "the Church" meant the traditional kind of institution which they knew best through Anglicanism of the older, plainer, less Anglo-Catholic kind.' In the non-Wesleyan branches, however, there was a greater affinity with Puritanism 'in which "the Church" meant a community open to the laity at all points.' [133]

A statement made in the early days of the Union Committee that 'the Wesleyans did not regard their ministers as the paid agents of the Church' exemplified a widely held Wesleyan view that Primitive and United Methodists had a 'low' view of the ministry. This statement caused A. S. Peake to 'ask himself in amazement what Methodist people entertained so grovelling a view of the ministry.' [134] It was true, however, that the non-Wesleyan branches attached less significance to ordination. Wesleyan ministers, especially superintendents, also had more formal authority than their Primitive and United Methodist counterparts.

As shown in Chapter 8 the non-Wesleyan branches also placed rather less emphasis on the sacraments of Baptism and the Lord's Supper, both of which could be administered by laymen.

Administratively, from 1878 to 1932 the Wesleyan Conference met in two sessions. The 'Pastoral', comprising ministers only, and the 'Representative', comprised of ministers and laymen in equal numbers. At the heart of the Conference was the 'Legal Hundred', a self-perpetuating band of ministers first appointed by Wesley in 1784. In contrast the Primitive and United Methodist Conferences had only one session. Representation at the Primitive Conference was on the basis of two laymen to one minister, while the United Methodist Conference comprised equal numbers of ministers and laymen. Both Primitive and United Methodists perceived the Wesleyan Pastoral Session and the Legal Hundred as a negation of democracy and evidence of a ministerial autocracy to which they were opposed.

Both the non-Wesleyan branches were nevertheless strongly committed to organic union. The main opposition was from a Wesleyan group led principally by Revd J. E. Rattenbury and Sir Henry Lunn, which became known as 'the Other Side'. The basis of their opposition was summarised in a manifesto signed by some 800 Wesleyan ministers in 1922 which stated:

> We hold that the viewpoint of Wesleyan Methodism is essentially different from that of the other Methodist Churches in regard to doctrinal standards, the Sacraments, forms of worship, the ministry, party politics and other matters of first importance. The proposed scheme of union involves a large accession of those whose sentiments and training will inevitably lead further and further away from the Wesleyan tradition and usages.[135]

The Primitive and United Methodists had also their own much smaller 'Other Sides'. A Primitive Methodist Defence League formed in 1924 issued a manifesto warning of the consequences of ministerial rule which prompted a considerable correspondence in the *Primitive Methodist Leader*.[136]

In 1925 the Union committee recommended that the agreement of 75 per cent of the members of each Conference should be obtained before Parliament was asked to enact an Enabling Act, which should contain a clause that union should only be implemented when 75 per cent of each of the three Conferences severally and unitedly agreed. Both the Primitive and United Methodist Conferences of 1925 voted overwhelmingly in favour of union but it was 1928 before the Pastoral and Representative Sessions of the Wesleyan Conference achieved the required majority.

A detailed account of the negotiations, which led to the resolution of the problems facing the Union Committee is outside the scope of this book.[137]

As Currie observes:

> The Methodist Church was made possible because the Wesleyans took a long step to meet Liberal Methodists and Liberal Methodists took a larger step still to meet the Wesleyans. Both surrendered much ground in hope.[138]

In fact Union was only achieved by the determination of prominent ministers and laymen in each of the three Churches. Among others, constructive leadership was provided by the Revds Aldom French, Scott Lidgett and J. Hornabrook for the Wesleyans, Revd Samuel Horton and Professor A. S. Peake for the Primitives and Revd R. Pyke for the United Methodists.

The Methodist Union Bill was enacted in 1929 and the final votes on a Scheme for the implementation of Union at the Conferences of 1931. Arrangements were made for a Uniting Conference to be held at the Albert Hall, London in September 1932.

The last Primitive Methodist Conference met from 15–22 June 1932 at Middlesborough under the Presidency of Revd William Younger. After the conclusion of its ordinary business the Conference adjourned its proceedings to the Uniting Conference in September. The development of Primitive Methodism in its 121-year history was well summarised in a statement adopting the Report on Methodist Union:

> Commencing with a small group of ten people we are entering the Union with 222,021 members, with 1,131

> ministers, 12,896 lay preachers, 377,792 Sunday school scholars and property worth upwards of seven million and a half pounds, after having made notable contributions to the Methodist Churches of Australia and New Zealand, Canada and South Africa.[139]

On the afternoon of Sunday, 25 September 1932, I vividly remember being taken by my parents to Lane Head, the head church of the Lowton Circuit, to take part in a commemorative service intended to enable all Methodist churches to share the same prayers, hymns and devotions as those at the Uniting Conference. The congregation listened to the service through a large loudspeaker, which had been installed in the church. I kept the Order of Service for many years. I recall that on the cover it had a verse from the school song of Charterhouse where, from 1714–20 John Wesley was a pupil. The verse has remained with me through the years:

> Wesley, John Wesley, was one of our Company,
> Prophet untiring and fearless of tongue.
> Down the long years he went,
> Spending, yet never spent,
> Serving his Lord with a heart ever young.

So I ceased to be 'a Little Primitive' and became a 'Young Methodist'.

During the next seven years little seemed to change at the local level. There were exchanges of pulpits between former Wesleyan and Primitive ministers. In 1932 we acquired a new hymn book and in 1936 a Book of Offices but it was some years before these were in full use. Primitive Methodism has, however, remained a life-long influence not only for the writer but also for the rapidly diminishing numbers of people who were born into its culture. It is in gratitude for that culture that this book has been written.

Part Two
A Circuit

5

Churches, Ministers and People

The last chapter outlined the national development of Primitive Methodism from sect to church. Most of the remainder of this book will attempt to relate various facets of Primitive Methodism as implemented or experienced in a typical Primitive Methodist circuit. Such facets will include beliefs, ethics, worship, church-chapel relationships and politics. It is, however, necessary to put such aspects into their context. The present chapter is therefore concerned with the origin and development in the Circuit and chapels with which I was associated; their Sunday schools, ministers and people.

The Lowton Primitive Methodist Circuit

The Lowton Circuit, situated between Wigan and Leigh in Lancashire, could trace its antecedents back to the first Primitive Methodist circuit in Tunstall. In 1819 John Wedgwood, who had the distinction of being the first Primitive Methodist to be imprisoned for open air preaching,[1] missioned a number of places including Nantwich, in Cheshire. Wedgwood, like Clowes a skilled potter, was No. 19 on the Tunstall Circuit Plan and was closely associated with Hugh Bourne. In June 1820, the Tunstall Circuit resolved to supply preachers to certain places which had become known collectively as the Cheshire Mission. These, in turn, became the Burland Branch and, later, the Burland Circuit. In 1820, Preston Brook, between Runcorn and Northwich, Cheshire, became a branch of the Burland Circuit and three years later, an independent circuit, Warrington, was created out of Preston Brook.

Missionaries from the Preston Brook Circuit first visited Lowton about 1827 and formed a society which dissolved because of the failure to obtain a suitable place of worship. Both the Preston Brook and Warrington Circuits seem to have been involved in the subsequent introduction of Primitive Methodism to Lowton.

In 1831, F. N. Jersey, then Methodist Missionary for the Preston Brook Circuit, wrote in his journal:

> October 24th. Went to Lowton, a distance of about twelve miles. We have preached at this place about nine months in a house occupied by a person of another community but with no success, so we thought it best to return to our old custom of preaching in the open air; when hundreds rallied round the standard. We sung down the town, and held a prayer meeting in a field belonging to a friend, the house being too small to contain the people.
>
> The weather being now too cold for worship in the open air, we preach in a large house belonging to one of our members. The house was crowded to excess. I felt the power of the Holy Ghost. The Word ran like fire among stubble. Held a meeting after preaching, several were in distress, and some found peace. I attempted to form a society, when about nine gave in their names. The work of God is still going on in this place.[2]

The above statement implies that indoor and outdoor Primitive Methodist services had been held in Lowton from the beginning of 1831. Yet it is recorded that in the same year, a Mr Cuthbert Oliver, who had visited Lowton in 1831 on business connected with the Manchester and Liverpool Railway, had, on enquiring for the Primitive Methodists, found none within a distance of five miles. Oliver therefore approached the Warrington Circuit asking that a 'cause' be established at Lowton. This request was granted and a 'Travelling Preacher' was sent from Warrington once a fortnight. A female preacher, Elizabeth Allen, is stated as having taken her stand in the open air and preached with 'remarkable power and acceptance'. A Society was formed in 1832. This event was followed by what is described as a great revival in which many souls were converted.

The new converts were persecuted. Some lost their employment, others were ill-treated. So called 'ungodly young men' attended the open air services to disrupt and deride. Yet, by 1834, the Society had fifty members and in 1833, the Preston Brook Circuit sanctioned the building of a chapel. This was apparently built but 'through the trickery of a certain individual', the Lowton Society was deprived of its use. Nine years later, another building, 27 feet long and 22 feet wide was erected costing £130. Although extended in 1843, the chapel was inadequate for a growing congregation and in 1881, a new edifice seating four hundred worshippers was built at a cost of £900. The former chapel remained in use as a Sunday school until 1914 when a new school was opened.[3]

Meanwhile, other Primitive Methodist Societies had been established at Edge Green, Golborne (1846), Bridge Street, Golborne (1847), Lowton Road, Golborne (1854), and Stubshaw Cross (1874). The Golborne societies were transferred from Preston Brook to the Leigh Primitive Methodist Circuit in 1868. Seven years later, the Leigh Primitive Methodist Circuit comprised eleven churches: Leigh, Bedford, Lowton, Glazebrook, Edge Green, Bridge Street and Lowton Road (Golborne), Platt Bridge, Stubshaw Cross, Cadishead and Chowbent. In 1884, a petition to the Manchester District to form a separate Lowton Circuit was accepted and ratified by Conference. When it began in 1885, the Lowton Primitive Methodist Circuit comprised five Societies, to which Ashton-in-Makerfield and Bamfurlong were added in 1893 and 1894 respectively.

The churches

The seven chapels of the Lowton Circuit were located in four parishes: Lowton St Luke's (Lowton); Golborne St Thomas's, (Bridge Street, Edge Green and Lowton Road); Ashton St

Thomas's (Ashton and Stubshaw Cross); and Abram, St Johns (Bamfurlong). By the Local Government Act of 1894, the four parishes were situated in the Urban Districts of Abram, Ashton-in-Makerfield and Golborne. From a sociological perspective, the Lowton Circuit provides an interesting study. The Lowton and Bridge Street chapels were in or on the edge of rural residential areas. The leading families in both churches were farmers while the memberships were predominantly middle or lower middle class and included a number of teachers, local government officers, clerks and other white collar workers. Several of the younger people attended local grammar schools either having won scholarships or being paid for by their parents. Some subsequently went on to university and professional occupations.

The Lowton Road chapel, attended by my parents, also had several small entrepreneurs. These included a wholesale fruit and potatoes merchant who was also a Justice of the Peace and County Councillor, a coal merchant and haulier who also served on the Urban Council, a grocer and baker and a travelling ironmonger who also kept a small sweetshop.

In contrast, the other four chapels were in mining areas and all had working-class memberships. Most members lived in 'two up and two down' dwellings bereft of such basic amenities as baths or WCs. Many dwellings had cracks in the brickwork due to mining subsidence and a few were held together by tie rods. Coal dust pervaded everywhere, often leaving dirty smuts on clean washing hung out to dry. Chip shops provided satisfactory but monotonous meals. Pubs challenged the temperance teaching of the chapels. The number of families with Welsh names such as Burgess, Davies, Jones, Pritchard and Roberts, together with a number of then still functioning Welsh Congregational, Calvinistic and Methodist chapels, evidenced an earlier influx of Welsh families to work in the Wigan area coalfields. Scholarships, few in number, awarded by the Lancashire Education Committee, were the only avenue by which the children of most families could go to grammar school. One of my second cousins won scholarships to the Ashton-in Makerfield Grammar School and subsequently to Manchester University. There was grudging admiration for his success. At Manchester, he lived in St Anselm's Hall and in those days was required to have a dinner suit. I recall Aunt Sarah's caustic comment: 'It looks weel, 'im 'avin' a dinner jacket an' 'is feayther in t' pit.'

Geographically, only a few miles separated Lowton and the Bridge Street end of Golborne from Ashton, Bamfurlong and Stubshaw Cross but environmentally, they were in different worlds. My Uncle James, who lived in the mining village of Stubshaw Cross, described almost with wonder a visit to a circuit meeting at Bridge Street. He travelled by rail from Bamfurlong to Lowton and walked to his destination. As he travelled through the open country with green fields on each side of the road, he felt transported into heaven.

Buildings and leadership were other manifestations of the relative affluence of the Lowton, Bridge Street and Lowton Road chapels.

The Bridge Street chapel was particularly beautiful. On a fine Sunday morning, it was impossible not to be spiritually uplifted as the sun streamed in through the high windows. It was the loveliness of the building that led me to move when aged about fourteen from the smaller and plainer chapel at Lowton Road. I never anticipated that, some fifty years later, I would preach at the last service held in Bridge Street prior to its demolition.

The Lowton chapel was also enhanced. I accompanied my mother in 1931 to a service at Lowton when a new stained-glass window was unveiled, a new organ opened and electric lighting switched on to replace the previous gas illumination.

The mining chapels were, by contrast, bare and spartan. Only Edge Green had a pipe organ, acquired second-hand, the other three relying on harmoniums or pianos for their musical accompaniment. Low wages and even lower strike pay during the 1921 and 1926 disputes together with high unemployment meant that although there was the will, there were no means to beautify the buildings. It was often difficult for them to raise their circuit assessments. On at least one occasion, the Circuit Steward paid the assessment of the Stubshaw Cross Society from his own pocket.

Leadership was also concentrated in the Lowton and Golborne chapels. Probably because of the independence of self-employment, acquaintance with business and local politics and standing in the wider community, the most important lay offices of Circuit Steward, Assistant Circuit Steward and Circuit Secretary were held by men from these Societies. They were also in closer proximity to the minister who resided in Golborne and who, until the late 1930s, had no telephone. This concentration of influence also extended to the local preachers. A 1941 Circuit Plan shows that six of the seven 'fully accredited' (i.e. Connexionally recognised) local preachers lived in either Golborne or Lowton. The other was a Golborne boy who, having obtained a primary school headship, had moved to Withnell near Chorley.

While theoretically a unity, the Lowton Primitive Methodist Circuit was effectively subdivided into three sub-groups. The largest related to Lowton and the three Golborne churches – Bridge Street, Edge Green and Lowton Road. The second group comprised Stubshaw Cross and Bamfurlong. Ashton was not closely connected with either group. These groupings were mainly due to their origins. The Lowton Society had missioned and founded Edge Green. Edge Green in turn had established Bridge Street and Lowton Road. Stubshaw Cross was the mother church of Bamfurlong. The origins of Ashton are difficult to discover. Sheard mentions that in 1846 the Society at Ashton in the Warrington Circuit was stated to 'have been broken up through drunkenness, backbiting etc.'[4]

In 1955, the Lowton and former Earlestown Primitive Methodist Circuits merged to become the Earlestown and Lowton Circuit; the Stubshaw Cross and Bamfurlong churches being transferred to the then Hindley Circuit. Stubshaw Cross subsequently closed in the 1970s. A further reorganisation took place in 1969 when the Earlestown and Lowton Circuit became the present Makerfield Circuit. One consequence was the union in 1972 of the former Wesleyan and Primitive churches in Ashton and the closure of the latter. Lane Head, formerly the head church of the Lowton Circuit, was demolished in 1985 although worship continued in the former Sunday school. The following year, the Golborne, Bridge Street Church suffered a similar fate.

The Sunday schools

Laqueur states that the proportion of the population attending Sunday school probably reached its peak during the 1880s and thereafter declined.[5] By 1930 it was approximately the same as it had been in 1833. As late as 1957, 76 per cent of those over the age of thirty had at some time attended Sunday school.[6]

In the 1930s, each of the seven churches in the Lowton Circuit had a relatively flourishing Sunday school. The Sunday schools had a wider influence in these respective localities than the chapels with which they were affiliated. Parents who never attended the churches themselves sent their children to Sunday school from mixed motives. Undoubtedly they enjoyed the temporary Sunday respite from parental responsibilities but equally, they were anxious that their offspring should receive a firm grounding in religion and morality. Since attendance at Sunday school involved such virtues as cleanliness, smartness and punctuality, it reinforced the discipline of weekday attendance at day school.

The Sunday schools, as Laqueur observes, 'formed part of a distinct sub-culture. It was on the periphery of church or chapel but organisationally and in style of operation, apart from it.'[7] Officially the Sunday school was regarded as a feeder to the chapel; the scholars of today being the members of tomorrow. Sunday schools were virtually independent organisations. The minister, normally conducting three services, had little opportunity to oversee his Circuit Sunday schools and responsibility for their conduct rested with the Sunday School Superintendent. At the morning and afternoon schools, this official announced the first and second hymns, offered prayers, dismissed the assembled scholars to their classes (often after a brief exhortation) and afterwards concluded the proceedings with a final hymn and the benediction. Some attempt to provide appropriate teaching in the classes, which were of half to three-quarters of an hour in duration, was provided by the Primitive Methodist Sunday School Union. After its establishment in 1874, the Primitive Methodist Sunday School Union published hundreds of graded lesson plans and other instructional aids in addition to organising annual examinations for both scholars and teachers. The main problem faced by most Sunday schools was not direction but staffing. In adolescence many scholars ceased to attend. Those whose attendance continued into their teens were virtually conscripted as Sunday school teachers. After the initial novelty had worn off, most of these pressed teachers had little commitment to the task. As mentioned earlier, my father took the Connexional Teachers' Examinations over a long period. I believe he was the only Sunday school teacher in the Circuit to do so. The general pattern was one of working-class teachers instructing mainly working-class children. In most cases, teachers were only slightly ahead of their scholars both in age and knowledge. Notwithstanding such imperfections, however, some Sunday school teaching had a lasting influence. Neville Cardus, doyen of cricket correspondents, related an incident in a Roses match concerning Dick Tyldesley of Lancashire fame. One of the Yorkshire batsmen was well set and seemed likely to amass a big score when Tyldesley, fielding at short leg, made an apparently brilliant catch close to the ground. The batsman was already 'walking' when Tyldesley signalled that the ball had touched the ground before being caught. The next day, Cardus congratulated Tyldesley on his sportsmanship. 'Thank you Mr Cardus,' Tyldesley replied. Then, with a twinkle in his eye, he added 'Westhoughton Sunday School tha' knows.'[8]

Attendance at Sunday school was encouraged by book prizes presented at an annual prize-giving. To qualify for a prize, scholars had to accumulate a prescribed number of 'stars' embossed into a 'star-card' with a rubber stamp. My first prize, obtained at the age of six, was a biography of a prominent Primitive Methodist minister, *Thomas Jackson of Whitechapel*. I did not choose the book. For several years, father scrutinised the catalogue of the Primitive Methodist Book Room to obtain, on the basis of my attendance, books he wanted to read. Although by today's standards the book was too advanced for a six-year-old, I nevertheless read it. One incident relating to Jackson's boyhood has remained with me. In a period of prolonged drought, the Primitive Methodists decided to pray for rain. Meetings were held in a little thatched one-storey cottage occupied by an elderly woman who always contributed to the petitions. Her prayers always ended: 'Lord, pour out Thy blessing upon us. Let it come in bucketfuls!' One night, Thomas Jackson, with two other boys, decided to lend a hand. One boy crouched under the window, listening; the other stood by with a bucket of water; young Thomas Jackson was on the ridges of the roof near the chimney. Loud and earnest were the voices within the cottage. When the boy nearest the window whispered, 'She's started', the second boy handed up the pail, and with the final petition: 'Send it down in bucketfuls', Tom emptied the bucket down the chimney, and more soot than blessing fell upon the worshippers.[9]

One year, prizes were presented by a Preston pugilist who fought under the name of Tommy Tucker. Afterwards, I followed Tucker's fortunes in the *News Chronicle*. I thought that such a godly man must, with the help of the Almighty, be invincible. I was somewhat disconcerted to read of a contest with an opponent named O'Malley. The newspaper reported that prior to knocking him out, O'Malley had chased Tommy Tucker round the ring.

My father subscribed to all the Primitive Methodist periodicals including the weekly *Primitive Methodist Leader* and the monthly *Christian Messenger* and *Aldersgate Magazine*. There was also a magazine for Sunday school scholars, titled *Morning*. After Methodist Union in 1932, this last periodical was renamed *Morning and Springtime*. One feature of *Morning and Springtime* was a 'Poetry Circle' to which readers were encouraged to send contributions for criticism and possible publication. One of the older girls at the Bridge Street Sunday School achieved local notoriety by having several of her poems published. At the age of sixteen I was deeply in love with her and have preserved one poem, 'The Silent Approach of Night', through the years.[10]

The Silent Approach of Night

The sky is shot with colour now –
  Amber and violet;
Soft shades of rosy light appear
  Deeper than at sunset;
The west is still a mass of fiery glow
From whence sad moaning night-winds
  breathe and blow.

So tranquilly the shadows fall
  And the night breezes cease;
Grey mist is thickening like a pall,
  While all around is peace;
Brown velvet dusk appears, and comes to cheer
My fainting heart, and dry my falling tear.

The heavens have changed to deeper tone –
  A dark blue of the sea.
Sweet poppy! Emblem of the night,
  Thy smell is greeting me.
The world is still and holy. Nothing deigns
To spoil serenity. The pale moon reigns.

Another important event was the annual Scripture examinations. These not only focused attention on a specified scriptural theme but also provided an introduction to examination technique. For most scholars in attendance at elementary schools, the Scripture papers were their only experience of public examinations. They also gave me my first acquaintance with written examinations when I obtained a second class pass in the Lower Junior Division in 'Nehemiah, the Man and his Work'. Thereafter, I took the examinations for some years, eventually obtaining passes with honours. Both before and after the actual sitting, the examinations gave rise to considerable parental interest. I recall a discussion between my mother and the parents of another examinee regarding whether we should memorise the prayer of Nehemiah 1.4–11.

The Sunday school achieving the best results in the Scripture examinations received a shield which it held for twelve months. The shield alternated between the Lowton, Bridge Street and Lowton Road Sunday Schools not only because these tended to have more entrants but also since more of the examinees were also in attendance at the grammar schools.

Sunday schools had many other facets. Scholars competed against each other not only in the Scripture examinations but also in collections for overseas missions. For this activity we were awarded medals and subsequently bars for the amounts obtained. There were plays and operettas. One such operetta, *The Magic Rose*, was performed by the Lowton Road Sunday School not only round the Circuit but for the edification of the inmates of the Leigh Workhouse. There were Sunday school outings to such places as Southport. One Sunday school, Bamfurlong, had a football team good enough to compete in the local Sunday School League and to visit, and beat, the students of Hartley College. Unlike their Anglican and RC counterparts, none of the Sunday schools of the Circuit had a walking day. I never hear the hymn 'The Church's one Foundation' to the tune of *Aurelia* without seeing in my mind's eye the annual procession of the Lowton St Luke's church, marching to the strains of the hymn played by the local band. At the head was the Rector, flanked by his Churchwardens. After the band came the banner and then a long stream of boys and girls in their best attire, followed by the Mothers' Union. The high spot of our Sunday school year was the anniversary but this is more appropriately considered in Chapter 8.

Ministers

Kent states that in 1924, 486 (71 per cent) of the 684 Primitive Methodist circuits were single minister stations.[11] Lowton was such a circuit. Between 1885 and 1940, fifteen men ministered in the circuit, of whom fourteen are listed by Leary.[12] As shown, no ministry exceeded five years:

Years in Circuit	Number of Ministers
2	3
3	4
4	5
5	3
	15

Two of the three shortest ministries were at the start of the Circuit's life as a separate station. No minister stayed long enough to significantly influence the Circuit's life.

I only knew the last three of the above ministers. The first two of these did not wear a dog collar or any distinctive clerical attire either on weekdays or Sundays and I recall wondering if they were 'proper' ministers like the local Rector or Congregational parson. Davies points out that among other reasons, the Puritans opposed the wearing of vestments because such attire upheld the priesthood of the clergy and, by implication, denied the priesthood of all believers.[13] Puritan emphasis on plainness of dress was stressed by early Methodists. Even before John Wesley's death, the practice had begun to break down in Wesleyan Methodism but it was re-emphasised by the Primitive Methodist Conference of 1819.

> Q 17. In what dress shall our Travelling Preachers appear in public?
>
> A. In a plain one: the men to wear single breasted coats, single breasted waistcoats and their hair in its natural form; and not to be allowed to wear pantaloons, trousers, nor white hats; and that the Female Preachers be patterns of plainness in all their Dress.
>
> Note: We strongly recommend it to our brethren, the Stewards, Local Preachers, Leaders and private Members, both Male and Female, in our societies to be plain in their dress.[14]

The following letter concerning the Revd R.W. Callin (1886–1951), a prominent Primitive Methodist minister, shows that this Puritan attitude still persisted in the 1930s:

> Primitive Methodists, myself included, were unashamedly nonconformist and looked askance at any of their ministers whose dress in any way resembled that of the Anglican clergy. When a new minister came to the circuit, we hoped that he would not be wearing 'the collar' and, in fact, in my recollection, for over thirty years at George Street (Chester) none of them did. While at Chester, Callin appeared in the pulpit wearing a stand-up collar and a black bow which was at any rate distinctive. Later on, when at the Bradford Conference in 1950, I found him wearing a clerical collar. I felt he had 'let the side down' – though I didn't dare say so.[15]

No one from the Lowton Circuit entered the Primitive Methodist ministry although one local preacher unsuccessfully candidated. Later he joined the Congregational Church and entered Paton College, Nottingham. As a theological student, he was invited to preach the Sunday School Anniversary of the Bamfurlong church. To the consternation of a predominantly mining congregation, he wore not only a dog collar but a preaching gown. His sermons were soon forgotten, but the gown was discussed for months.

The Primitive Methodist objection to clerical attire was a protest against Anglican episcopacy. It also symbolised that the Primitive Methodist interpretation of the priesthood of all believers emphasised that there was no ministerial role, including the highest of all, that of President of Conference, that could not equally be undertaken by a layman. Controversy over this view, as stated later, was one of the principal obstacles to Methodist Union. The objection to this 'low view of the ministry' was answered by Kendall:

> Lastly, in regard to ministerial prerogative being at a minimum amongst us – ministers themselves may speak

> out here. There may be very little of doing this, that or the other, 'by virtue of office' amongst us, but there is a very great deal done and accorded by virtue of the moral influence which the minister will do and should always wield.[16]

Ministers were also held in esteem because Primitive Methodist was a working-class church and ministers were drawn largely from the working classes. A survey in 1894–6 revealed that 75 per cent of Primitive Methodist chapels and most of their preaching places were in villages.[17] Many such villages as in Durham and, in the Lowton Circuit, Stubshaw Cross and Bamfurlong, were in mining communities. It is therefore not surprising that, as Brown shows, between 1900 and 1929 and earlier, miners and farm labourers figure predominantly among Primitive Methodist ministerial candidates.[18] Entry into the ministry offered a working class lad a professional future but the road to that future was long and involved preparation, candidature, college, probation and thereafter an arduous life. We respected ministers and Hartley College students because we knew that their status had been achieved by a high degree of dedication, self-help and improvement.

Preparation, candidature, training and probation[19]

Preparation had to begin early for only Conference could sanction the calling into the Primitive Methodist ministry of a married man, widower with children or a single man over twenty-five. The first step was to become a local preacher. Following an examination by the circuit regarding his 'religious experience, devotional habits and knowledge of the Scriptures', an aspirant was given the status of 'Exhorter' and permitted to take services. This probationary period lasted between one and two years during which the aspirant was required to undergo regular oral examinations conducted by the circuit. In 1904, the Connexion, anxious to improve the training of local preachers, introduced a training course, including prescribed books and the provision of correspondence courses.[20] Take-up was, however, relatively poor and in 1932, it was 'a cause for regret that approximately only one third of our budding lay preachers take the training course.'[21] Those who were recommended to be placed on 'full-plan' were publicly recognised as fully accredited local preachers at a circuit service.

Candidature for the ministry began at the September Quarterly Meeting at which the recommendation of at least two-thirds of those voting by ballot was required. The next hurdle was the District Examining Committee prior to which candidates sat five written papers based on prescribed books. The papers, each of two hours' duration, were (1) Contents of the Old and New Testaments; (2) Biblical Introduction; (3) The Life and Teaching of Jesus; (4) English Language and Composition; (5) History divided into (a) English History and (b) Primitive Methodist Church Principles and Polity. Candidates who had matriculated were exempted from the English Language and part (a) of the History paper. The District Candidates' Committee also examined applicants orally and arranged for them to preach a trial sermon at an ordinary service. At the Liverpool District Synod held at Ellesmere Port in 1914, the two candidates each conducted an early morning service at 7 a.m. The maximum marks for the whole examination was 800 comprising 250 for the oral examination, 100 each for the five written papers and 50 for the sermon preached at the district meeting. The pass mark was 560; those obtaining at least 645 marks were placed on an Honours List.

Those candidates recommended by the district appeared before a Candidates' General Examining Committee. In the interim, a candidate had to provide an original written sermon of not more than 2,500 words for evaluation and marking by 'at least three examiners'. At one of the General Examining Committees meeting in London, Leeds and Birmingham, candidates were subjected to further oral and written tests and a medical examination. The oral testing included: (a) The Holy Scriptures with (b) reading aloud a passage selected by the Examiners; (c) writing a paragraph from dictation (style of writing, punctuation and orthography to be considered in deciding its value). Those deemed to have passed took further written tests in English grammar, geography and arithmetic. The Committee was however, warned:

> not to reject young men who though found lacking in educational advantages, give evidence of deep piety and great promise, have good natural gifts and more than average preaching ability.[22]

These tests must have been a formidable ordeal for young men, most of whom had only an elementary education. It is significant that in 1923, only 9.1 per cent of the school population in England attended grammar schools.[23] By 1938 this had risen to 10.9 per cent.[24] In 1932, only 42 (2.3 per cent) of the 898 Primitive Methodist ministers in active work were graduates.[25]

College training must also have been anticipated by most accepted candidates with some trepidation. While not a condition of acceptance, students were expected to contribute what they could to first- and second-year fees. During his lifetime, the fees of all third-year students were met by Sir William Hartley. There was also the sudden transition from work to study. The Revd Robert F. Wearmouth, who subsequently obtained the degrees of MA, BSc and PhD, entered Hartley College in 1906. In his autobiography he records:

> The last days of my pitman's career were unforgettable. In the period leading up to my final examinations for the ministry ... I had to hew and fill coal in a place two feet six inches high and six feet wide, with intensely cold water trickling ceaselessly from the roof and almost filling the place.
>
> The last place in which I laboured before going to College was dangerous to health and strength. The air was impure and almost non-existent ... Every fifteen minutes it was necessary to leave the place to refresh the lungs with purer air or be rendered unconscious.[26]

The next week he began a three-year course at Hartley College:

> The training at Hartley College, Manchester, reached a very high standard. To me it was a great uplift. I had nothing to do but study. In addition to the theological and Biblical subjects, others were added such as Greek, Hebrew, Latin, German, Economics and Elocution. Most of us took a course on Education at the Manchester University and were successful in the Examinations.[27]

Each of the three ministers who served in the Lowton Circuit between 1928 and 1940 had sat at the feet of Professor Peake. All paid tribute to Peake's influence as a teacher and a man. After Peake's death in 1929, the high standard of training was maintained. At the time of Union, the staff of the College comprised the Revd W. L. Wardle MA DD, Revd A. L. Humphries MA, Revd H. G. Meecham MA BD PhD and Mr Atkinson Lee MA. These were augmented by the staff of the former United Methodist Victoria Park College including the Principal, Revd J. T. Brewis BA BD.

The College staff occasionally preached at special services in the Lowton Circuit. I still recall Anniversary sermons preached in the Lowton chapel by Brewis on Colossians 3:2 and, at the beginning of the Second World War, by Meecham on Psalm 50:21. Students also preached regularly in the Circuit both as 'supplies' and for 'specials'. Student appointments were especially popular with the younger ladies of a congregation.

Probation in a Circuit appointment was related to the period in college in such a way that the two periods together amounted to seven years. Normally, students spent three years at College and four on probation. Probation was, if anything, more demanding than College. In addition to the oversight of a number of churches, probationers had to take yearly examinations on 'selected portions of the Old and New Testaments in the original languages of Hebrew and Greek' embracing grammar, translation and retranslation, introduction and interpretation. Alternative studies were prescribed for those who had not taken Hebrew at College. An annual appearance before the District

Probationers Committee was also required. During probation, no man was permitted to marry and his stipend, out of which he had to pay for accommodation, was only two-thirds of that of a minister on the 'Approved List'.

Admission to the approved list of Ministers at the end of the probationary period was marked by ordination.

The Wesleyan Conference of 1836, presided over by Jabez Bunting, had introduced the ordination of all candidates for the ministry by the laying on of hands alongside reception into full Connexion. [28] In Primitive Methodism up to 1932 Primitive Methodist candidates were individually 'admitted to the approved list' at district level and not collectively at Conference as with the Wesleyans. The 'Prims' had no formal service. The typical pattern seems to have been a statement by each candidate of his Christian experience and call to the ministry; an address or charge by a senior minister and in some cases the celebration of the Lord's Supper at the end of the service. There was no laying on of hands.

The title 'Ministerial Recognition Service' was first used at Norwich in 1866 when six probationers were received. Burdon records that at the end of his charge, the Revd T. Swindell left the pulpit for the pew occupied by the young men and said 'I have no ordination hand to place on your heads; if I had I would not care to do it, but I can give you my hand as a Christian minister and brother.' Burdon also records that the first time when Primitive Methodist candidates were presented with a Bible was at the Sunderland District Meeting in 1869. [29]

It is noteworthy that the title 'Ordination Service' was used. After this date the title seems to have passed into general use for the admission of probationers to the Primitive Methodist 'Approved List'. It is significant, however, that in 1922 Primitive Methodist Rules make no reference to Ordination.

The work of the ministry

After successfully completing his probation, a Primitive Methodist minister could anticipate a further thirty-six years of itinerancy in circuit work. Apart from preaching and the administration of the Lord's Supper and baptism, dealt with in Chapter 6, the pastoral work of a single minister station such as Lowton demanded long working days that imposed considerable strain on both the minister and his wife. Theoretically, ministers spent mornings in their studies, afternoons on visitations and evenings at meetings or week-night preaching services. In practice, much of the morning was spent on correspondence and callers. A circuit of seven churches involved considerable clerical and administrative work relating to property matters, plan-making and general correspondence. In Lowton, the minister also acted as Circuit Book Steward, Missionary Treasurer and Corresponding Secretary on Connexional Affairs. Since they were the only time when the minister was likely to be at home, mornings were frequently interrupted by callers. Preparation of sermons and addresses and for business meetings left little time for private reading or studies.

Primitive Methodist General Rules laid down that:

> A superintendent minister must visit weekly at least thirty families and a non-superintendent forty families. Otherwise they must not be regarded as general family visitors; nor must these numbers suffice when they can visit more without setting other important ministerial duties aside … The Conference urges on all ministers the vast importance of attending to this duty.[30]

In practice, the above rules were counsels of perfection. Ministers had no cars and none of the three known to me possessed a bicycle. Though the Circuit manse was centrally located, the most distant church was some three miles away. Five others involved walking distances from the manse of between one to two miles in each direction. It was also a considerable walk to the nearest bus stop. It is interesting to speculate how much ministerial time must have been spent on travelling. Visiting sick members in the two local infirmaries based in Wigan and Leigh involved catching a bus, journeys of about thirty minutes in each direction and lengthy walks from the bus termini in the two towns to the hospitals. A hospital visit, often to one member, would therefore absorb a whole afternoon. Each Sunday, the minister conducted three services. Because the bus services only began at noon, he had to plan himself at the nearest chapels in the mornings and the furthest in the afternoons and evenings. Often on both weekdays and Sundays he cut down on travelling time by having tea at the home of a member before proceeding to the evening meeting or service. Most members considered it an honour to have the minister to tea. A telephone was not installed in the manse until 1939. In any event, few members had telephones. Visitation was the only way in which the minister could keep in touch with his flock. Even so, the ministers were criticised for 'never visiting'.

On Tuesday, Wednesday and Thursday evenings, the minister conducted a fortnightly preaching service at one or other of the Circuit chapels. Additionally, he had to conduct the Circuit Quarterly and Local Preachers' Meetings, Local Leaders' and Trustees' meetings. On Saturdays, there would usually be an evening 'effort' such as a social or concert at one or other of the chapels which the minister was expected to attend. Most evenings, he would not be home at the earliest before 9 p.m., often after leaving the manse eight hours before.

Some involvement was also expected from the minister's wife. This ranged from dispensing tea to manse visitors to speaking at Women's Meetings and opening bazaars or sales of work. The versatility expected from the minister and his wife is humorously described below:[31]

Wanted!

A Minister is wanted for a Circuit in the North,
And he must be a first-rate man, a man of solid worth.
The Congregations are not good, 'the Cause' is rather low,
And they must have a man that knows the way to make them grow.
In judgement sound, in counsel wise, in disposition kind.
The man they want must perfect be in body and in mind.

He never must be bilious, and never have the tic;
They can't afford to keep a man who now and then is sick.
It will not do for him to have just common flesh and blood;
No, he must have unbroken health, or he will be no good.
Within the pulpit he must be an eloquent divine,
And on the platform, 'midst his peers, a radiant star must shine,
He also must, as Visitor, from house to house proceed,
And seek, as Pastor of the flock, the sheep and lambs to feed.
If he has been a Lawyer's clerk he will the Circuit please,
For he may save the Trust accounts the cost of lawyers' fees.
If he has been a Doctor once, still better he will do,
For he can then the wants supply of soul and body too.
His wife must be a model wife, and perfect in her way,
Must meet a class, of course – or two, and in the meetings pray.
Collector for the Mission Fund, she cheerfully must roam,
Superior to the smaller claims of children and of home:
Must visit, in the town at least, and work for each bazaar,
And speak at every love feast, too, whate'er her feelings are!

* * *

Come, angel bright, from glory-throne, and with this people dwell,
And hold the wondering worshippers entranced beneath your spell,
But no! 'Tis better you should stay in your own sphere of light,
Your presence might be all too fair for merely mortal sight,
And 'ere a year had passed away, though seeming passing strange,
Some folks might say, 'At Conference we'd better have a change!'

As with most matters, there was another viewpoint:

Wanted!

A Circuit, Sir, is wanted for a minister precise:
'The Cause' must be a healthy one, the people must be nice,
The congregations must be good, intelligent, and kind,
Their preacher's virtues they must praise, to all his faults be blind.
A country circuit will not do – the people are so rough,
The work, too, is so very hard, one cannot do enough,

The visiting would kill a man, then travelling besides!
This pastor is a student, Sir, and not used to long rides.
Oh no! The country will not do: his 'charming little wife',
In loneliness and misery, would fret away her life.
The children, too, 'poor little dears', would have to go away,
Or else attend the village school, with common children play.
Oh dear no! Not the country, then; but come now, let us see,
Surely a London circuit, Sir, the very thing would be.
But then there are Committees there – too many of them too;
And more or less, all preachers there financial work must do.
The congregations, too, are stiff, and given to criticise;
Though some say even they are tired of varnish, starch, and size;
Our student-pastor will not do; they want there men of might,
To visit darkest alleys, and to wave the torch of light.
Stay; have you thought a sea-side place might suit our preacher friend?
To South, or West, or Eastern coast, this learned man we'll send.
But what's the stipend there? I ask; he must be amply paid;
Such genius is worth paying for as that of which he's made.
I fear I cannot find a place to suit the gentleman.
The Missionary Committee will do wonders if they can;
The country circuits are too wide; the town ones are too small;
Too much society in some, in others none at all.
The Northern circuits are too hard, the Southern ones too poor,
The villages want visiting; the large towns want much more.
Some people are so rough and loud, they shout, and sing, and rant,
Others are formal, cold, and dry – their piety is 'cant'.

* * *

Oh open! Heaven, and take him in, this precious man of ours,
And let him join your holy throng, O ye angelic powers!
But no; is it not possible of Paradise to tire?
To weary of the constant praise, and of the golden lyre?
Might not the very rest itself become a ceaseless pain
To one who whilst in circuit work would never 'stay again?'
Might he not be constrained to say – though seeming passing strange –
'If I were an itinerant, I think I'd have a change?'

Yet, notwithstanding its labours, the work of the ministry had its compensations. While there was some slight truth in the saying that in their first year ministers were 'idolised', in their second year 'tantalised', and in their third year 'scandalised', all the ministers known to me were regarded not merely with respect but also affection. In 1924, stipends of Primitive and Wesleyan Methodist ministers of six years' standing who were not superintendents were equal at £240 to which was added the value of a furnished manse and incidental fees from funerals and weddings. Additionally, each married minister was allowed £2.10.0d per quarter for each of his children aged under eighteen. This remuneration compared unfavourably with that in 1930 of the Rectors of Golborne (£545) and Lowton St Luke's (£470).[32] They were, however, substantially better than the average male earnings in 1924 of 58 shillings weekly or £150.16s yearly.[33] My father used to say that Primitive Methodist stipends 'ensured humility on the one hand and saved from poverty on the other.' Ministers also tended to live long. Leary's biographical details enable the ages at death of the fourteen Lowton Circuit ministers listed to be calculated within one year and are given below:[34]

Age at Death	Number of Ministers
90+	1
80–89	4
70–79	5
60–69	3
50–59	1
	14

The average age at death was 74.75 years. This is closely in accord with the 74.6 years reported by Brown in respect of Primitive Methodist ministers dying between 1900–1929.[35] In 1901, the average male life expectancy at birth was 45 years. By 1931, this had risen to 58 years.[36] Actuarially, Primitive Methodist ministers were a good risk!

People

Some of the social characteristics of the Lowton Circuit chapels and their members have been discussed earlier in this chapter. A number of factors made the chapels and the Circuit itself into close-knit communities. These factors included the social conduct expected from Primitive Methodists, transport and the denominational exclusiveness prevailing before 1939. The social conduct that emphasised temperance and prohibited dancing and negative attitudes to the theatre and the cinema which persisted among older members into the 1930s is considered in Chapter 7. Such attitudes meant most members had only limited social contacts outside the chapel and circuit communities. Up to 1939, travelling for most people meant public transport. Probably not more than five families in the whole Circuit had a car. There were some contacts with other Nonconformist bodies, particularly the Independent Methodists but, notwithstanding Methodist Union, minimal association with the Wesleyan Methodists. There was also little association with Anglicans who tended to denigrate 'Ranters' and virtually none with Roman Catholics. In any case, the chapels were numerically small, the memberships in 1941 being:[37]

Society	Membership
Lowton	59
Edge Green	56
Golborne	38
Lowton Road	45
Stubshaw Cross	30
Ashton	43
Bamfurlong	60
	331

These figures would, of course, be augmented by 'adherents' or attenders who were not members. The influence of the chapels would also be extended through their Sunday schools.

Compared with the total populations of the areas served, the impact of the chapels on the communities in which they were located was comparatively little. At the 1931 Census, Ashton and Golborne (including the two Lowton parishes of St Luke's and St Mary's) had respective populations of 20,546 and 7,321. Assuming a combined total of approximately 75 for the Ashton and Stubshaw Cross churches, the Primitive Methodist membership would be only 0.36 per cent of the Ashton population. An assumed total of 200 for the Lowton, Edge Green, Golborne and Lowton Road churches would give only 2.7 per cent of the Golborne population.

The factors contributing to the close-knit chapel communities also increased this insularity by intermarriage. I recall several marriages between young people attending the Lowton and three Golborne chapels but none between attenders at these four chapels and those connected with the Ashton, Bamfurlong and Stubshaw Cross societies. When persons of different churches married, the convention was that the wife should attend her husband's place of worship. A non-Primitive Methodist girl marrying an active Primitive Methodist husband was warmly welcomed because she was a potential new member. Less popular were marriages of Primitive Methodist girls to 'outsiders' since, conversely, this could mean membership losses. Such marriages were carefully scrutinised. In diminishing order of approval were marriages to husbands from other Primitive Methodist chapels, different Nonconformist denominations and Anglicans. Roman Catholics were beyond the pale. Marriage to a non-churchgoer was almost preferable because it was more likely that afterwards the bride would continue to attend her chapel and might even induce her husband to do likewise.

A consequence of intermarriage was that in all the chapels there were strong informal organisations based on kinship. Every chapel had a dominant family or personality, so much so that one society was popularly referred to as 'X's Chapel'. A chapel with two dominant but considerably inter-related families was widely known as 'X, Y and Co'.

A sociological analysis of the people attending each chapel would have identified formal and informal leaders, cliques, 'in and out' groups and isolates. Such an analysis of a Methodist church by Dempsey, places the members along a continuum ranging from 'the politically powerful' to the 'politically insignificant'.[38] The categories identified by this analysis were labelled Key Leaders, Secondary Leaders, Formers of Opinion and, as mentioned 'the Politically Insignificant'. Key Leaders having the most ability to influence events would normally be the Society Stewards, Treasurer, Sunday School Superintendent and, possibly, the Organist. Secondary leaders might include the Property Trustees, Senior Sunday School Teachers, Local Preachers attending the church, and even the Caretaker. Formers of Opinion were persons holding no official position but who, because of their financial support, social position or education, excited influence by acting as 'channels of communication, initiators of dissent or support, interpreters of decisions in which they may or may not have participated and moulders of consensus'. The Politically Insignificant were those new to a society, lacking knowledge of Primitive Methodist polity, strong kinship affiliations or ability to contribute financially or in other ways. Because chapel memberships were small, one person might hold several positions. Such a person might be Society Steward, Trustee, a local preacher and emergency organist. Once appointed, holders tended to retain their positions for many years irrespective of ability. Senior positions were almost always held by men even though women members probably outnumbered men by a ratio of at least five to one.

In chapels with several key leaders or strong personalities, comparative trivialities often caused bitter and prolonged conflicts. I recall heated disputes over whether the Lord's Prayer should be said or sung and the use and choice of a vesper. Sadly, such controversies were sometimes conducted on both sides in a spirit alien to the professed Christianity of the contenders. Connexional rules laid down that the appointed preacher was in sole charge of the service. A considerable furore was provoked when a local preacher requested that the Lord's Prayer should be said rather than sung, only to be told by the organist: 'Get on wi' th' preachin' and' leave t' Lord's Prayer to me.'

The vesper controversy was whether this adjunct to the evening service was required and, if so, what words should be sung. The eventual choice was:

Lord keep us safe this night,
Secure from all our fears
May angels guard us while we sleep
'Till morning light appears.

The anti-vesper party, with some logic, pointed out that the words implied that God's protection was only required through the night: when morning light appeared the petitioners could care for themselves! A better theological argument was that the preceding benediction had commended the congregation to the 'Grace of the Lord Jesus Christ, the Love of God and the Fellowship of the Holy Spirit.' Protected by 'the strong name of the Trinity' the additional guardianship of angels was somewhat superfluous.

Kinship was an important factor in such disputes. Whole families would cast a block vote supporting the views of a relative so that logical and democratic decision-making was compromised. Sometimes the impossibility of an unbiased hearing or loss of face caused a defeated leader to resign all offices and transfer his allegiance (accompanied by his family and friends) to another chapel or even denomination. Both sides endeavoured to enlist the support of the minister, who was placed in a no-win situation and was sometimes influenced more by the likely effects of a decision on the society than considerations of justice or the strengths of the competing arguments. Ministerial appeals to resolve disputes in a spirit of Christian love and fellowship or for reason and compromise were often dismissed by the protagonists as weakness. Yet the lives of most members centred on the chapel. Forman quotes a 'local preacher' who, referring to the Westfield Street Primitive Methodist Chapel in the neighbouring town of St Helens, stated:

> Most of the people who attended there – it was almost like a village – worked from the church and centred their lives round it. That started from childhood. The children always seemed to be practising for something – either an operetta or a Sunday when the kids did their own service. We had a lot of mid-week activity. A young ladies' parlour, a men's union, a young men's union. A ladies' guild met regularly, at least once a week. We had a Boys' Life Brigade which specialised mainly in ambulance work, a football team and a very, very good cricket team.[39]

In the early 1920s, the Westfield Street Chapel had a membership of about 220 and a Sunday school of over 300 scholars and 40 teachers. It was thus far bigger and had a greater range of activities than any chapel in the Lowton Circuit. Yet, some weekday activities were common to the Westfield Street and Lowton Circuit chapels. In both, children were always practising for something. All the chapels had some sort of meeting for women. All had a week-evening preaching service or Christian Endeavour meeting. The Bamfurlong church had a very good soccer team. Socials and 'hot-pot suppers' were happy convivial entertainments where friend met friend. No Lowton Circuit chapel, however, boasted a cricket team or a Boys' Life Brigade corps.

For some chapel-goers the spiritual side of chapel life was subordinate to the social. Brown quotes from a writer, W. R. Kent, who in his book *Testament of a Victorian Youth* (1938), observed that 'Jack Jones goes to chapel to have a talk with Bill Smith. Mrs Robinson goes not to meet her God but Mrs Brown.'[40] While not without substance, the observation is somewhat harsh. For most people I knew, the spiritual and secular aspects of chapel life were inter-related. Jibes such as,

> They're praising God on Sunday
> They'll be alright on Monday
> It's just a little habit they've acquired.[41]

or,

> Their worship's done; their God returns to heaven
> and stays there till next Sunday at Eleven.[42]

certainly did not apply to chapel life as I knew it. All the Circuit chapels were open on several evenings each week although the various activities tended to be insular rather than expressions of outreach. In my home and the homes of most members that I knew, chapel pursuits, people, preaching and politics were perennial topics of weekday conversation. Chapel was associated with life's significant events; birth, marriage, death and for all these it provided the appropriate rite of passage. Ministers were persons who could be relied upon to give appropriate counsel, guidance and practical help with both spiritual and secular problems. Chapel provided a fellowship in which members could share their joys, receive support in their sorrows and participate in a lifestyle which, although in some respects narrow, saw religion not as an adjunct to but something that permeated the whole of life, so that sacred and secular were not compartmentalised but almost imperceptibly merged. One of the most used hymns owed its popularity to the fact that it expressed the aspirations and experience of those by whom it was sung:

> Fill Thou my life, O Lord my God,
> In every part with praise
> that my whole being may proclaim
> Thy being and Thy ways.
> Not for the lip of praise alone
> Nor e'en the praising heart
> I ask, but for a life made up
> Of praise in every part.
>
> Praise in the common words I speak
> Life's common looks and tones;
> In intercourse at hearth or board
> With my belovèd ones.
> Not in the temple crowd alone,
> Where holy voices chime;
> But in the silent paths of earth
> The quiet rooms of time.

Fill every part of me with praise.
Let all my being speak
Of Thee and of Thy love, O Lord!
　Poor though I be and weak.
So shall Thou, Lord, from me, e'en me
　Receive the glory due
And so shall I begin on earth
　The song for ever new.

So shall each fear, each fret, each care
　Be turned into a song,
And every winding of the way
　The echo shall prolong.
So shall no part of day or night
　From sacredness be free
But all my life, in every step,
　Be fellowship with Thee.[43]

6
Beliefs

This chapter is not concerned with an academic discussion of theology. After an introductory section setting out the official doctrines of Primitive Methodism I shall try to describe how those beliefs were understood by the writer and most lay members of the churches in the Lowton Circuit in the period with which this book is concerned.

Primitive Methodism and its doctrines

At the 1829 Primitive Methodist Conference held at Scotter, Lincolnshire, a Deed Poll was signed and sealed by Hugh Bourne, James Bourne and William Clowes. The Deed Poll listed the following eleven (actually thirteen) Articles of Faith:

1 The being of God, including the Holy Trinity.
2 The Deity of the Lord Jesus Christ.
3 The innocence of our first parents when they were created.
4 Their Fall and that of their posterity.
5 General redemption by the Lord Jesus Christ.
6 Repentance including godly sorrow for sin and corresponding reformation.
7 The justification by faith of the ungodly on their turning to God.
8 The witness of the Holy Spirit to their adoption into the family of God.
9 Sanctification by the Holy Spirit producing inward and outward holiness.
10 The resurrection of the dead both of the just and the unjust.
11 The General Judgement and eternal rewards and punishments.

Kendall points out that the above Articles of Faith were merely specified, not defined.[1] The Deed Poll, however, specified that the doctrines would be interpreted agreeably to the teaching of John Wesley as contained in his first five volumes of sermons (often called *The Fifty-Three Sermons*) and *Notes on the New Testament.*

In 1921, the doctrinal statement in the Deed Poll was revised and the reference to the teaching of John Wesley removed. Mews suggests that this deletion might have been construed as provocative since it was only in the previous year that the joint committee of Wesleyan, Primitive and United Methodists, set up to explore the possibilities of union, had specifically referred to Wesley in their own draft doctrinal statement. Mews, however, attributes the 1921 Primitive Methdist decision as being:

> not so much a move in the protracted chess game which was to lead to Methodist Union in 1932 so much as the culmination of thinking which went back to the 1890s, back to the Connexion's one case of heresy, back to the courageous ministry of John Day Thompson.[2]

Prior to entering the Primitive Methodist ministry, John Day Thompson had been apprenticed to a firm of analytical chemists and had developed a questioning and critical outlook. In 1892 he was appointed by Conference to Adelaide in South Australia. The heresy charge was based on a published address delivered by Thompson in Adelaide in 1894 on 'The Simple Gospel' in which he attacked the view that it was the duty of ministers to proclaim 'the Simple Gospel and leave on one side critical questions' and what came to be called 'the Social Gospel'. This view was attacked as a deviation from Methodist doctrine in the *Primitive Methodist World*, one of the then two Primitive Methodist weekly periodicals, the other being *The Primitive Methodist* which had commenced publication in 1883. Day's main opponents were two former principals of the Primitive Methodist Theological Institution, James Macpherson and Joseph Wood. Mews suggests that it may have been partly their sense of outrage at the direction in which the College was going under their successors that lay behind the chagrin of Macpherson and Wood.[3] In 1896, the Primitive Methodist Conference meeting at Burnley was asked to adjudicate on the matter as the final Connexional Court of Appeal where, by an overwhelming majority, it was resolved that no action be taken on the matter. Thompson went on to become President of the Primitive Methodist Conference in 1915. The case represented a watershed in the transition from the early Primitive Methodist evangelism based on the inerrency of the Scriptures and the cultural revolution in the attitude to biblical interpretation that followed the appointment of A. S. Peake as tutor to the Manchester Theological Institution in 1892.

Fundamentally, Primitive Methodist doctrine and that of Wesleyan Methodism were identical, although as Kent shows, the main obstacles to Methodist Union were disagreements about the doctrines of the ministry and sacraments. [4]

Theology at the local level

Apart from the better-read local preachers, probably few lay people in the Lowton Circuit were more than vaguely aware of Primitive Methodist doctrine. In this respect they differed little from lay people of most denominations. Wilson rightly observes that 'the man in the street has not the permanent commitment to enquiry of the intellectual' but wants only 'assurance and certainty'. [5] Most members were Primitive Methodists by heredity rather than conviction. Their allegiance was often less to the denomination or even circuit than to the local church building in which they had been nurtured. The Bible was the authority for faith. Most members if asked to vindicate their beliefs would probably have begun by saying 'the Bible says'. Few knew anything of the enlightened critical approach to the Bible given by A. S. Peake both in his writings and lectures to Hartley College students. As shown in Chapter 4, the appointment of Arthur S. Peake MA, Fellow of Merton College, Oxford and lecturer at Mansfield College as Tutor in Biblical Introduction, Exegesis, Theology and History of Doctrine at the Primitive Methodist Theological Institution in Manchester revolutionised ministerial training in the Connexion. His avowed aim was to produce ministers who were 'cultured evangelists' and he succeeded. During his thirty-seven-year tenure of the post, during which he also became the first Rylands Professor of Biblical Criticism and Exegesis in the University of Manchester, Peake almost single-handedly helped Primitive Methodism to avoid the worst effects of fundamentalism. Not that the fundamentalists were silenced. Hooker quotes several examples of their fury, of which the following extract from a letter appearing in the *Christian Herald* for 1 July 1920 is typical:

> We used to be told that Bible science and history were faulty, but now we learn that its ethics and theology and its teaching on social and economic subjects are all quite unreliable. Then the world is much poorer than we thought. We have lost much, and what does Dr Peake offer to supply the loss? According to him, the Bible is wrong; Christ, His apostles, the prophets and fathers of the Church are all wrong; Creeds and Confessions, Standards and Prayer-book are all wrong; and all we have left on which to rely for spiritual and eternal truth is – Dr Peake! What he approves is right. He is the 'Truth Controller'. We have no infallible Christ now, but we have Dr Peake! He is the light of the world! Even his own critical compeers disagree with him widely, but still he is our new infallible Pope. We must stand in a queue at his door, and take our Peake-controlled doles of doctrine and be thankful.[6]

I recall many disparaging references by lay preachers to 'Peake', 'modernism' and 'the Higher Criticism'. Huxtable, a Congregationalist, tells how, in 1929, when staying with his Methodist grandparents, he exclaimed when reading the *News Chronicle*: 'A. S. Peake's dead.' His grandmother, peeling potatoes in the adjacent kitchen, ejaculated: 'Thank God.' When asked to explain herself, she said: 'He's upset the faith of so many people. It's a mercy he's gone.'[7] On occasion, the gulf between the informed and the uninformed knowledge and use of the Bible by ministers and lay people respectively was a source of conflict between the two.

There were, however, other sources of authority. Luke Wiseman, famous Wesleyan minister, observed in a sermon that for most people the second line of a popular children's hymn should not be:

> Jesus loves me this I know
> For the Bible tells me so.

but rather: 'For my mother told me so.' This was certainly true for me. It was my father, however, with his stirring stories of Gideon, Samson, Elijah, Elisha, David, Esther, Daniel and the Maccabees that made the Old Testament and Apocrypha come alive.

Unfortunately then, as now, many people never progressed in their theological thinking from the simple ideas learned at their mother's knee or in Sunday school. Most were content with a Peter Pan religion that never grew up. Pressed to state the Articles of Primitive Methodist doctrine to which they subscribed, the majority of members would probably have mentioned God, Jesus Christ, The Holy Spirit and the Last Things.

God

In the inter-war years, the majority of people, both church and non-church, professed some kind of belief in God. Avowed atheists such as Bertrand Russell and the Huxleys (T. H. the biologist, J. S. the zoologist and Aldous the writer) were frequently castigated in Primitive Methodist pulpits by preachers of inferior intellect who had probably never read, or were incapable of reading, the books they condemned. Local atheists were regarded with suspicion and pulpit anecdotes of how they had been confounded were related with relish. Father's contribution was the story of an atheistically minded miner. One day, there was a fall of coal. The miner cried out: 'Lord save me!' A fellow collier, hearing the cry remarked shrewdly, 'Aye, there's nowt like cobs o' coal fer knockin' th' atheism out of a mon.'

Arguments from design, such as Paley's Watch, were the most commonly cited 'proof' of God's existence. Paley, writing in 1802, made use of an argument which philosophers have traced back to Cicero's *De Natura Deorum*:

> In crossing a heath, suppose I pitched my foot against a stone, and were asked how the stone came to be there, I might possibly answer, that for anything I knew to the contrary, it had lain there for ever: nor would it perhaps be very easy to show the absurdity of this answer. But suppose I found a watch upon the ground and it should be inquired how the watch happened to be in that place, I should hardly think of the answer which I had before given, that for anything I knew, the watch might have always been there ...
>
> The inference we think is inevitable that the watch must have a maker; that it must have existed, at sometime, and at some place or other an artificer or artificers, who formed it for the purpose which we find it actually to answer; who comprehended its construction, and designed its use.[8]

Paley went on to drive home his argument with other examples, beginning with the human eye which he compares with a designed instrument such as a telescope and concluded that 'there is precisely the same proof that the eye was made for vision, as there is that the telescope was made for assisting it. Both the eye and the telescopes must have had designers.'

This was an argument that was easy both to grasp and quote. It was also an argument that physicists and biologists such as Richard Dawkins[9] have not found difficult to refute. But most religious people then, as now, wanted certainty and conviction, not questioning and doubt.

Much emphasis was correctly placed on the principle that God could never be fully apprehended by reason but only by experience and faith:

> Where reason fails with all her powers
> There faith prevails, and love adores.[10]

My early ideas of God were anthropomorphic. This was understandable. A family Bible in my home had pictures of God in human form walking in the Garden of Eden in the cool of the day, appearing from the clouds to divide the waters of the Red Sea for the escaping Israelites, and, throned in heavenly splendour, opening the books on Judgement Day. Such pictures were reinforced by religious language, asking God to 'open his *ears* to our cries', reminding us that 'the *eyes* of the Lord are in every place' and giving assurance that 'his *hands* are outstretched to save'. I suspect that few people interpreted such language metaphorically and that, more than today, the inadequate concepts of God listed by Phillips were widely prevalent. These inadequate concepts included 'The Resident Policeman', 'The Grand Old Man', 'Absolute Perfection', 'Heavenly Bosom', 'God-in-a-Box', 'Managing Director' and 'Perennial Grievance' or 'the God who lets us down'.[11] All these mental images of God were prevalent both in chapel preaching and Sunday school teaching. God, of course, was indubitably male.

As expounded in Sunday school and sermons, God had also many roles and attributes. He was Father and Friend but also King, Judge and Creator – 'the maker of all things near and far.' Because he was the 'Giver of every good and perfect gift', we offered our thanksgivings. Every meal in my home was prefaced by a Grace:

For what we are about to receive
Make us truly thankful.

Before every chapel tea, we sang the Doxology:

Praise God from whom all blessings flow
Praise Him all creatures here below.
Praise Him above ye heavenly host
Praise Father, Son and Holy Ghost.

God's attributes included omnipotence, omniscience and omnipresence. Few members of the Lowton Circuit chapels had these words in their vocabularies but they knew that God is all-powerful, all-knowing and everywhere present.

Because God was all-powerful and personal – 'the Sovereign King over all the Earth' – he could answer prayer. Apart from being taught to kneel, close my eyes and put my hands together and repeat a simple petition and the Lord's Prayer, I never recall being systematically taught anything about the pattern, principles and perplexities of prayer. Adoration, thanksgiving, confession, petition and intercession were aspects of prayer that were caught rather than taught. Small wonder that many people had a somewhat crude and magical concept of prayer. Preachers quoted many examples of the power of prayer, sometimes both theologically and philosophically dubious. I recall one example of answered prayer related by a visiting lay preacher who was involved with the cricket team of the Primitive Methodist Sunday school in a neighbouring circuit. The team played in one of the lower divisions of the West Lancashire League and were drawn in a cup competition against Bickershaw Collieries, who were then indisputably champions of the League's First Division. Not only did the Colliery team employ a professional but, by virtue of the ability to offer employment, it was able to cream off the best cricketing talent in the locality. (By the same process, the Bickershaw Collieries Brass Band became a household name, regularly competing in – and winning – the National Brass Band Contest.) The cricket match in football terms was the equivalent of a Premier Club against a virtually unknown minor league side. Bickershaw batted first and were surprisingly dismissed for the low score of 82. The chapel side, however, were soon in trouble. At 36 for 7, drastic action was required. The preacher went behind the pavilion and prayed for victory. On his return, he found that, due to lusty hitting and missed catches, the score had advanced to 60 without further loss. The big hitter was bowled but the umpire had previously called 'no-ball'. Several appeals for 'lbw' were turned down. Eventually, the chapel team won by one wicket. Such was the power of prayer. The preacher failed to mention, however, that in the next round, his team were slaughtered by a much less formidable team than Bickershaw. When prayers went unanswered, we were told that the reason was lack of faith or even that 'No' was still an answer.

Only much later did I recognise the difficulties of faith raised by the concept of omnipotence, such as the argument that if God was all good, he would not allow innocent suffering. If he were all powerful, he would prevent it.

I was constantly reminded of God's all-seeing eye by the framed text 'Thou God Seest Me' hanging in my bedroom. So far as I recall, it did not cause me to have a sense of guilt or think of God in a negative way as a snooping policeman who noted every misdemeanour. Rather, I thought of the words positively as an incentive, in Milton's words, 'to do all as in my great Task-Master's eye.'

God's omnipresence was the attribute which caused the least intellectual difficulty. Pure eyes and open hearts could find God everywhere, not only in church but in the beauty of the earth, the splendour of the skies and the joy of human love. No part of day or night from sacredness was free and God could be found in every duty and deed no matter how small and mean. I remember hearing the reading of Psalm 139, 'whither shall I go from Thy presence?' and reconciling it with the words of Whittier, the meaning of which, with passing years, have deepened by experience:

I only know I cannot drift
Beyond His love and care.

Above all, God was love. We were reminded of this so often in sermons that the statement could easily become a platitude, oblivious to the contradictory evidences of 'nature red in tooth and claw' or human suffering. When I was thirteen, however, an incident changed the platitude into an experience. One glorious spring evening, my parents and I arrived home from chapel. For some reason, I remained outside after my parents had gone indoors. The sun was setting, a glorious ball of fire in the west. The last line of the closing hymn, 'Sun of my soul; Thou Saviour dear' echoed in my mind:

Till in the ocean of Thy love
We lose ourselves in heaven above.

Suddenly, I knew what the lines meant. I had a vivid sense of being enfolded by God's love. To try to describe the experience is like attempting to convey the beauty of a sunset to a blind person or the majesty of a symphony to someone totally deaf. At that moment, I *knew* peace, security, and joy and the warmth of God's love. The experience was probably only momentary but it was an eternal moment. I never told my parents of the experience. Retrospectively, I realise that the experience was not dissimilar to Wesley's warmed heart, Fox's inner light or the realisation of Julian of Norwich that 'all things have being through the love of God.'

Psychologists might dismiss the experience as the heightened religious consciousness of early adolescence. But the fact is that sixty years later, the experience is still vivid and inspiring. In the intervening years, I have known intellectual doubt, war, suffering and some of life's darker places. Nothing, however, has shaken the certitude of the spring evening that the ultimate reality is love. When the lamp of faith has burned dim, I have always managed to keep the flame aglow. Because of that evening, I have always been able to declare with Browning's Paracelsus:

> God Thou art love;
> I build my faith on that.

Jesus Christ

The year after the experience described above, I was received into membership of the Methodist Church at Bridge Street. The minister, T. H. Champion, gave me the right hand of fellowship and a card which stated that I had accepted Jesus Christ as Lord and Saviour.

At that age, my acceptance of the Gospel biographies of Jesus was, of course, uncritical. Such problems as the Virgin birth, the authenticity of the Christmas stories, the feasibility of miracles, the significance of Christ's death and the meaning of the resurrection and ascension lay in the future. Looking back, it seems that between the ages of roughly five to sixteen, my thoughts of Jesus gradually progressed from Jesus as the Friend of little children, Redeemer, Revealer of God to the Human Jesus – 'Our Hero Strong and Tender'.

The Friend of little children

Like most people, my earliest concept of Jesus was that of the Friend of little children. This concept was imparted in the home, continued in Sunday school and reinforced by pictures, hymns and prayers. The walls of my Sunday school were adorned by pictures of Jesus. Visually, he had a long white robe and was surrounded by children of all colours. Significantly, Jesus himself was white. Every night, I prayed to 'Gentle Jesus, meek and mild' and sang the same words, by Charles Wesley, in Sunday school. I was in my teens before I realised the inadequacy of this idea of Jesus. Many years later, I read Bruce Barton's book *The Man Nobody Knows* in which he relates how he had been alienated by such concepts of Jesus.

> Love Jesus! The little boy looked at the picture which hung on the Sunday School wall. It showed a pale young man with flabby forearms and a sad expression. The young man had red whiskers.
>
> Then the little boy looked across to the other wall. There was Daniel, good old Daniel, standing off the lions. The little boy liked Daniel. He liked David too, with the little sling that landed a stone square on the forehead of Goliath, and Moses with his rod and his big brass snake. They were winners those three …
>
> But Jesus! Jesus was the 'Lamb of God'. The little boy did not know what that meant but it sounded like Mary's little lamb. Something for girls – sissified. Jesus was also 'meek and lowly', 'a man of sorrows and acquainted with grief'. He went round for three years telling people not to do things …
>
> The little boy was glad when the Superintendent thumped the bell and announced 'We will now sing the closing hymn'. One more bad hour was over. For one more week, the little boy had got rid of Jesus.[12]

Jesus the Saviour and Redeemer

This was the second concept. The Primitive Methodist doctrines of the innocence of Adam and Eve, their Fall and that of their posterity and their general redemption by Jesus Christ were often expounded in the first Sunday school I attended at Lowton Road. We never considered what the consequence for the world would have been had they not fallen. Neither did most scholars understand the nature of the sin for which they had been cast out. For some years, I believed that they had been expelled from Paradise for wearing no clothes. Between the wars, nudism was regarded in chapel circles not just as an offence against decency but sinful. We were often told that Jesus had died to save us. This salvation was still interpreted as salvation from hell so that 'we might go at last to heaven saved by his precious blood'. As children, we listened politely but were not impressed. For young boys and girls, hell and heaven were a long time into the future.

From memory, what is termed the 'substitutionary theory' of redemption was proclaimed from most pulpits. This asserted that God's attitude to sinners is necessarily one of anger because justice demands that sin should be punished. Christ agreed to become the sinners' representative or rather substitute and, as such, bore on the Cross the punishment for the sins of the whole world. The demands of justice were therefore satisfied and God's wrath was turned away. The theory was perhaps better expressed in a hymn from the *Primitive Methodist Hymnal*:

> Jesus, who lived above the sky
> Came down to be a man and die
> And in the Bible, we may see
> How very good He used to be.
> He knew how wicked man had been.
> And knew that God must punish sin.
> So out of pity, Jesus said
> He'd bear the punishment instead.

That hymn was expunged from the 1933 *Methodist Hymn Book* but the substitutionary theory still survives in lines such as:

There was no other good enough
To pay the price of sin.

or in the verse by Phillip Bliss:

Bearing shame and scoffing rude.
In my place condemned he stood;
Sealed my pardon with his blood:
Alleluia! What a Saviour.

In the Parable of the Prodigal Son, however, the Father did not require to be placated before receiving the wanderer back home. As Macquarrie wrote:

> The parable stresses the unchanging character of God's attitude and work which is always one of reconciliation …
>
> No historical event changes God's attitude, or makes him from a wrathful God into a gracious God, or allows his reconciling work to get started – such thoughts should be utterly rejected.[13]

By the 1930s, preachers, apart from the most fundamentally evangelical, were discarding the substitutionary doctrine. Other approaches included the 'moral theory' that Christ's death should be seen in the light of his life as a revelation of God's love. That love is revealed in the Cross, which not only reveals the exceeding sinfulness of sin but also the lengths to which love can go, and, when apprehended, moves us to repentance.

Primitive Methodist preachers, like all other Methodists except the Calvinists, echoed the Armenian confidence of Charles Wesley:

For all, my Lord was crucified
For all, for all my Saviour died.

My father often sang:

At the Cross, at the Cross! When I first saw the light,
And the burden of my heart rolled away.
It was there, by faith, I received my sight
And now I am happy all the day![14]

Those words expressed the experience of many Primitive Methodist converts, yet my impression is that in both early and later Primitive Methodist revivalism, the Cross was mentioned much less than in Anglican or Roman Catholic evangelism. Even in the 1930s, most Primitive Methodists who sang the above verse would probably have rejected out-of-hand any proposal to place a Cross on their communion table as 'Going to Rome'. In my experience, Primitive Methodist observance of Good Friday was virtually non-existent.

The 'scheme of salvation' set out in the Primitive Methodist Deed Poll which traced the progress of the Christian life from conviction of sin to repentance, justification by Grace through faith in Christ's saving work, adoption into God's family and finally sanctification, or growth into holiness, the goal of the Christian life, the essential mark of which was love or agape as revealed in Jesus, was, in my experience, also not widely known. Some of the older local preachers still preached for conversions. Conversion, however, was thought of as a once-and-for-all experience. Older people used to tell me when, where and by whom they were saved – the latter usually being the evangelist rather than Christ. Fred, my half-brother, told me how he had been converted at a mission held in the Stubshaw Cross church by a travelling evangelist popularly known as 'Happy Jack'. The following year, Happy Jack made a return visit. In response to his appeal, Fred again went forward but before he could join the penitents at the communion rail, he was intercepted and turned back by my Uncle James, who reminded him, 'You were done last year.' At the Lowton and Bridge Street churches, conversions were dismissed as 'emotionalism'.

Jesus the Revealer of God

As stated above, Jesus as Redeemer revealed the love of God so that redemption was an aspect of the incarnation. In Sunday school and sermons we were told that Jesus is God but not in a way that was easy to understand. Even as an adolescent, I found it difficult to comprehend how the Jesus who walked in Galilee and Judea, often weary, footsore, hungry and homeless, could be the Creator of all things. Only much later did I realise that it is possible, as Blake says:

> To see the world in a grain of sand.
> And Heaven in a wild flower.
> Hold infinity in the palm of the hand.
> And eternity in an hour.[15]

And also, to find ultimate reality, the meaning of existence and the same Spirit that moves the sun and stars in one incomparable life of heroic loveliness.

Our Hero Strong and Tender

By 1939, much emphasis was being placed on a better understanding of the personality and teaching of Jesus. At the Bridge Street Sunday school, the senior class, of which I had become a member, met in a vestry on Sunday afternoons to read and discuss books. It was probably the only Sunday school in the Circuit at which such readings and discussions took place and retrospectively, I regard those Sunday afternoons among my most formative educational experiences. Among the books read were some which opened my mind to the human and credible Jesus. Among such books were *The Jesus of History* by T. R. Glover and a number of the works of Leslie Weatherhead.

Glover, classical scholar and Cambridge don, published *The Jesus of History* in 1917. The book had a phenomenal success, running through twenty-five editions and 124,000 copies in thirty years. Glover's approach is summed up in his first chapter:

> The central figure of the Gospels must impress every attentive reader as, at least, a man of marked personality. He has his own attitude to life, his own views of God and man and all else, and his own language.[16]

Weatherhead was minister of London's City Temple from 1936 to 1960. As indicated by their titles, his early books, *Psychology and Life* (1934), *Psychology in the Service of the Soul* (1929) and *The*

Mastery of Sex through Psychology and Religion (1932) were concerned to apply psychological insights to Christian living. Other books, however, such as *The Transforming Friendship* (1928), *Jesus and Ourselves* (1930) and *It Happened in Palestine* and *His Life and Ours* (1932) were concerned:

> to work out in the light of the twentieth century the significance for us today of the main happenings in that life of lives and to express that significance as far as possible in ordinary everyday language.[17]

Both Glover, a Baptist, and Weatherhead, a Wesleyan Methodist, were the objects of considerable disapprobation, often vitriolic, within their respective denominations. Within Methodism, Weatherhead was criticised by fundamentalists as a 'modernist' and by evangelicals as 'having no gospel'. He was even arraigned on a heresy charge before the Disciplinary Committee of the Wesleyan Methodist Church. Yet for many, as for the writer, his books made Jesus come alive. In the books of both Glover and Weatherhead, Jesus was not only a 'man of sorrows, acquainted with grief' but a man of joy who could make the rafters ring with laughter as he sat at dinner with his friends.

Those afternoons in the Bridge Street vestry were the beginnings of my theological education. It was not, however, books but a sermon that opened my eyes to the heroic Jesus. On a Passion Sunday at Bridge Street, Revd T. H. Champion preached on Mark 10.32.

> And they were on the way going up to Jerusalem; and Jesus went before them and they that followed were afraid.

The general theme was Jesus, the Leader who went ahead. Leadership is the power to influence by words or example. It was the influence of Jesus that kept the disciples following even though they were apprehensive about where and to what he was leading them. It was not just the courage of Jesus shaming them out of their cowardice so much as love overcoming fear. The disciples felt it worthwhile to be with Jesus no matter where He might go. They were afraid; but they followed. Years later, I discovered a hymn that summed up the picture of Jesus given to an impressionable boy on that Sunday morning:

> I have a Captain, and the heart
> Of every private man
> Has drunk the valour from his eyes
> Since first the war began.
> He is most merciful in fight
> And of his scars, a single sight
> The embers of our failing might
> Into a flame can scan.[18]

In the 1930s there was also a greater emphasis on the teaching of Jesus relating to the Kingdom of God as the royal rule of God in the hearts of people. Christ's concept of the Kingdom is primarily a gospel rather than a social and economic programme. It is essentially concerned with the relation of sinful people to the love of God and only secondarily, and by inference, with the social conditions under which they live. A good case can, however, be made for the assertion that the principles of socialism are in harmony with Christ's teaching.

In Primitive Methodism especially, the traditional evangelical concept of salvation was expanded to relate not only to matters spiritual, futuristic and individual but also to temporal, present and social concerns. It is doubtful whether any of the local and auxiliary preachers in the Lowton Circuit had heard of the German theologian Adolf Harnack who in his book *What is Christianity* (1900) emphasised the centrality of the idea of the Kingdom of God in the teaching of Jesus and advanced the thesis that the Kingdom was to be realised in the achievement of a just social order here on earth. However, it is possible that some were aware of F. D. Maurice and the Christian Socialists of the 1850s who suggested that the Kingdom of God encompassed nothing less than the whole of creation and religion was concerned with the whole of life both sacred and secular. They very likely knew of R. J. Campbell who, in a sermon preached in the City Temple in 1906 on 'Christianity and Socialism', had equated the latter with the former. While such preachers disapproved of Campbell's theological views as declared in the *New Theology* (1907) many would be in sympathy with his politics.

The concept of the Kingdom as realised in a new social order was popularised in Primitive Methodist congregations by some of the 295 hymns included in the *Hymnal Supplement* issued in 1912.

The section on 'The Lord Jesus Christ – His Kingdom' contained twenty hymns including:

> These things shall be: a loftier race
> Than e'er the world hath known shall rise
> With flame of freedom in their souls
> And light of knowledge in their eyes.
>
> – *John Addington Symmonds, No. 78*

The section on 'National and Civic Hymns' had fifteen items, two of which were:

> England, arise! The long, long night is over,
> Faint in the east behold the dawn appear;
> Out of your evil dream of toil and sorrow
> Arise, O England, for the day is here.
>
> – *E. Carpenter, No. 2*

> When wilt thou save the people?
> O Lord of mercy, when?
> Not kings and lords, but nations!
> Not thrones and crowns but men!
> Flowers of thy heart, O God, are they;
> Let them not pass, like weeds away –
> Their heritage a sunless day,
> God save the people!
>
> – *Ebenezer Elliot, No. 279*

Particularly in the Bamfurlong and Stubshaw churches of the Lowton Circuit where the people knew at first hand about long hours and sub-human conditions in the mines, the Kingdom of God was equated with an approved social order. No preacher could go wrong in choosing 'When wilt thou save the people?' and 'These things shall be' – the latter to the tune of *Arizona.* Both hymns have been expunged from modern hymnals, the latter on the grounds that it is entirely humanistic in outlook and only incidentally mentions God. It was, however, sung fervently by both congregations who read into its verses a vision of the Kingdom of God on earth. Whatever its demerits the hymn probably contained nobler ideals than the *Red Flag.*

Two of the members of the Lowton Road church, as mentioned in Chapter 4, were Labour Councillors. Neither of them stressed class conflict and, in fact, exhibited a wide tolerance of other political opinions and an ability to be 'all things to all men'. Both were criticised by chapel members because their political work necessitated visiting the Labour Clubs where beer was sold even though they themselves were temperance stalwarts. Their Christian service also extended to being members of Boards of Guardians, School Managers and service to voluntary hospitals. They regarded such service as the 'Service of the Kingdom'.

The Holy Spirit and the Trinity

At the local level, the Holy Spirit and the Trinity were comparatively neglected aspects of Primitive Methodist doctrine. We celebrated Whitsuntide in a perfunctory way. We never observed Trinity Sunday or Ascension Day. The sections on the Holy Spirit and the Trinity in both the Primitive Methodist and Methodist Hymn Books contained some of the best-loved and most used hymns including 'Breathe on me, Breath of God,' 'Spirit divine, attend our prayers' and Heber's 'Holy, holy, holy, Lord God Almighty' with its reference to 'God in Three Persons, blessed Trinity'. We were taught that all Scripture is inspired by God and sang lustily:

> Come, Holy Ghost, for moved by thee
> The prophets wrote and spoke.

Yet, along with probably most members, I found it difficult to understand the doctrines of the Holy Spirit and Trinity.

Writing much later in 1974, Hans Küng states that:

> We cannot overlook the fact that any talk of the Holy Spirit is so unintelligible to many today that it cannot even be regarded as controversial.[19]

One reason, as Küng suggests, was because then, as now,

> When theologians did not know how to justify a particular doctrine, a dogma or a biblical form, they appealed to the Holy Spirit. When mild or wild fanatics did not know how to justify their subjectivist whims, they invoked the Holy Spirit.

As a boy, I noticed that although the guidance of the Holy Spirit was invoked at the start of church meetings, the subsequent discussions and dissensions seemed to indicate that the Holy Spirit was leading different people in different ways.

Another problem was the term 'Ghost'. Even when in the doxology we sang:

> Praise Him above ye heavenly host
> Praise Father, Son and Holy Ghost.

I felt somewhat 'spooky'. The word suggested an apparition like that of Jacob Marley in Dickens's *Christmas Carol.* The thought of a 'ghost' sent a shiver down the spine.

With both the Holy Spirit and the Trinity, however, the main difficulty was the word 'persons'. Like lawyers, most people construe words in their literal sense and a 'person' was a human figure or bodily presence. The doctrine of the Trinity therefore suggests tritheism like the boy who, when asked to name the three persons of the Trinity, replied Mr Jones, Mr Smith and Mr Brown, who respectively were the Vicar and his two curates at the local parish church. We thought of the Trinity as three distinct beings. Even words like 'In the name of the Father, and of the Son, and the Holy Ghost' reinforced this view, as did other religious language such as 'Seated on the right hand of God.' The latter words caused me to imagine a Divine Tribunal with God as the Chairman sitting in the middle flanked on the right and left by the Son and the Holy Ghost. The problem with this concept was the difficulty of visualising a 'seated' incorporeal person.

Not until I was much older did I understand that the doctrine of the Trinity is concerned to affirm a unitary rather than tritheistic view of God and that Father, Son and Holy Spirit are three aspects of the same personality. God in history and nature, God as revealed by Jesus and God in our own experience and God in the experience of the Church inspiring, enlightening, strengthening, comforting. As a homely illustration of the essential meaning of the Trinity, it is difficult to improve on that of William Sangster who overheard a conversation between two children after a Trinity Sunday service.

> 'I don't understand this three in one and one in three business,' said the first child.
>
> 'Neither do I', said the other, 'but I think it must be something like this. Mummie is Mabel to Daddy, Mummie to us, and Mrs Smith to the people next door.'

The Last Things

To my knowledge, no church in our Circuit ever associated the four Sundays in Advent with the themes of Death, Judgement, Hell or Heaven. I am sure, however, that most people, including my parents, interpreted both their personal resurrection and the imagery of the Book of Revelation literally. Few Primitive Methodists had read the Fourth (or any) of the Church of England's Thirty-Nine Articles but they believed implicitly that 'Christ did truly rise again from death and took again his body, with flesh, bones and all things appertaining to the perfection of Man's nature.' This belief in a bodily resurrection was reinforced for me by pictures in the Family Bible of people emerging from their graves at the sound of the Last Trumpet. Belief in the resurrection of the body was regarded as essential to the hope that, in heaven, we would be reunited with those whom we had loved on earth. There was little understanding of Paul's distinction between the natural or animal body and the spiritual or 'glorified' body, fit for the life of heaven.

There was a similar lack of understanding that the imagery of the Book of Revelation is picture language, used by the writer to express the inexpressible. I can never recall any attempt to explain that the description of the Heavenly City as four square with five gates on each side is simply a means of saying that life in heaven is a harmonious complete existence, that gold suggests the timelessness of heaven since gold does not rust or that heaven is filled with music because, for most people, music is synonymous with happiness and joy. Although some evangelical preachers referred to the flames awaiting the unsaved, I doubt if many people believed with Spurgeon and Jonathan Edwards that 'There is real fire in hell.'

There was, however, a general belief that, at death, the deceased had 'gone to a better place'. This belief was implicit in a hymn sung regularly at the funerals, which as a child I attended with my parents:

Rejoice for a brother deceased
Our loss is his infinite gain;
A soul out of prison released
And freed from its bodily chain;
With songs let us follow his flight,
And mount with his spirit above.
Escaped to the mansions of light
And lodged in the Eden of love.[20]

In adolescence I facetiously reworded the second line as

His loss *our* infinite gain.

The 'great assize' at the end of time conflicted with the popular belief, supported by Christ's parable of Dives and Lazarus, that a person's destiny is determined at the moment of death.

This belief gave inadequate consideration to the possibility that the deceased might be unready for heaven. The need for an intermediate state between death and the Final Judgement in which the soul might move from the near-annihilation of sin to the closest union with God is met by the doctrine of Purgatory.

Probably because of its association with the sale of masses and indulgences, the doctrine received little serious consideration in Primitive Methodist circles and was dismissed as a Roman Catholic superstition. Neither was there any understanding of the theories of conditional immortality and universalism. Conditionalism holds that immortality is not a necessary attribute of the soul but is conditional on its behaviour during life in the body. Universalism stresses that because God's ultimate purpose is the redemption of the world, which is the object of his love, no soul will be finally lost. I suspect universalism was and still is the popular choice not because of reasoned argument but from the basic optimism expressed by Omar Khayyam:

> They talk of some strict testing of us – Pish!
> He's a Good Fellow, and 'twill all be well.[21]

Simple and reasoned faith

The beliefs of the members comprising the Lowton Circuit, like those of most churchgoers today, could probably have been statistically represented by a bell-shaped normal curve. At one extreme were those who read about and questioned their beliefs. These would include the small group with whom I was associated at the Bridge Street Sunday school and some of the better educated local preachers. The overwhelming majority of members, clustered round the mean, would, I suspect, accept Primitive Methodist doctrines without much questioning or reflection. Writing in the 1940s, Cyril Joad, the Oxford philosopher, observed cynically that 'not more than ten per cent of the population attend church and the majority of these are elderly and comparatively ill-educated women.' The statement, though hurtful, was largely true of the memberships of the Lowton Circuit churches. Most such members had not the leisure or inclination to read abstruse theological books or the capacity to understand them. In any event, we sang lustily a hymn which reminded us that:

> To doubt would be disloyalty
> To falter would be sin.

Nevertheless, such people found that their beliefs gave meaning to life, comfort in sorrow and guidelines for conduct based on the ethics of the Ten Commandments and the Golden Rule.

At the other extreme were a small number of mainly elderly persons, who, although unaware of it themselves, were well on the road to sanctification. The changing scenes of life had deepened their religious experience. Through prayer, reading the Bible and religious classics including the *Pilgrim's Progress*, pondering the words of hymns and in the fellowship of the church, they had achieved a deep spirituality. These lived by faith and literally walked with God.

Bernard of Clairvaux, in a much loved hymn, declares:

> The love of Jesus, what it is,
> None but his loved ones know.

The people about whom I am writing were those who *knew*. Their memory constantly reminds me that many Christians have entered into salvation without the intellectual capacity to understand the Creeds.

Yet, in my early teens, I realised that more than a simple faith is required. One of our near neighbours worked at a local engineering works. In his early life, he had been a member and organist at a Primitive Methodist church. Later, he had left in disillusionment and became a militant Communist. He had a standing weekly order for half a dozen eggs which I delivered on Saturday mornings. Sometimes, he sent my father copies of a publication, *Russia Today*, filled with pictures of newly erected state hospitals, model factories and happy workers. I found it difficult to reconcile the utopia of *Russia Today* with the stories of church persecution which regularly appeared in the religious press.

One Saturday, I found the Communist arguing at his garden gate with one of our auxiliary local preachers. The Communist was too involved to be bothered with the eggs, so I listened to the argument. It was a one-sided contest. The Communist had reasons for his beliefs and could adduce numerous reasons to support his contention that religion is so much 'pie-in-the-sky when we die'. In contrast, the local preacher, not now 'raised six foot above contradiction' was out of his depth. A chance conversation can have consequences not contemplated by the participant. John Bunyan, for example, was converted by overhearing the conversation of 'three or four poor women sitting at the door in the sun, talking about the things of God.'[22] The conversation between the Communist and the local preacher marked another milestone in my religious development. That morning I realised that when arguing with those who do not share Christian convictions, it is essential to have rational grounds for faith. At first I read apologetics simply to defend the faith more convincingly than the local preacher. Later, I recognised the truth of Tennyson's lines:

> There lives more faith in honest doubt
> Believe me, than in half the Creeds.[23]

Over a lifetime I have realised that while theology is the systematic critical clarification of the historical beliefs of the Church, it deals with hypotheses rather than verifiable conclusions which, of course, would make faith unnecessary and that consequently, on many of the issues raised, we must adopt an attitude of reverent agnosticism. In the final chapter of *Christianity and History*, published in 1950, Herbert Butterfield, then Cambridge Professor of Modern History, points out that 'there are times when we can never meet the future with sufficient elasticity of mind, especially if we are locked in the contemporary systems of thought.' For such times, Butterfield suggests a principle 'which both gives us a firm Rock and leaves us the maximum elasticity for our minds: Hold fast to Christ, and for the rest be totally uncommitted.'[24]

7
Ethics and Moral Theology

I was in my late teens before the word 'ethics' became part of my vocabulary. An academic knowledge of moral theology or the study of Christian character and conduct was an even later acquisition. Preston distinguishes Christian ethics from moral theology. Christian ethics is concerned with the general character of the Christian life. Moral theology is the relating of Christian ethics to particular circumstances.[1] From a very early age, however, I knew what conduct was acceptable or otherwise and what, in Primitive Methodist circles, was permissible or the converse.

Primitive Methodist ethics and moral theology were related to the Protestant Ethic and the Nonconformist conscience as exemplified in the wider Methodist movement. It is probable, however, that the predominantly working-class Primitive Methodist church interpreted certain aspects of moral and ethical conduct more stringently than some other middle-class denominations such as the Congregationalists and the Unitarians or even, in some instances, the Wesleyans. Primitive Methodist ethics and moral theology were firmly based in the Bible especially the Ten Commandments. They were, however, also strongly influenced by the Protestant ethic and expressed themselves in the Nonconformist conscience.

The Protestant ethic

Nothing contributed more to the reputation of the German sociologist Max Weber (1864–1920) than his book *The Protestant Ethic and the Spirit of Capitalism.*[2] Weber set out to show the close relationship between religious belief and economic development with particular reference to the capitalist society which had arisen in the Western World. Weber argued that the capitalism of the West, with its vast industrial and commercial empires, cannot be attributed solely to the acquisitive instinct since people everywhere are acquisitive. Neither can it be accounted for by the possession of raw materials, since many undeveloped areas are richer in natural resources than the West. Capitalism is not wholly explainable in terms of technical 'know-how' since technology tends to follow rather than precede industrial development. How then can we account for the rise of Western capitalism? Weber began by stating an obvious but overlooked fact, that in countries like America, Britain and Germany, captains of industry were overwhelmingly Protestant and that, historically, American, Dutch and English Puritans were the pioneers of commercial enterprise. Weber therefore concluded that the Reformation was not only of religious significance but had profoundly influenced the values that govern economic action.

Before the Reformation, the three values emphasised by the mediaeval Church were poverty, chastity and obedience. Far from looking on poverty as a misfortune, the Church elevated it, providing that, as with St Francis, it was voluntary, into a mark of saintliness. At the Reformation, however, the whole outlook changed. Protestantism asserted the importance of the individual approach to God and, in place of the withdrawal from the world advocated by the monasticism of the Middle Ages, taught that people should strive to lead lives of holiness in the midst of worldly activity. Accordingly, in its Puritan and Nonconformist forms, Protestantism laid great stress on hard work, thrift and abstinence from worldly pleasures. Poverty ceased to be a virtue and was regarded as evidencing lack of character and divine disapproval. Conversely, riches, when earned, were looked upon as a sign of God's favour. By the time of the Industrial Revolution, therefore, the emphasis on individualism in religion had paved the way for complete individualism in industrial and commercial enterprise.

Tawney has shown how Puritanism gradually moved from the mediaeval idea of a Church-civilisation which, under Calvin, had sought to make Geneva 'a pattern, not only of doctrinal purity, but social righteousness and commercial morality' to one which 'found in the rapidly growing spirit of economic enterprise, something not uncongenial to its own temper and went out to welcome it as an ally.' [3] What, in Calvin, had been a qualified concession to practical exigencies, appeared in some of his later followers as a frank idealisation of the life of the trader, as the service of God and the training ground of the soul. Money making was something that could be done for the greater glory of God.

Tawney states that the concept bridging the gulf between the spiritual and the temporal 'sprang from the very heart of Puritan theology.' That concept was 'the calling'. This theology held that every person had both a spiritual and a temporal calling:

> It is the first duty of the Christian to know and believe in God; it is by faith that he will be saved … The second duty of the Christian is to labour in the affairs of practical life and this second duty is subordinate only to the first. 'God' wrote a Puritan divine 'doth call every man and woman to serve him in some peculiar employment in this world, both for their own and the common good.' [4]

This Puritan thinking is well expressed in some of Charles Wesley's best-known hymns:

> To serve the present age,
> My calling to fulfil;
> O may it all my powers engage
> To do my Master's will! [5]
>
> The task Thy wisdom hath assigned
> O let me cheerfully fulfil,
> In all my works Thy presence find
> And prove Thy acceptable will. [6]

The Protestant ethic of hard work, enterprise, individual responsibility and independence, and the achievement of affluence was exemplified not only by industrial and commercial empires but also in small local businesses. The small businesses associated with the Lowton Road church have already been mentioned in Chapter 3. It is not without significance that my father, who was also a minor entrepreneur, had on his shelves a copy of *Self Help* by Samuel Smiles, first published in 1859. Father had recognised what Samuel Smiles advocated, that self-help through adult education was one means by which working-class people might be able to secure some measure of personal and social advance. There were, in my locality, many small and even larger concerns that had been founded and developed through the application of such Puritan principles as hard work, careful living, thrift, enterprise, self-improvement and the desire for financial independence. They had discovered, as Tawney says in a critique of *A Tradesman's Calling, being a Discourse concerning the Nature, Necessity, Choice etc of a Calling in General* written by Richard Steel in 1684, that:

> By a fortunate dispensation, the virtues enjoined on Christians – diligence, moderation, sobriety, thrift – are the very qualities most conducive to commercial success. The foundation of all is providence and prudence is merely another name for the 'Godly wisdom [which] comes in and puts due bounds to his expenses, and teaches the tradesman to live rather somewhat below than at all above his income.' Industry comes next and industry is at once expedient and meritorious. It will keep the tradesman from 'frequent and needless frequenting of taverns' and pin him to his shop 'where you may most confidently expect the presence and blessing of God.' [7]

The Nonconformist conscience

The Nonconformist conscience was both a narrower and wider concept than the Protestant ethic. It was narrower in that while the Protestant ethic embraced Protestantism irrespective of denomination in the world's developed industrial countries, the Nonconformist conscience was applied to UK dissentients from the Church of England such as Baptists, Congregationalists, Methodists, Presbyterians, Quakers, Unitarians and many minor sects who, while differing from each other on issues of belief and church government, also demonstrated sufficient commonality of outlook on social and political issues to form a distinctive community.

The Nonconformist conscience was also a wider concept. The Protestant ethic was primarily a theory based on the proposition that, while capitalism had existed throughout most of history, a particular *spirit* of capitalism, that of methodical wealth accumulation, is found after the sixteenth century in Protestant countries or among Protestant sects within Catholic countries. The Nonconformist conscience, however, embraced many aspects of social and individual living.

The term Nonconformist conscience was applied to two situations. As coined by the Wesleyan leader, Hugh Price Hughes in 1890 in relation to the adultery of the Irish leader Charles Stewart Parnell, it related to the political influence of Nonconformity on national issues. Critics asserted that in relation to the Parnell case, the Nonconformist conscience had spoken out only because it was realised that if Parnell did not go, the Liberals would lose votes at the next election. As Bebbington states: 'the phrase was used to suggest that Nonconformist moralising on political themes was no more than hypocrisy.'[8]

Matthew Arnold in *Culture and Anarchy* also pointed out that because of their Puritan antecedents, Nonconformists shared a tendency to emphasise rigid codes of personal behaviour, which identified 'sin' in what others regarded as harmless and pleasurable amusements.[9] Currie mentions that:

> A Bible Christian catalogue of sins in 1850 consisted of 'the ballroom, the card-table, the village wake, the racecourse, the bowling green, the cricket ground, the gin-palace, or the ale house.' A comparatively moderate New Connexion article on dangers of the Christian life listed, among other items, 'undue fondness of dress, fashionable

> evening parties ... and games of amusement.' A Primitive Methodist, now fighting a losing battle, announced in 1894 that:
>
> 'The associations of the football field ... are impure and degrading ... Let us take the advice of the Word of God, "And come out from among the ungodly and be separate from sinners" ... As Primitive Methodists, let us take the lead in this matter and renounce this great evil.' [10]

Even earlier, in 1819, the Primitive Methodists had declared:

> No person shall be continued a member of our Society who visits public or worldly amusements; nor those who waste their time in public houses. [11]

Yet the Nonconformist conscience had its strong points. As Bebbington states, in its political application, it was based on three convictions. First, that religion and politics could not be kept apart; second, that since politics is primarily a matter of taking moral decisions, power should only be entrusted to men of sterling personal qualities; third, that legislation could improve the character of the nation. [12]

As exemplified by the Primitive Methodist jam manufacturer, Sir William Pickles Hartley, the Nonconformist conscience also influenced improved employment conditions and commercial probity.

Hartley became a jam manufacturer by accident. A local supplier failed to honour a contract to supply Hartley's Colne grocer's shop with jam. Hartley therefore decided to make jam himself. The popularity of this home-made product caused Hartley to abandon his grocery business and concentrate on jam manufacture. In 1874 he built a factory in Palm Grove, Bootle, and later moved to Aintree, Liverpool. A London factory at Tower Bridge Road was also established in 1901.

Hartley had been brought up a Primitive Methodist and, for a time, was organist at the Colne Primitive Methodist church. His Nonconformist conscience impelled him to care for his employees and practise stewardship with regard to wealth. On 1 January 1877 Mr and Mrs Hartley made a written vow to 'devote a definite and well considered share of their income for religious and humanitarian work.' This, Hartley conceived to be one of the best checks to that natural selfishness which is inherent in human nature.[13] In response to an allegation that the low wages forced some of his female employees into immoral living, Hartley asserted that his wage rates for women were 'from 20 to 40 per cent more than those of his Liverpool competitors'. Further, being desirous to crush selfishness in some measure, 'he had three times voluntarily increased the wages of all his employees even though he had not received "a single complaint from any person".' Hartley's concern for his workforce was also evidenced by free medical care for all Aintree employees and a profit-sharing scheme introduced in 1889. He also provided housing at rentals of between 3s 6d and 4s 6d weekly, inclusive of rates, taxes and water in a model village built at Aintree which the Industrial Law Committee stated ranked with Port Sunlight and Bournville in the 1890s.

As for probity, Hartley's biographer relates how a grocer rebutted a customer who was voicing his resentment of the Free Church's influence in national affairs. 'The Nonconformist conscience,' sneered the customer, 'What is the Nonconformist conscience?' The grocer turned to his shelves, selected a jar of Hartley's jam and placed it, none too gently, on the counter. He let it stand there a moment while he looked his customer straight in the eye. 'That's the Nonconformist conscience,' he said decisively. 'Full weight and absolute purity.'[14]

Only in later life was I able to understand how much of my upbringing was related to the concepts of the Protestant ethic and Nonconformist conscience. The Protestant ethic was expressed in my father's strivings for independence and self-improvement and emphasis on enterprise and the stewardship of money and time. As a boy, I had little comprehension of the influence of the Nonconformist conscience on national political and social life. I did hear much about Hartley, both as employer and Primitive

Methodist benefactor. Father rarely interfered with mother's housekeeping but he insisted that Hartley's jam be purchased in preference to Robertson's competitive product. My experience of the Nonconformist conscience in action was confined to the Puritan-derived Primitive Methodist attitudes to Sunday observance, temperance, gambling, novel reading and dancing.

Sunday observance

Wigley has provided a useful summary of five ways, based on Old Testament references, the Puritans endeavoured to keep a holy Sabbath:

> First, by preparing themselves on the previous day (Exodus 16:22–3). Secondly, by avoiding work such as harvesting (Exodus 34:21) and gathering fuel (Numbers 13:15–22; Jeremiah 17:19–27) and in some cases by refusing to cook (Exodus 16:29). Lastly, they took Isaiah's phrase 'turn away from doing thy pleasure on my Holy Day' to mean that an absolutely integral part of keeping the Sabbath 'holy' lay in proscribing all forms of worldly enjoyment.[15]

Wigley also lists five 'convictions' held by the Sabbatarians:

> First, that because the day was holy and had been blessed and sanctified, it had an inherently sacred nature. Secondly, that its nature was desecrated and profaned when men engaged in worldly labour or pleasure or neglected the positive religious duties of worship. Thirdly, that God would punish Sabbath breaking. Fourthly, that Sabbatarians should restrain their countrymen as Nehemiah had done; and fifthly, that the English were God's chosen people, whose national success depended on pleasing him by keeping the Sabbath.

Three hundred years later, I encountered the same convictions in the Primitive Methodist milieu to which I belonged.

Domestically, as much Sunday work as possible was done on

the preceding Saturday. This included preparation of Sunday lunch which, with its roast beef, potatoes, carrots, sprouts and Yorkshire pudding, followed by an apple, gooseberry or blackberry pie was the major meal of the week. Mother refused to knit or sew and even school homework was proscribed. Chapel members ostracised those non-churchgoers who dug their gardens or hung out their washing on the Sabbath.

The Commandment to 'do no manner of work' was scrupulously observed, sometimes at considerable cost. The farmers connected with the Lowton and Bridge Street churches were strongly opposed to Sunday hay-making. If a field of hay was ready for stacking on a Saturday, they would refuse to do the work on a Sunday, even if heavy rain was forecast for the Monday.

Sunday observance also extended to pleasures. Toys were put away on Saturday evenings, playing out was forbidden and even reading was restricted to 'Sunday books'. Sunday newspapers were also *verboten*. Notwithstanding his opposition to such publications, however, Father could not resist a surreptitious glance at the previous day's cricket scores if an opportunity arose of looking at someone else's Sunday paper.

Games on Sunday were roundly condemned. In Sunday school, the refusal to play tennis on Sundays by Dorothy Round, Wimbledon Singles Champion in 1931, 1934 and 1937 was greatly acclaimed. One of the largest local employers, Harbens, provided a sports ground on a farm adjoining ours. Their cricket team began to play Sunday fixtures and approached Father to umpire, offering a fee of £1 per match – four times the amount he received from West Lancashire League clubs on Saturdays. I was present when the offer was made and I recall his response: 'Ah wouldn't umpire on Sundays if th' were t' give me t' mill and everything in it!'

By the end of the 1930s, cheap cars such as the Austin 7 and Ford 8 were making motoring available to the masses. For many people, however, the cheapest form of transport was the tandem bicycle immortalised by Gracie Fields in her song 'Daisy' with the lines:

You'll look sweet,
Upon the seat
Of a bicycle made for two.

On fine summer Sunday evenings, the East Lancashire Road between Liverpool and Manchester would have a constant stream of tandem riders making their way home, oblivious of the criticisms of chapelgoers taking a post evening service walk. Such criticisms centred not only on Sabbath breaking. Women, I noticed, commented caustically on the amount of bare leg revealed by the girls' shorts.

Barclay points out that the fourth commandment is not primarily a religious regulation and makes no mention of worship or religious services. It is, however, 'a great piece of social and humanitarian legislation ordering a weekly rest day on which, from sunset to sunset, no work would be done by man, woman or beast.' [16] Over time, however, the Jewish Scribes reduced the general principle to incredibly detailed regulations. Thirty-nine categories of work were forbidden on the Sabbath, further divided into thirty sub-classes. By Christ's time, there were 1,521 things a person could not do on the Sabbath including rescuing a drowning man. These petty rules devised by the Scribes were enforced and kept by the Pharisees. This is the background to the incident recorded in Mark 2 in which the disciples were criticised for plucking ears of corn and rubbing them between their hands – actions tantamount to reaping and threshing. The reply of Jesus, 'The Sabbath was made for man not man for the Sabbath,' was equivalent to saying that the usefulness of an institution is the extent to which it is beneficial to people.

With Christianity, the Jewish Sabbath became 'The Lord's Day'. Strict Puritanism, however, transformed the day of joyful celebration into a day of sullenness and fear. This was probably due to two reasons. At a time when all parts of the Bible were regarded as of equal value, the Old Testament was over emphasised at the expense of the New. There was also fear of Divine retribution for Sabbath breaking. Aged about nine, I once stopped en route for afternoon Sunday school to talk to some children. An ice cream cart came by and the mother of one of the children bought us all a wafer. I recall two reasons why this act of kindness perturbed me. First, how to eat the wafer, unobserved by any chapel people before arriving at Sunday school. Secondly, the dread that God would in some way mete out punishment. One of our local preachers declared, in all seriousness, that the outbreak of the Second World War was divine retribution for Sunday cricket.

Some of my contemporaries blame their alienation from the Church on the endless, dull, bleak Sundays endured in childhood. That was not my experience. With morning and afternoon Sunday school and afternoon and evening chapel, Sunday was hardly a day of rest but it was never dreary. Sunday school and chapel were places where there was a weekly reunion of friends and there was often fun. I enjoyed hymn singing and learned how to listen to sermons. Sometimes we had the excitement of having the preacher for tea. After service, we often went for walks in the summer and in winter, visited or were visited by friends. Probably because I had known nothing but a Sabbatarian environment I did not find the discipline irksome. I learned early that:

> A Sabbath well spent
> Brings a week of content

and if, in addition to worship, my Sabbath now includes the Sunday newspapers, an occasional Sunday lunch at a friendly pub, a cricket match, a good TV drama or a live concert, I have no reason to quarrel with that couplet.

Temperance

Harrison states that nineteenth-century temperance reformers liked to think only of the Puritans as their predecessors.[17] The Puritans, however, had no monopoly of temperance enthusiasm and from Henry VII onwards, English monarchs, including the Stuarts, legislated against drunkenness both to preserve order and conserve grain. The Puritans advocated temperance, or moderation in the use of beer and wine, not abstinence. It could hardly be otherwise. Trevelyan, writing about the period 1702–27 points out that 'except in the cider counties of the West, ale had been unchallenged in former ages as the native drink of English men, women and children at every meal and was only beginning to feel the rivalry of strong spirits on the one hand and tea and coffee on the other.'[18]

No temperance organisations appeared in the seventeenth century specifically to attack drunkenness and it was the consequences of the 1830 Beer Act that were the immediate cause of the change in emphasis from moderation to abstinence.

Though teetotalism did not originate in Preston, the cause of abstinence was most vigorously propagated by advocates from that town. From my father, who, because of his association with Preston, was well versed in the history of the total abstinence movement, I learned about Joseph Livesey and the Seven Men of Preston who, on 1 September 1832, publicly signed a pledge to abstain from all intoxicating liquors for a trial period of one year. I also knew that the word 'teetotal' originated from an incident at a meeting of the Preston Temperance Society when one of the seven men, Richard Turner, who had a slight stutter, declared that he would 'be reet down and out t-t-total for ever and ever.'

Although in May 1743, Methodist Rules made membership conditional on the avoidance of both drinking and selling spirituous liquors, Wesleyan enthusiasm for teetotalism was tepid. At the Manchester Conference of 1841, opponents of teetotalism succeeded in passing three resolutions:

1 That unfermented wine be not used in the administration of the Sacrament.
2 That no chapel be used for total abstinence meetings.
3 That no preacher go into another circuit to advocate total abstinence without first obtaining the consent of the superintendent minister of the circuit to which he may have been invited.[19]

Earlier, in 1839, the Preston Circuit Superintendent, Revd Benjamin Frankland, had attended a meeting of the Wesleyan

Methodist Branch Temperance Society held in the Edgar Street School Room and informed the members that they could not continue to use the premises for teetotal meetings on the ground that 'John Wesley's rules were sufficient for any temperance society.'[20] Edwards relates that in 1840 two ministerial candidates who confessed to being teetotallers were told either to abandon their opinions or withdraw their candidatures. The two men abandoned their opinions.[21] Mainly due to the influence of the Revd Charles Garrett, elected President of Conference in 1882, the Wesleyan Church gradually adopted a more favourable approach to teetotalism. In 1889, it was stated that the Church furnished hundreds of workers and thousands of members to total abstinence and gospel temperance societies.[22] The following year, it was reported that the whole of the students in the four Wesleyan theological colleges were total abstainers.[23]

Support for teetotalism in its early days was much stronger in such Wesleyan offshoots as the Primitive and Calvinistic Methodists and the Bible Christians. Three of the seven men of Preston were Primitive Methodists namely John King, Joseph Richardson and Richard Turner. The latter, as mentioned earlier, is credited with originating the word 'teetotal'.[24] The Primitive Methodist Conference recommended temperance societies as early as 1832 and in 1841 ordered the use of unfermented wine at communion.[25] By 1932, the Primitive Methodist Church claimed to have nearly 1,000 Bands of Hope with 52,000 members exclusive of Inter-denominational Bands of Hope with upwards of 14,000. There were also 381 Abstainers League Branches, with nearly 19,000 members.[26]

The Band of Hope movement, aimed at educating children in temperance principles, originated in Leeds in 1847. In that year, a Mrs Anne Carlisle, widow of an Irish Presbyterian minister, visited Leeds at the invitation of Revd Jabez Tunnicliffe, a Baptist minister. Mrs Carlisle advocated the establishment of a movement entitled 'The Bond of Hope'. This title was subsequently changed by Tunnicliffe to 'Band of Hope'. Closely associated with the Sunday schools, the Band of Hope movement at its height had a membership of several hundred thousand child tee-totallers who had signed a pledge which, as framed by Tunnicliffe, promised not only to abstain from 'intoxicating liquors' but also 'tobacco in all its forms'.[27]

There were, to my knowledge, no Bands of Hope associated with the Sunday schools in the Circuit to which I belonged. There was, however, much exhortation to total abstinence. Some of this was through the national and denominational temperance pressure groups. In the 1930s the brewing industries launched a massive poster campaign with such slogans as 'Beer is best' or 'My goodness, my Guinness!' The temperance movement re-joinders were 'Beer is best *left alone*!' and 'My goodness, my guineas!'

The virtues of temperance which, in Primitive Methodist circles was synonymous with teetotalism, were enjoined in both chapel and Sunday school. Frequent reference was made to the perils of the first glass and many examples were given of how drink had resulted in personal ruin and domestic unhappiness. One preacher frequently quoted a verse aimed at the 'bar' or that part of a public house where drink is actually sold, which began:

A bar to heaven,
A gate to hell,
Whoever named it
Named it well.

Conversely, temperance was extolled as the path to prosperity. Father's favourite temperance anecdote was about a reformed drunkard whose teetotalism and chapel going were ridiculed by his workmates. 'Surely,' they asked him, 'you don't believe that Christ actually turned the water into wine?' 'I don't know about water into wine,' he answered. 'I do know that for me he has turned beer into furniture!'

Not everyone was impressed by this argument. Harrison[28] points out that some socialists believed with Robert Blatchford that 'the better economic condition of the abstainer is only possible by reason of the continued degradation of his fellows.'[29] The

Socialist case was that in a free market, wages would fall to the lowest subsistence level so, as long as most workers drank, the sober minority could use the money saved to acquire luxuries. If temperance became universal, however, employers would conclude that workers could subsist on lower incomes, wages would be reduced and profits rise. This argument failed to recognise that increased spending power would lead to an increased demand for goods and services thus benefiting both employer and employee.

In Sunday school, temperance issues could be more freely debated. Older and more articulate scholars sometimes challenged their teachers by citing Christ's miracle at Cana and Paul's advice to Timothy, 'Drink no longer water, but use a little wine for thy stomach's sake' [30] as strict scriptural evidences against teetotalism. Young as I was, I did not always find the attempts to show that such incidents did not negate total abstinence convincing. I was reminded of them when, much older, I read the comment of a former Dean of Rochester who opposed the use of unfermented wine at communion. 'I verily believe that they [total abstainers] would have us read that the Good Samaritan poured in oil and water and took the poor wounded Jew to a temperance hotel.'[31]

In addition to exhortations, there were temperance songs and hymns. Songs included the ditty:

My drink is water bright,
Water bright, water bright.
My drink is water bright
From the sparking rill.

Of course, we really drank tea and 'pop'; water came from the tap.

As for hymns, the *Primitive Methodist Sunday School Hymn Book* and the 1912 *Supplement to the Primitive Methodist Hymnal* contained 12 and 9 hymns respectively under the heading of 'Temperance'. I can recall singing only one of these hymns which had a particularly rousing tune:

Yield not to temptation, for yielding is sin,
Each victory will help you some other to win. [32]

Not even on the annual Temperance Sunday did we sing such Victorian banalities as:

> Look not on the wine-cup bright,
> Flashing in its purple light,
> Lift not thou the goblet high
> With the sons of revelry;
> Ruin yet that draught shall bring,
> Deadly as the adder's sting.[33]

or,

> Touch not the cup, though 'tis bright and fair,
> For a serpent lurks within;
> It will poison your heart like a canker there.
> With its bitter curse and sin.[34]

On one Temperance Sunday when aged about fourteen or fifteen, I signed the pledge. Subsequently, I have enjoyed the occasional sherry in academic circles and a glass of wine at dinner. I have never, however, cultivated any taste for beer or spirits. Empirically, I concur with the Methodist declaration that:

> Considered individually, alcoholic indulgence … impairs conscience, judgement and the sense of responsibility. Considered socially, alcoholic indulgence inflicts heavy loss and damage on the community in deterioration of character, diminution of health and efficiency, discord in domestic life, neglect and suffering of children, public disorder, the creation and intensification of poverty and economic waste, and in the undue influence of the liquor trade in public affairs.[35]

I also concur with the view that the early temperance advocates concentrated too much on drunkenness and too little on its social causes. It is, however, true that the increased affluence and greater leisure of today is attended by an increasing drink-and-drug culture, especially among the young. To slightly amend a wise observation of Harrison's I believe that excessive recreational drinking (and drug taking) often results from the possession of funds without an accompanying tradition which ensures their constructive application, and from the possession of leisure without the interests and education to ensure its rational recreational and constructive use.[36]

Gambling

Primitive Methodism was implacable in its opposition to all forms of gambling. This opposition can be discerned in the Puritan values expressed in the Protestant ethic. The word 'luck' was proscribed in my home. I recall that when I referred to some event or other as being 'lucky', my father told me abruptly 'we make our own luck'. One objection to gambling was that it was at variance with an acceptance of the divine will and providence. As a later Methodist Declaration stated 'Belief in luck cannot be reconciled with faith in God.'[37] Gambling was also the antithesis implied by the Protestant ethic of work, merit and reward and such imperatives as effort, routine, thrift, prudence, conservatism, discipline and stewardship. By the time I was ten, the combined teachings of home, Sunday school and chapel equipped me to state some of the arguments against gambling. I knew, for example, that the essence of gambling is that gain for one party involves loss for the other and is therefore the negation of loving one's neighbour. I had also heard many lurid stories of how avarice as manifested in gambling had resulted in the ruin and sometimes suicide of the persons concerned.

In 1936, the Methodist Church identified four categories of gambling: gaming, betting, lotteries and sweepstakes and speculation.[38]

Gaming or playing a game of chance for money, including bridge and whist, was banned on church premises. Playing cards were also banned in my home. We had a dice, used for playing snakes and ladders or Ludo, but Father had reservations about dominoes since this was a 'pub game'. He dubbed cards and dice 'the devil's books and the devil's bones'. Only many years later did I discover that this was not an original saying.[39] At chapel socials, the substitution for the whist drive was the beetle drive in which players rolled a dice to obtain six for a body, five for a head, four for a tail, three for the two eyes, two for the antenna and one for each of the six legs. The first person to assemble a beetle received a small prize such as a bar of chocolate or jar of jam. A purist would have pointed out that even such small prizes were still money's worth. After the war, attitudes softened. When, in 1949, the Revd Benson Perkins was asked about his attitude to whist drives, he replied that the Methodist Church 'had no objection to whist drives but that on church premises, it should be played only as a game without a prize.' He added, however, that Methodists:

> were not prepared to have our church funds benefit from that kind of thing, though there are some people who will pay half-a-crown for the purpose of church funds and play whist, but without having prizes associated with it. They make these payments for the pleasure of the evening.[40]

Betting or the staking of money on a doubtful or uncertain event was mainly associated with dog and horse racing and football pools. From an early age, I knew that the only ultimate winner is the 'bookie'. Neither my parents, nor I suspected, any chapel members, had any truck with these sports. Football pools, however, were a different matter. Pools began in the early 1920s when national newspapers ran competitions offering a £1,000 prize for a correct forecast of twelve selected matches. A Birmingham bookmaker named Jervis also issued a coupon inviting clients to forecast for guaranteed prizes the correct results of prescribed matches such as 'eight homes' or 'four aways'. Pools began in earnest, however, in February 1923, when three young men, Colin Askham, Bill Hughes and John Moores opened an office in Church Street, Liverpool, under the name of Littlewoods. Littlewood was the real name of Askham who, on adoption by his aunt, had taken her surname. Their beginnings were inauspicious. Only 35 of the 4,000 coupons distributed outside Manchester Football Ground in the first week were returned. The following week, only one out of 10,000 coupons came back. Askham and Hughes were glad to accept Moore's offer to buy them out. Afterwards, the tide turned. By 1926, the weekly return was over 20,000. Within the next nine years, some half dozen pools promoters were in business, including Vernons, also of Liverpool, and Zetters and Empire Pools.[41]

Few Primitive Methodists would be seen entering a betting shop but pools coupons could be posted surreptitiously. In a neighbouring circuit, a Primitive Methodist had a pools win of several thousand pounds. A special Leaders' Meeting was convened at the chapel where he was a member. It was resolved that the minister should inform him that he could either forego his winnings or his membership. He kept his winnings. Most of his family also resigned their memberships.

Lotteries and sweepstakes included raffles which were also forbidden as a means of raising money for church funds. In this respect, Methodism differed from most other Protestant denominations. A 1950 Report to the Church Assembly stressed some positive aspects of raffles. Raffles provide a fair and democratic method of raising money on an article of some value for which no individual visiting a bazaar or sale of work can afford to pay. Selling the article at a price well below its true worth can deprive the 'cause' of a fair profit, favour the affluent, and possibly distress the donors. The raffle provides a means of obtaining an amount approaching the true value and 'provides the slenderest purse with an equal chance of acquiring a desirable possession.' In addition to the general arguments against gambling, Methodists held that raffles weaken the Christian attack on gambling and also adversely affect direct giving. Direct giving, however, is largely restricted to those committed to an organisation and, as the members decline, may be inadequate to meet the amount required.

Speculation

Speculation is popularly associated with easy profits made by wealthy men who differ from gamblers by their dealings in shares and commodities rather than in racing or at the casino.

Speculation has good and bad aspects. Well-informed Stock Exchange speculation based on underlying market conditions stabilises share values, reflects public demand for different types of capital and encourages new enterprise where it is needed.

The adverse aspect is when the sole purpose is price gain or share speculation independent of any expert or informed appraisal of yield prospects or the soundness of the company concerned. Essentially, the difference between speculation and gambling is that speculators take risks arising naturally from the uncertainties of a dynamic economy. Gamblers bear artificially created risks arising from the game.

There were several reasons why the Primitive Methodist chapel members whose thrift had enabled them to buy shares were not speculators. Their holdings were normally small investments in well established companies such as the LMS Railway Company Limited, the Manchester Ship Canal Company and the Mersey Docks and Harbour Board. They were also 'ethical' investors. Shares in breweries, casinos or tobacco companies were anathema. When some, including my father, deviated slightly from these principles, they paid the penalty. Encouraged by the short-lived, post First World War boom in the cotton industry and advised by the Nonconformist manager, Father and some other chapelgoers invested in a local mill. Within a year, due to Eastern competition and lower production costs, the mill was in liquidation and their shares worthless.

My first seeds of doubt regarding the wisdom of the rigorous Primitive Methodist and later Methodist attitudes to gambling were sown as a small boy. A frequent theme in Sunday school and on Temperance Sunday was the importance of 'witnessing'. One could, for example, 'witness' by refusing to participate in a raffle. When about eight, I had an ear infection which required a visit to a specialist at Wigan Infirmary. In those days, most hospitals relied heavily on voluntary contributions. While we, along with a dozen others, were waiting to see the consultant, a nurse came selling raffle tickets. Everyone bought a ticket except Mother. I could sense the freezing of an atmosphere that a minute before had been cordial. When mother went to get a cup of tea, there was a chorus of condemnation of her 'meanness'. Meanness was foreign to her character. Hawkers often called at our farm. Often they were unemployed men trying to make a living by travelling on foot from house to house selling cheap drapery or household goods out of heavy portmanteaux. She never liked to send them away without making a purchase and seldom did. Often from compassion at their tiredness, she would make them a cup of tea. To an unscrupulous person, she was 'a soft touch'. At the hospital, she believed she was witnessing for a principle. Actually, her refusal to buy a ticket achieved nothing. She was misjudged, her critics misinformed and the Infirmary deprived of a trifling amount of no significance to its finances.

Gradually, attitudes changed. In 1992, a Statement adopted by the Methodist Conference recognised that since the earlier Declaration of 1936, much had changed in British society, 'both in the areas of recreational gambling and Stock Exchange activity.'[42] While the Methodist Church still viewed gambling with concern, minor gambling such as raffles were, subject to specified conditions, allowed on church premises.

The novel

There were several reasons why until well into the nineteenth century the Nonconformist conscience regarded novel reading as 'worldly activity'. Not without reason was it believed that 'where novel reading comes in, Bible reading goes out'.[43] There was the fear that novel reading might stimulate imaginations to meditate on sinful pleasures that would otherwise never have been contemplated. Time wasting on novel reading was also contrary to the Protestant ethic. The latent Puritanism of Primitive Methodist thinking regarded most pleasurable activities with suspicion. The reasons why parents should not encourage novel reading were stated in the *Primitive Methodist Magazine* for 1870:

> Novel reading narrows the intellect, enfeebles the character, and gives the heart a distaste for the simple realities of life. The novel reader lives in an ideal world which his

> imagination has created around him. He cannot grapple with difficulties. He has no sympathy with real sorrows. He can weep over the fictitious sufferings of the hero or the heroine of the tale he reads but he turns away from the struggles and battles of life which are going on around him ...
>
> Naturally, books of fiction have a great charm for the susceptible, imaginative mind of youth; but what false views do tales and novels generally give of that world into which the young are just entering ... Their hopes are bright and buoyant, the path of life seems to them strewn with flowers and they expect, like the heroines of whom they have been reading that the sunshine of prosperity will ever gild their days. Then how obvious it must be to those who look beneath the surface of things that novels are dangerous books for youth ...
>
> Light reading will not advance them in the scale of intellect. If our children are mere novel readers we may rest assured that they will never attain to anything great or good. Their minds will be stunted at the very time when they should be expanding to sacred influences and invigorating principles. [44]

In 1867, the *Methodist New Connexion Magazine* had opined that 'novel reading feeds the passions and pollutes the heart'. Four years later, the same periodical stated that 'all the proprieties would be shocked if it published fiction'. Yet, in 1877, both the *Primitive Methodist* and *Methodist New Connexion Magazines* were inviting fictional contributions. [45]

Cunningham points out that the Unitarians and Congregationalists were in the van of this liberalisation followed by the Baptists and Methodists. [46] Yet even in the 1930s, Primitive Methodist suspicion of the novel lingered on. I remember a visiting minister describing how, when making an unexpected pastoral visit, he had surprised a lady member in the act of hiding a novel under a chair cushion.

The term 'novel' can, of course, be applied to any fictitious story from a paperback romance of ephemeral significance to a 'classic'. Our bookshelves had plenty of the latter and none of the former. My father had been nurtured on earlier Primitive Methodist attitudes to novel reading and for much of my childhood, had fairly fixed ideas regarding what constituted acceptable or unacceptable fiction. Approval was extended to many classics and novels with religious or social themes by Nonconformist writers. Our library included works by Bunyan, Jane Austen, the Brontë Sisters, Dickens and George Eliot. We also had Harriet Beecher Stowe's *Uncle Tom's Cabin*. There were also a number of novels by the brothers Joseph and Silas Hocking. The respectability of the Hocking stories was enhanced because prior to becoming full-time authors, the brothers had both been United Methodist ministers.

Joseph Hocking (1860–1937) wrote fifty-three novels, the religious content of which is evidenced by such titles as *The Woman of Babylon*, *The Purple Robe* and *The God that Answers by Fire*. The only Joseph Hocking book I read was *Jabez Easterbrook* written in 1921. Jabez, the hero of the story, was a young minister in love with a lady in his congregation who was beset by doubt regarding the faith espoused by the chapel. One chapter reported a powerful sermon by Jabez (probably one of the author's in his ministerial days) on Psalm 42:2: 'My soul thirsteth for God, for the Living God.' By the end, the heroine's doubts have been dispersed. Whether she had become or was about to become Mrs Easterbrook, I can't remember. Joseph Hocking achieved the distinction of a place in the *Dictionary of National Biography*.

Silas Hocking was denied similar recognition, although he was by far the more prolific writer who, as Drummond records 'from about 1880–1904 sold an average of 1,000 copies weekly to the Methodist public.'[47]

Dr Clifford, the champion of Nonconformist opposition to the 1902 Education Bill and Act, was presented with a complete set of Silas Hocking's works. These comprised one hundred and ninety-three volumes. By far the best known of Silas Hocking's novels was *Her Benny*. This book, which appeared in 1879, was first serialised in the *United Methodist Free Church's Magazine*. In the Preface to the book edition, the author states:

> My pastoral work during a three years' residence in Liverpool called me frequently into some of the poorest neighbourhoods of that town, where I became acquainted with some of the originals of this story ... The grouping of the characters ... is purely fictitious but not the characters themselves. Benny and Little Nell, Perks and Joe Wrag, Granny and Eva Lawrence were drawn from life. [48]

When, as a young boy, I read the story, the description of the death of Little Nell moved me to tears. An edition of *Her Benny* was reprinted as recently as 1985.

Cunningham concludes that 'Primitive Methodists and Baptists, with their relatively high density of lay preachers and working class members, generated the least number of Nonconformist literary men.'[49] Although Primitive Methodist novelists were few and comparatively obscure, three writers, Joseph Ritson (*d.* 1932), Samuel Horton (1857–1949) and John George Bowran (1869–1946) who wrote under the pseudonym of Ramsey Gutherie, were well known throughout the Connexion. Ritson's best known novel was *Hugh Morrigill: Street Arab* (1905) based on the life of a prominent Primitive Methodist Minister, Hugh Gilmore (1842–91).[50]

Gutherie's titles included *Dave Graham: Pitman* (1904), *The Canny Folks of Coal Vale* (1910) and *The Old Folks at Home* (1919). All had a background of pit-village Primitive Methodism.

Horton became President of the Primitive Methodist Conference in 1921. Both these writers published stories in Primitive Methodist periodicals and also as books. A selection of their titles was on the bookshelves of most Primitive Methodists.

Unacceptable fiction according to Father's canons related to novels with plots or characters offensive to Primitive Methodist moral susceptibilities. Novels presenting trivial or superficial views of life were also frowned upon. I was never allowed to have a story book as a Sunday school prize. I was also sensitive to what I might or might not read. When aged about eight, my parents asked a neighbour to sit with me while they went to a meeting. To pass the time, she brought with her a novel. The author was Nat Gould who, in the 1930s, was a widely read writer of horse racing stories. She finished the book and I picked it up to read. Seeing my interest, the neighbour said I might borrow the book. I was in a quandary. I knew that if caught reading such 'trash', I would be in serious trouble. Not only was it a novel but even worse, it was a racing novel with a garish dust wrapper showing jockeys and racehorses. My first problem was how to hide the book before my parents returned home. As a temporary expedient, I secreted it behind some other books. Next day, I smuggled the novel into the loft above our shippon where I could read it in comparative safety. The penalties for possessing such pernicious literature, however, weighed on me heavily. I was anxious that it would be discovered. My anxiety lifted only when I had successfully effected the book's surreptitious return to its owner.

Unacceptable novels also included those by authors known to be unsympathetic to Christianity or whose lives and morality were, from a Primitive Methodist perspective, suspect. These authors included Aldous Huxley (1894–1963), D. H. Lawrence (1885–1930) and H. G. Wells (1866–1946). Novels such as Walter Greenwood's *Love on the Dole* (1933), James Hilton's *Goodbye Mr Chips* (1938) and Winifred Holtby's *South Riding* (1936) were, however, acceptable.

Latterly, I noticed a mellowing of my father's attitude to novels. This liberalisation was largely because the opening of a branch of the Lancashire County Library introduced both of us to a wider selection of fiction. He found pleasure in J. B. Priestley and joy in W. W. Jacobs but frankly disapproved of my wasting time on P. G. Wodehouse.

Dancing

Dancing had greater potential for titillating sexual interest and imagination than the novel since it provided the additional stimuli of physical observation and touch. For these reasons, the waltz, imported into England from Germany in 1812, was particularly condemned. Fryer relates how Dr J. H. Kellogg and the Revd Herbert Lockyer both quoted American opinions to support their views that waltzing led to immodesty, promiscuity and adultery.[51]

Kellogg, in his *Ladies Guide* (1890), quoted a Philadelphia dancing master who regarded waltzing as immoral because:

> the ladies that danced it were hugged by gentlemen hitherto unknown to them, who had seen couples so tightly interlocked that the man's face was in contact with the palpitating girl in his arms and had watched kisses being exchanged in the whirl of the maddening waltz. Dr Kellogg did not even approve of dances where the participants were members of the same family. Many innocent young women had begun the downward course to shame and utter ruin in the dancing school.

Lockyer, writing in 1930, claimed that as the waltz had originated in Parisian brothels, it was not an amusement for any child of God. The attraction of dancing, he suggested, would disappear 'if by Act of Parliament, women were only permitted to dance with women and men with men.' 'Is it a comely thing', he asked, 'to see a man's wife pressed to the bosom and whirled around in the arms of another man? Is it a pleasant thing to see a Christian girl in the embrace of a young man who has no thought of God?'

While extreme, these views were not without substance. Much scorn has been poured on the Puritan gloom that banned dancing round the Maypole. Yet there is ample evidence that the Maypole preparations were frequently an excuse for promiscuity.

The above, while not specifically Primitive Methodist views, would have been endorsed by the overwhelming majority of chapel people, most of whom had never seen, much less attended, a dance. In the late 1930s I remember the concern and shock when it became known that three young ladies who attended the relatively liberal Bridge Street chapel were taking dancing lessons at a local *palais de dance*. My mother was told by one disgusted member that 'the minister should speak to them about it.'

When asked 'Can Methodists dance?', Donald Soper is reputed to have replied, 'Some can – some can't.'[52] In 1939, it is probably true that hardly any members of the Lowton Circuit chapels could dance. At the time of Union, all three branches of Methodism had rules forbidding dancing on church premises. After Union, this prohibition was not modified until in 1964 Standing Order 304 was modified to read:

> Dances arranged as social functions for the members and friends of members of organisations meeting on Methodist Trust premises may be held on Methodist Trust premises. Public dances are not permitted on Methodist Trust premises.[53]

Morals and change

Paradoxically, the constant element running through this chapter is that of changing ethical views. Preston, however, points out that:

> The rethinking of many hitherto strongly held Christian ethical positions (as of doctrinal ones) is not a sign of weakness but the vitality of a Christian Community which is always reflecting on its Christian resources at the same time that it uses them.[54]

Preston also states that reasons for changes in ethical positions include:

1 changing situations producing new empirical information;
2 critical reflection on methods of ethical reasoning producing better ones;
3 more attention to the ethical thought of confessions besides one's own as a result of the Ecumenical Movement.

Changing situations are exemplified by the contrast between the social conditions in which Primitive Methodist and Nonconformist ethical concepts were developed and those of today. Primitive Methodist ethics were influenced by earlier Puritan attitudes to Sunday observance, alcohol, gambling and dancing. During most of its 111 years of history, working-class people who formed the majority of Primitive Methodist members had limited leisure, or opportunities for education or travel. Indoor entertainment was largely confined to either the public house or the chapel. Most importantly, as Preston mentions, in 1900 about 96 per cent of weekly wages was spent on 'necessities'. Expenditure on drinking and gambling was therefore at the expense of 'necessities' and could only lead to poverty and destitution. Changed attitudes to Sunday observance, drinking and gambling on the part of the general population which, in turn, has influenced the thinking of the churches, are partly attributable to changed social conditions. These include increased leisure, wider educational opportunities, improved housing, reduced domestic drudgery and the influence of technology, especially computers, the car and television. Most importantly, however, although the scope of items designated 'necessities' has widened, the balance of income remaining has, for most people in work, also increased. There is also the fact that in an industrial society work, morals, religion and leisure were all of a piece with the work ethic. In a post-industrial society, however, people compartmentalise their lives and do not necessarily perceive any relationship between the 'techno-economic realm' of employment and the 'cultural realm' of pleasure, play, consumption or religion.

Critical reflection on ethical reasoning has also contributed to modified attitudes. Older, Puritan-derived attitudes saw 'sin' in what many people regarded as innocent recreation. The way to prevent 'sin' was through prohibition. For inadequate, immature people, gambling, alcohol and, today, a wide range of other drugs may become addictions. Preston, however, rightly states that 'we cannot run society in general on prohibitions designed for the benefit of addicts and we would have a horribly paternalistic and unworkable society if we tried.' Either, as with the Prohibition experiment in the USA, drink and gambling would become underground activities or simply ignored. It is not possible to make people good by Act of Parliament or the rules laid down in Methodist Constitutional Practice and Discipline. A survey carried out in one Methodist circuit found that a third of Methodist members gambled and distinguished very clearly between gambling as a harmless social activity and the desire to gain at the expense of others. [55] A similar survey would probably indicate that recreational drinking is more widespread among Methodists than is officially acknowledged.

Attention to the ethical thoughts of confessions besides one's own has assumed greater importance with the rise of ecumenicalism. If Anglican-Methodist unity is achieved, it will be difficult for Methodists to retain even their modified official attitudes to alcohol and gambling both in private and on church premises.

Preston, adapting an earlier idea by A. D. Lindsay, points out that Christians live under two moralities: 'everyday morality' and 'the morality of grace'. [56]

Everyday morality is based on 'the ethics of reciprocity' – doing good turns to those who do good turns to us. It is derived from 'the social customs, conventions and laws where Christians live together in the strictures of life with people of varying levels of faith, other faiths and no faith.' In this area, Christians are concerned 'that the institutions of the common life should work in a humane and just way, and are prepared to advise and influence others to that end. Even within the churches, many people equate everyday morality with 'Christian morality'.

The 'morality of grace', in contrast, is non-reciprocal and unconditional. Grace is God's active favour and mercy to people irrespective of their deserts. In the Synoptic Gospels, 'grace' is the coming of the Kingdom of God in the life and deeds of Jesus Himself which calls forth a unique ethical teaching. This is exemplified in Christ's teaching. Not the reciprocity of 'an eye for an eye and a tooth for a tooth' but the turning of the cheek and the second mile. Not forgiveness seven times but seventy times seven. The morality of grace is also exemplified in such parables as the Prodigal Son and the Labourers in the Vineyard. Thus, the morality of grace gives everyday morality a deeper perspective and challenges it to a more searching exploration of what reciprocity means.

Preston states that the virtues that should guide all social ethics are proportion and prudence. These virtues apply generally today. The early Primitive Methodists, however, saw at first hand the moral and material degradation brought about by the drinking and gambling of which the middle and upper classes were largely ignorant or attributed to the 'undeserving poor'. In the light of these experiences, it was therefore difficult for them to take a balanced view. Many of the people involved were also incapable of understanding the concept of temperance and for them, abstinence was the safer and simpler rule. Nevertheless, as many contemporary Methodists need to recognise, moral codes evolve.

As Harrison says, moral codes, in part, are like the white skin of the polar bear or nocturnal habits of the owl, in that they have developed unplanned and been accidentally selected by circumstances unenvisaged and unforeseen. [57] Codes, however, are also partly like the design of the motor car or the rules of Parliamentary procedure in that they need to be adapted or modified in the light of experience of their disadvantages and insight of ways in which they can be improved. 'Time makes ancient good uncouth.'

8
Worship

Before I was sixteen my experience of worship was mainly limited to the chapels of the Lowton Circuit. My mother once took me to the Anglican Lowton St Luke's church harvest festival. Father disapproved and the visit was not repeated. For a time my half-brother, Fred, was organist at the Old Meeting Congregational Church, Uxbridge. On two of his visits to the north I went with him to the Golborne Congregational Church where I first heard and enjoyed the chanting of the psalms. In Buxton I paid a single visit to the Wesleyan Methodist church. With my parents I had attended several Sunday School Anniversaries of the Golborne Independent Methodists. Apart from the Anglican service and the chanting at the 'Congs' the above services were very similar to those I habitually attended. Even as a boy, however, I noticed a difference between worship at the Lowton and Bridge Street chapels and others in the Circuit. Long before my time, these two societies had replaced the emotional evangelicalism characteristic of earlier Primitive Methodism with a more ordered worship. Older members of the Bridge Street chapel recalled that, before the First World War, their choir also chanted the psalms and regularly sang the *Te-Deum*. Several members of each church were known sermon connoisseurs.

My recollections and reflections on Primitive Methodist worship fall under three headings:

1 Feasts and festivals
2 The elements of worship
3 Sacraments

Feasts and festivals

Apart from Christmas, Easter and Pentecost, the latter being referred to as Whit (White) Sunday, Primitive Methodism as I knew it gave little attention to the Christian Year. I never recall any recognition of Advent. I was in my twenties before I knew of Epiphany. Attendance at an Anglican school gave an awareness of Lent particularly since, on Ash Wednesday, some of my class-mates went to church and returned with what, to me, was a dirty mark on their foreheads. The thought of practising any self-denial in Lent was as alien as abstaining from meat on Fridays. I cannot recall any of the seven chapels ever celebrating Good Friday. Ascension Day was mentioned at school but appeared to have no significance in the chapels. Trinity Sunday, All Saints' Day and all other saints' days were disregarded. This Primitive Methodist neglect of the Church calendar was a perpetuation of seventeenth-century Puritanism when the accepted festivals and saints' days of the Church year were rejected as belonging to the hated Catholic tradition and condemned as superstitions. Until Methodist Union, few Primitive Methodists had heard of John Wesley's magnificent Covenant Service, although a much inferior Covenant Service was included in the Primitive Methodist Form of Service issued in 1860.

Apart from Christmas, Easter and Pentecost, Primitive Methodism had other festivals and Sundays to mark the passing of the Church year. Minor Sundays included those prescribed by the Connexion including Overseas Missions and Temperance. Locally, we had the New Year's Eve 'Watch-Night' service, Flower Sunday and Christian Endeavour, Hospitals, Choir, Men's and Ladies' Sundays. I enjoyed the Watch Night Service because I could stay up later than usual. There was also the eerie atmosphere of waiting for the Old Year to die and the greeting of the New Year by singing Charles Wesley's hymn:

Come, let us anew
Our Journey pursue,

Roll round with the year,
And never stand still till the
Master appear.[1]

On Flower Sunday, the Sunday school scholars would bring bunches of flowers to chapel. They entered the church while the congregation sang a hymn beginning:

Here, Lord, we offer Thee all that is fairest,
Bloom from the garden, and flowers from the field.
Gifts for the stricken ones, knowing Thou carest
More for the love than the wealth that we yield.[2]

The flowers would be received either by the preacher or some special person. My mother seemed to be in some demand for the role of receiver and was expected to give a short address relating to flowers. Afterwards, the flowers were taken to the sick or sent to the local infirmaries or workhouse. The three major events of the chapel year were, however, the Sunday School and Chapel Anniversaries and the Harvest Festival.

The Sunday School Anniversary

Planning for the Sunday School Anniversary began up to two or three years ahead with the preparation of a shortlist of possible preachers. If none of those approached were available, the 'fall-back' was a student from Hartley Victoria College. As the time approached, other decisions were made by the Sunday school officials, in consultation with the organist, regarding hymns, items to be presented by the Sunday school scholars and choir anthems. Several weeks before the hymn sheets and posters were ordered and practices commenced. There were also domestic preparations. Ladies often used 'the Anniversary' as a reason to buy a new hat or other attire. Children taking part and therefore 'on show' had to have a new dress or shirt.

On the day, the chapel would be packed at each service. The congregation would be swollen by proud mums and dads making their once yearly attendance to see their offspring 'perform'.

Especially in the Sunday School Anniversary and Harvest seasons, there would be a substantial influx of visitors on a reciprocal basis, from other chapels. My father referred to this reciprocity as 'fill chapel, empty chapel'. He had little reason to criticise. In addition to our own Sunday School Anniversary, we always visited the Stubshaw Cross, Bamfurlong and Lane Head Anniversaries and, occasionally, others such as the Independent Methodists. None of the chapels had a choir large enough to sing the chosen anthems. Members with good voices might be invited to augment other choirs, so that they could be absent from their own chapel for several consecutive weeks.

The main feature of the Sunday School Anniversary was the singing and recitations of the Sunday school scholars. These sat on a tiered platform, usually under the pulpit, and faced the congregation, the smallest children being on the top and the oldest on the bottom rows. Sitting on the platform through a long service was uncomfortable. By devious means, I succeeded in being conscripted on only two occasions. On the first, I sang a verse which began:

> Like a little rambler rose
> Sweetly smiling where it grows.

On my return appearance twelve months later, I contributed a verse from Frances Ridley Havergal's hymn, 'Take my life, and let it be'. In retrospect, most pieces sung by the children were poor poetry set to poor tunes. Due to the large demand from Sunday schools throughout the country, some minor music publishers specialised in producing such trivia. To reduce costs, chapels sometimes exchanged anthems. On occasion, the choice of anthem was unfortunate. I remember one choir giving a stirring rendering of the chorus 'Baal we cry to thee' from Mendelssohn's *Elijah*. The incongruity of a northern Primitive Methodist choir invoking a heathen deity went unnoticed. The difference between worship at the Lane Head and Bridge Street chapels and other societies in the Circuit has already been mentioned. This extended to the hymns chosen for Anniversaries. Hymns at the two chapels were more decorous than at Stubshaw Cross and Bamfurlong where the emphasis was on 'a good sing' and the Sunday School Anniversary hymns and tunes could be predicted with some certainty. These would include 'And can it be' to *Sagina*, 'All hail the power of Jesu's name' to *Diadem*, 'Guide me, O Thou great Jehovah' to *Cwm Rhondda* and 'Jesus, the name high over all' to *Lydia*.

The preacher was expected to deliver two rousing sermons and also two addresses ostensibly to the children but which would also instruct and edify their elders.

The Sunday School Anniversary, however, was more than a religious service which cynics declared to be less to the glory of God than for the entertainment of the attenders. It was also an occasion for fund raising and the reunion of families and friends. The expectation was that the Sunday School Anniversary collections would be sufficient to make the Sunday school solvent for the ensuing year and perhaps also contribute to chapel funds. Each year the Stubshaw Cross and Bamfurlong churches invited a number of persons 'to collect' at one of the two Sunday School Anniversary services. It was expected that a collector would acknowledge the honour by putting a substantial amount in the offertory. This sometimes required sacrificial giving. Men, sometimes unemployed or on low pay in the mines, would save for twelve months to contribute an amount which might be the equivalent of two weeks' wages. At the evening service, the collection was usually taken after the sermon and the collectors would all disappear into the vestry. Afterwards, there would probably be a hymn, pieces by the children or an anthem, all put into the service to give time for a quick counting of the collection. Before the final hymn, a note would be passed to the preacher so that he could announce the total collections for the day. This announcement was eagerly awaited and there would be elation or disappointment according to whether the amount was greater or less than the previous year.

The Sunday School Anniversary was also an occasion for reunions. At Bamfurlong, the tradition was that my Aunt Sarah

Jane entertained the visiting preacher. She also provided tea for visiting relatives including my parents and myself. Up to a score of people crowded into her small living room where most of us sat on borrowed Sunday School forms. The tea was always a sight to behold. There was meat, ham and tongue, supported by mustard, pickles and other condiments. Plates were piled high with white and brown bread. There was also peaches, cream and home-made trifle, at least one large apple pie, and a variety of cakes. I recall my aunt addressing one preacher who must already have been wondering how he could possibly preach after all he had eaten, and saying, 'Now come on, Mr—, have some more trifle, *you mustn't stop eating because you're full!*'

My aunt's toilet was an earth privy at the end of her backyard. Before going to the evening service, her guests, who had drunk endless cups of tea, would begin to form a pee-queue in which the preacher was given priority. After service, some people would return for a supper comprising the afternoon's left-overs. There is, however, another side to this story. My aunt's husband, a former miner, had been seriously injured in the pit. Their main income was a small weekly compensation payment that had no margin for luxuries. For the rest of the year, their staple diet was bread, jam, chips and eggs from a few hens kept on an allotment. The Sunday School Anniversary spread was only possible because, throughout the year, my aunt had skimped and saved to provide the anniversary tea. For her, like the collectors and the mums who bought new clothes for their children, the Sunday School Anniversary involved sacrifice.

The Chapel Anniversary

Apart from a special preacher and an anthem sung by an augmented choir at the evening service, Chapel Anniversaries were little different from the normal Sunday service. Congregations were much smaller than at the Sunday School Anniversary, although they would be larger than usual, especially if the preacher was what we termed 'an attraction'.

The Harvest Festival

This was my favourite festival, especially after I joined Bridge Street where, as stated earlier, the most prominent families were farmers. The chapel was always beautifully decorated and redolent with the smell of the produce displayed. The centrepiece on the communion table was always a large, specially baked loaf, symbolic of both earthly bread and the 'bread eternal' of which we sang. [3] A lump of coal also symbolised that miners also harvested the earth's riches. Primitive Methodism generally had a Puritan suspicion of symbolism but the bread and the coal spoke of the spiritual in the material. There was also realism in the hymns. Many of the worshippers had actually ploughed the fields and scattered the good seed on the land. When they sang 'All is safely gathered in ere the winter storms begin', they were describing what they had accomplished. Other harvest hymns, some now forgotten, also spoke of unseen realities and moved me to tears by their imagery:

> Now sing we a song for the harvest;
> Thanksgiving and honour and praise,
> For all that the Bountiful Giver
> Hath given to gladden our days;
>
> For grasses of upland and lowland,
> For fruits of the garden and field,
> For gold which the mine and the furrow
> Do delver and husbandman yield.
>
> But now we sing deeper and higher,
> Of harvests that eye cannot see;
> They ripen on mountains of duty,
> Are reaped by the brave and the free. [4]

Yet our harvests were somewhat introspective and unquestioning. We sang lustily that 'all good gifts around us are sent from heaven above' but we had little concept of countries where what people have around them are not good gifts but hunger, famine, malnutrition, drought and death. We confidently declared: 'He only is the maker of all things near and far.' We were blissfully unaware that logically this assertion led to lines such as those of *Monty Python*:

> All things dull and ugly
> All creatures short and squat
> All things rude and nasty
> The Lord God made the lot.
> Each little snake that poisons
> Each little wasp that stings
> He made their brutish venom
> He made their horrid wings.[5]

That we were untroubled by such considerations was not due to selfishness or naivety. On Harvest Festival Sunday, we were glad to express our thankfulness for our life, our health and especially our food. Thanksgiving has been defined as 'happiness reaching out beyond itself, seeking to make contact with its cause.' Our happiness was expressed in the joyousness of our singing, and our whole worship was directed to making contact with the God whom we had no doubt was the source of all good gifts around us.

The elements of worship

The usual Primitive Methodist Sunday service was a 'sandwich' in which prayers, lessons, sometimes a children's address, notices, offertory and sermon were interposed between normally five hymns. The service ended with the benediction and often, in the evening, a vesper. Each of these elements is now briefly considered.

Hymns

Hymns were the most participative aspect of Primitive Methodist public worship. We also sang frequently at home accompanied by my father on an American organ he had bought secondhand. We had a wide selection from which to choose. As indicated in Chapter 2, the *Primitive Methodist Hymnal* contained 1,052 hymns.

Another 295 were available in the *Hymnal Supplement* published in 1912. The sociological significance of hymns has received insufficient attention. Hymn books reflect the religious and social concerns current at their time of publication. The number of hymns in the sections of the 1887 *Primitive Methodist Hymnal* headed 'Death and resurrection', 'The Judgement' and 'Final Awards' were thirty-eight, twelve and eighteen respectively and are evidence of the Victorian obsession with eschatology. By 1932, the *Methodist Hymn Book* had reduced the number of hymns in the section 'Death, Judgement and the Future Life' to twenty with an additional six for use at funerals and memorial services. In *Hymns and Psalms* published in 1983, both the headings and all but three of the hymns were expunged.

As indicated in Chapter 6, many of the hymns included in 1912 reflected Edwardian optimism and humanism. A number were representative of R. J. Campbell's *New Theology* with its emphasis on God's immanence as distinct from his transcendence and the establishment by human effort of the kingdom of God on earth. Such liberal hymns were in juxtaposition with more evangelical items including a judicious selection from Moody and Sankey. The *Supplement* also contained a section of thirty-one good, bad and indifferent 'Hymns for the Young'. Preachers and congregations found many of the *Supplement* hymns refreshingly modern. Some became congregational favourites and their omission from the post-Union *Methodist Hymn Book* was regretted. These included 'Christ shall lead us in the time of youth', 'Courage, brother, do not stumble' and 'Day is dying in the west'. The latter was probably more popular than 'The day Thou gavest, Lord, is ended'. In the *Supplement*, both the last two hymns appeared in a Primitive Methodist hymnal for the first time. Some *Supplement* hymns, however, were unworthy of use. Sellers notes 'the weird clarion call of lines from a temperance hymn, "The boys and girls of England":

> To God each true heart sends a cry
> And each the "Amen" adds.
> As Jacob, when about to die,
> Exclaimed – "God bless the lads!"' [6]

Martin suggests that religious culture patterns can be identified by a division into 'those who sing carols, those who sing hymns and those who sing choruses' and 'can be located to some extent at different intellectual and status levels.'[7] Carols are aligned with Bach, Byrd and Britten and had an insignificant influence on Primitive Methodist hymnody. Hymns date from apostolic days but in the Middle Ages disappeared from public worship to the services of the monastic orders until, at the Reformation, Luther revived their public use. In England, their widespread use owes much to the work of Watts and the Wesleys in the first half of the eighteenth century. It was, however, the chorus or the hymn used as a chorus by the repetition of verses to express the emotion of worshippers that best expresses the culture of early Primitive Methodist evangelical zeal. This revivalism was expressed in two hymns, sung at the Final Primitive Methodist Conference in June 1932: one at the beginning of the Service of Commemoration, Thanksgiving and Rededication and the other at the last session. The first was 'Hark the Gospel news is sounding' by William Sanders. Sung to the tune *Grace*, this was known as the Primitive Methodist Grand March. Strangely, I never remember it being sung at a service, although my father often sang it at home. The second 'And can it be ...' by Charles Wesley which, sung to the tune *Sagina*, was regarded as the Primitive Methodist National Anthem.

By the middle of the nineteenth century, the culture of martial evangelism expressed in such Primitive Methodist verses as

> Apollyon's armies we must fight
> And put the troops of hell to flight.

had begun to wane. The later evangelism (1873–5) of Moody and Sankey was reinforced by their *Sacred Songs and Solos*. These, as Kent points out, were not predominantly concerned with sin and salvation but the reassurance of 'the reunion of families and the pleasures of a bourgeois heaven.'[8]

Many Primitive Methodist churches bought copies of *Sacred Songs and Solos* for use alongside their Connexional hymn books.

The copy in my home was extensively used. My father sang 'Let the lower lights be burning', 'Hold the fort for I am coming' and 'There were ninety and nine' with great gusto and feeling.

The liberalism of the 1912 *Supplement* also sat uncomfortably beside the *Primitive Methodist Mission Hymnal for use in Evangelistic Services* published in 1923. The two books are indicative that by the 1920s, the Primitive Methodists had two cultures. The chorus culture lingered on in pit villages and country chapels. In many Primitive Methodist chapels, especially in the towns, however, the chorus had become a source of social and intellectual embarrassment. This difference is exemplified in the choice of hymns for Sunday School Anniversaries mentioned earlier in this chapter.

Hymns do more than reflect culture. They are also vehicles through which theological beliefs and individual and corporate aspirations can be succinctly expressed. For many Primitive Methodists their hymn books were also prayer books and a means through which they could sing their creed. My father, as indicated, had a strong revivalistic tendency. Yet he told me that his mother's and his own deepest spiritual aspirations were expressed in the verses of one of Charles Wesley's hymn:

> Jesus, if still the same Thou art,
> If all Thy promises are sure,
> Set up Thy kingdom in my heart
> And make me rich, for I am poor:
> To me be all Thy treasures given,
> The kingdom of an inward heaven. [9]

He claimed, and I believed him, that his faith gave him an experience of 'an inward heaven that nothing could destroy.'

Probably hymns were often sung without regard to the words. Often singing, almost irrespective of what was sung, became an activity in itself. Moore, in a study of the effects of Methodism in a Durham mining community, suggests that singing 'may at times fulfil some of the functions of alcohol, enabling the miner to escape temporarily from the consciousness of the limitations of his way of life.'[10] But disregard for the words was not always the case. Within the unlovely mining chapels of the Lowton Circuit, there was often a deep spirituality. The husband of one of my paternal cousins, a strapping young miner who attended the Bamfurlong church, told me how, in the darkness and danger of the pit, assailed by the profanity and obscenity of some workmates, he sustained his faith by meditating on the words of a now forgotten Primitive Methodist hymn:

Play thy part and play it well
Joy in thy appointed task
And, if pride or flesh rebel
Courage of thy Father ask.

Shrink not from thy daily task,
Murmur not at toil or pain,
'Tis to purge thy spirit's dross
All must toil and not complain.

Take the task thy Father gives,
Bind it to thy cheerful breast,
He who suffers doubly lives,
He who suffers well, lives best.

Courage then! and nobly meek
Let thy love thy sorrows quell.
Honour in obedience seek,
Play thy part and play it well.[11]

The hymn can be easily criticised as advocating resigned acceptance of that 'state of life into which it shall please God to call me.'[12] Karl Marx might have cited both miner and hymn in support of his thesis that religion is the 'opiate' of the people. Yet the converse was also true. The miner's simple religious faith enabled him to transcend rather than succumb to his dehumanising working environment.

A hymn, of course, never consists in its words alone, but in the successful combination of words and tune. As Walford Davies stated, a hymn tune should be 'beautifully fitting and fittingly beautiful'. 'Ranting' did not pay too much attention to the musical merit of tunes but rather whether they were popular, well known and a vehicle for emotional release. Often, secular tunes, and even words were adapted to spiritual purposes as instanced by Kendall in his description of the entry of Primitive Methodism to Leicester where in the 1840s Chartism was rife.[13] The Chartists marched through the streets singing:

> The Lion of Freedom is come from his den;
> We'll rally around him, again and again.
> We'll crown him with laurel, our champion to be:
> O'Connor the Patriot for sweet liberty.

William Jefferson, the Primitive Methodist Missioner, adapted both tune and words so that the Primitive Methodists also took to the streets singing:

> For the Lion of Judah shall break every chain,
> And give us the victory again and again.

My father still sang the hymn in the 1930s.

In the opinion of experts, not all settings satisfied the criteria of fitness laid down by Walford Davies. This is especially true of 'And can it be' to the tune *Sagina*. Erik Routley, no mean authority on hymns, concluded that *Sagina* 'leaves the same impression that a sermon containing much shouting and thumping but little rational discourse leaves. It is oppressive, suffocating of imagination, stultifying of true response, and pretentious. It is, I fear, vulgar.'[14] Another writer, Foury, states that 'the danger of strongly eloquent tunes like *Sagina* is that their heartiness makes us "feel good" as we sing. Herein lies their danger and seduction: that we will sing an "exciting tune" to obtain this result without attending to the real message and meaning of the words.'[15] 'And can it be' is a meditative, confident, but not a boasting hymn. It starts with a diminuendo and ends on a crescendo. Such reflections never occurred to my father. I doubt if they occur to many who sing the hymn today.

Prayers

Primitive Methodist services, as I experienced them, normally had three prayers: the 'preacher's prayer', the Lord's Prayer and the Benediction. The last two are self-explanatory. The 'preacher's prayer', so called because its length, content and phraseology were at the discretion of the preacher, had two characteristics.

First, it was an extempore prayer. Chapel congregations had a strong prejudice against read prayers, which was Puritan in its origins. Puritan objection to the *Book of Common Prayer* was partly based on the imposition by the Establishment of set forms of prayer, which was regarded as an infringement of their liberty of conscience to 'worship God according to the dictates of conscience.' Horton points out that liturgical and free prayer reflected two differing concepts of the Church:

> The former stresses the corporate nature of the Church in 'Common Prayer', the latter emphasises the need of individuals in a family church. If liturgical prayer adequately reflects what is held in Common in its Creeds, its General Confession, its abstract Collects praying for graces required by all Christians, then free prayer meets the individual's particular requirements. And moreover, liturgical prayer does not demand that the minister should know the members of his congregation; free prayer implies a smaller, more compact community, all of whom, theoretically, are known to the minister.[16]

Horton further shows that Puritan objections to set prayers were both theological and practical. Theologically, set prayers were at variance with the teaching of Romans 8.26: 'Likewise, the Spirit also helpeth our infirmities; for we know not what we should pray for as we ought; but the Spirit itself maketh intercession for us with groanings that cannot be uttered.' Read prayers implied human self-sufficiency in being able to identify our wants rather than our needs.

The practical objections were not that set forms of prayer deprived both minister and people of the gift of prayer; they made Christians satisfied with hearing prayers instead of encouraging them to pray themselves and set prayers could not meet the varying needs of different congregations and occasions. It was also objected that the constant use of set prayers was conducive to hypocrisy and vain repetitions and that the imposition of set prayers by the Church was a form of persecution.

In one form or another, I heard all these objections. As a small boy, largely unacquainted with the glories of the *Book of Common Prayer*, I believed that Anglican clergy did not know how to pray. I was also taught that Anglican congregations do not know how to sing!

The second characteristic of the Primitive Methodist preacher's prayer was that it was normally of the 'omnibus' variety. We did not have separate prayers of adoration, confession, thanksgiving, supplication and intercession but included all these elements in one comprehensive prayer that, with some preachers, might be up to fifteen minutes in duration. In retrospect, such prayers had several deficiencies. Preachers were sometimes 'over pally with the Lord' or, conversely, confused adoration with providing the Almighty with a lot of miscellaneous information about his attributes and character. Intercession and supplication often comprised a catalogue of non-specific persons and places: 'the sick, the sad and the sorrowing', 'the trouble spots of the world', 'all labourers in Thy vineyard'. The range could literally be from Battersea Dogs' Home to 'darkest Africa'. No one that I heard approached the remark of the apocryphal preacher who prayed: 'Lord, you have no doubt read in this morning's *Guardian* ...' but some came perilously near. As Willey observed of Wesleyan worship: 'The prayers, especially the "Long Prayer", were embarrassing because in their approach to the Almighty [Methodist ministers] commonly used a tone of easy familiarity, as of the leader of a deputation interviewing a trusted but not too well-informed chief.' [17]

In some prayers, penitence and confession were relegated to the closing sentence: 'These things we ask, with the forgiveness of all our sins, through Jesus Christ our Lord.' Such prayers overlooked two of the fundamental teachings of Jesus about prayer: his statement that 'Your Father knows what your needs are before you ask him' (Matthew 6.8) and 'In your prayers, do not go babbling on like the heathen, who imagine that the more they say, the most likely they are to be heard' (Matthew 6.5).

Too frequently, preachers, both ministerial and lay, confused extempore prayer with unprepared prayer. This danger was, as Davies mentions, recognised by two Puritan critics of extempore prayer, Jeremy Taylor and Matthew Henry. Taylor pointed out that extempore prayer might be the result of mental laziness:

> I consider that the true state of the Question is only this, whether it is better to pray to God with consideration, or without? Whether is the wiser of the two, he who thinks and deliberates what to say, or he that utters his mind as fast as it comes?[18]

Henry also recognised the need for ordered prayer:

> And it is requisite to the decent Performance of Duty, that some proper method be observed, not only that what is said be good, but that it be said in its proper place and time; and that we offer not anything to the Glorious Majesty of Heaven and Earth, which is confused, impertinent and undigested.[19]

Not all Primitive Methodist prayers were slovenly or ill-prepared. I remember an evening service when a local preacher simply repeated, with great sensitivity and feeling, the verses of Henry Twells' hymn 'At Even when the sun was set'.[20] Several worshippers who might have objected to a more formal read prayer were much moved. There was another local preacher of whom it could be truthfully said that in his pulpit prayers, he addressed God simply and unaffectedly 'as a man speaketh with his friend'. My father said of one minister who was an above-average preacher that his pulpit prayers were even greater blessings than his sermons. As I discovered much later in life, there are three fundamental conditions for effective pulpit prayers: preachers must know God and their congregations and prepare their prayers after meditating imaginatively on both.

The lessons

Scripture readings followed the second and preceded the third or fourth hymns according to whether a hymn intervened between the first and second lesson. Primitive Methodist services did not follow the pattern of Old Testament lesson, Epistle and Gospel but normally were restricted to readings from the Old and New Testament. Neither did we use any lectionary. One of the chosen readings would usually provide the context in which the sermon text would be found. Up to 1939, pulpit Bibles were mainly the Authorised Version but sometimes preachers would read from other translations. For the Old Testament, this was mainly the Revised Version of 1885. Several translations of the New Testament were available, including those of Weymouth (1902) and Moffatt (1913). The latter's translation of Paul's hymn of love in 1 Corinthians 13 was often used. Some preachers had cultivated the art of good reading and from them I almost unconsciously learned how to read expressively, paying due regard to pace, emphasis and punctuation. Few things irritate me more than someone who cannot thrill to such words as 'Comfort ye, comfort ye my people, saith your God' or 'O be Joyful in the Lord, all ye lands: serve the Lord with gladness, and come before his Presence with a song.' Some preachers read such words (and some still do) in the same tone that one would expect a company chairman to read an Annual Report to a company meeting. Only rarely did readers announce the lessons with the bidding 'Let us hear the Word of God.' The closing formulary, 'The Lord bless to us the reading of his Word,' was, however, often used.

The children's address

The inclusion of the section, 'Hymns for the Young' in the 1912 *Supplement to the Primitive Methodist Hymnal* reflects an increased concern shared with other denominations for children in church. Almost all such children had already attended Sunday school.

Some, like the writer, joined their parents for the chapel service and sat in the parental pew. Children of non-churchgoers usually sat in a group in the front pews accompanied by some Sunday school teachers who had cajoled them into attending. The third hymn at the morning or afternoon service was 'the children's hymn', followed by a lesson and/or the 'children's address'.

The children's address, usually of five to ten minutes in duration, took several forms. Some preachers related a personal experience. A local preacher, who was a farmer, spoke of taking his plough horses to the blacksmith for shoeing. Immediately the white-hot metal was taken from the furnace, it was beaten into shape. The moral was 'strike while the iron is hot' or 'do it now!' Another preacher used fables such as Aesop's story of a man, his son and a donkey, and added a spiritual dimension to the original moral that if we try to please everybody, we please nobody by asserting that we should therefore only seek to please God. Some preachers simply retold a Bible story. Others used incidents from history or literature such as the story of the Welsh prince, Llewelyn, who returned home to find his dog, Gelert, with jaws dripping blood. Llewelyn's son, who had been left in Gelert's care could not be found. In his distress, the prince slew Gelert but then found his son alive and untouched beside the body of a wolf that the faithful hound had killed. This story was used to drive home the lessons either of faithfulness or that acting in haste can cause us to repent at leisure.

Preachers, especially ministers who were regularly in the same pulpit, must have found the task of finding new and striking children's addresses demanding. Not surprisingly, religious book publishers discovered a lucrative demand for books of addresses. A problem was that addresses 'lifted' from such books could be given, unknown to each other, by different preachers. I remember this taking place to the consternation of the preachers and the amusement of the congregation three times in a single quarter. The address was based on a young farmhand, John the Yorkshireman. When interviewed by a farmer for employment, John offered two attributes: the abilities to 'sleep on a windy night' and 'to invite his master's friends for dinner'. The address told how John could 'sleep on a windy night' because he had done his duty by making all the stacks and buildings secure before going to bed. When, after a bad harvest, he invited his master's friends to dinner, he asked them to bring their cheque books with them. There were few acceptances but those who did so were the farmer's true friends whose friendship was there in bad days as well as good. A friend, as the Book of Proverbs says 'loveth at all times'.

Many years later, I found the book from which the stories were taken in a secondhand bookshop. I bought it for nostalgic reasons.

In retrospect, the children's addresses I heard had three main characteristics. These lessons were predominantly moral rather than spiritual. Because they were brief, sometimes humorous, and conveyed 'truth embodied in a tale', they tended to be remembered. A good children's address was enjoyed as much, if not more so, by the adults. As Coffin wisely observed: 'A children's talk may aid a grown-up to become as a child, and according to our Lord, he will then be far better prepared to enter the kingdom.[21]

The notices and offering

These normally preceded the hymn before the sermon and were often announced by the Senior Chapel Steward. At Anniversary and Harvest seasons, chapels inundated each other with details of forthcoming services. There would also be local announcements relating to church meetings, 'hot pot' suppers, socials, jumble sales, services of song and the like. The notices often took at least ten minutes to read and usually ended with such words as: 'The offering for Church and Circuit funds will now be taken.' These words were the signal for the appointed collectors to take round a collecting box, bag or plate into which worshippers would place their 'offering'. Etiquette required that irrespective of the receptacle used, the collector would avert his gaze to avoid noticing the amount contributed. When the collectors had completed their task, they would place the bag, box or plate on the communion table and return to their seats.

The more orderly and reverent procedure by which collectors marched together to the communion rail where the offerings were received and dedicated by the preacher was only implemented in most Lowton Circuit chapels at a considerably later date.

The notices and offering had the effect of breaking the unity of worship and interrupting its movement. Many worshippers regarded this part of the service as a kind of half-time interval in which, protected by the volume of the organ voluntary, they could have a whispered conversation, cough, blow their noses, unwrap a sweet and pop it into their mouths in preparation for the sermon.

The sermon

The sermon was the high point of Primitive Methodist worship. Often the preceding hymns, prayers and lessons were referred to with unintentional disrespect as the 'preliminaries'. The first question asked about a potential new minister was 'Can he preach?' The emphasis placed on the preaching potential of candidates for the ministry was also indicative of the emphasis placed on 'The Ministry of the Word'.

The importance accorded to the sermon was in the Puritan tradition. Davies states that 'the opening of the Scriptures' occupied the 'central position in Puritan worship', its supremacy consisting in the fact that it was 'the declaration by the preacher of the revelation of God, confirmed in the hearts of the believers by the interior testimony of the Holy Spirit.'[22] A leading Puritan author, William Bradshaw, quoted by Davies, declared:

> They hould that the highest and supreame office and authorite of the Pastor, is to preach the Gospell solemnly and publickly to the Congregation, by interpreting the written word of God, and applying the same by exhortation and reproof unto them. They hould that this was the greatest works that Christ and his Apostles did.[23]

In contrast, the Establishment view was that the excessive importance attached by the Puritans to the sermon usurped the position of the prayers and sacraments.

The typical Primitive Methodist sermon of my youth derived many of its characteristics from Puritan practice. It also differed from many of its modern Methodist counterparts in respect of length, the lectionary, exegesis, divisions, illustrations and delivery.

Sermons were longer in duration. Congregations had a greater time span of attention, anything under twenty-five minutes being considered 'short-weight'.

There was, as stated, no lectionary of lessons and themes. Here again there was an affinity with Puritan preachers such as Richard Baxter, who, as Davies shows, objected to prescribed subjects or homilies on the ground 'that they failed to meet the conditions of the local congregation which the minister alone knows.'[24]

> If I know my hearers to be most addicted to drunkenness, must I be tyed up from preaching or reading against that sin, and tyed to Read and Preach only against Covetousness or the like, because it seemeth meet to Governours to tye me to a constant course.[25]

Sermons were invariably based on a text announced at the commencement of the sermon. With ministers especially, the influence of A. S. Peake was often manifested in careful exegesis and, as appropriate, the nuances of New Testament Greek. Texts caught the attention of sermon tasters. Some preachers realised this and preached on unusual texts. I recall hearing sermons on the 'flies in the ointment' mentioned by Ecclesiastes (10.1), the grey hairs of Hosea (7.9), the jawbone used by Samson (Judges 15.16), the measuring rod of Zechariah (21), the sundial of Ahaz (Isaiah 38.8), the potter's wheel of Jeremiah (18.3) and several on the dry bones of Ezekiel (37.1).

Most sermons were structured on the pattern of introduction, two or more divisions (usually three) and an application. This again followed the Puritan pattern of 'Doctrine, Reason and Use'. Some teachers of homiletics deprecate the use of divisions on the basis that the skeleton should not show through the flesh. Even in a comparatively short sermon, however, divisions provide 'resting places on the way' and assist recall. Elspeth MacFadyen, in Ian MacLaren's now forgotten book *Beside the Bonnie Brier Bush*, could recall all the seventy-four headings of John Peddie's sermon on total depravity based on the text: 'Arise, shine, for thy light is come.' The sermon took approaching two hours to deliver.[26]

Preachers also made greater use of illustrations. W. E. Sangster gives seven reasons why apposite illustrations increase sermon effectiveness, one being that 'they make sermons remembered'.[27] I recall a minister visiting the Bridge Street chapel three times in about five years. Each time, he preached the same sermon based on 1 Kings 20.40: 'And as thy servant was busy here and there, he was gone.' He might have got away with it but for one of his illustrations. A police inspector had said that the time when his force had to be particularly alert at the Grand National horse race was when the leading horses were approaching the finishing post. Spectators would be leaning over the rails, craning to see the winner. It was then, when everyone's attention was diverted, that the pickpockets got busy. While you were watching for the winner, your wallet could walk. Preachers were always looking for illustrations. A fruitful source in the 1920s and 1930s was the books of a Baptist minister, Frank W Boreham, who, after training at Spurgeon's College, ministered in New Zealand and Australia. Boreham wrote over forty books. When, in 1936, he was invited to address the General Assembly of the Church of Scotland, the Moderator, Professor David Lamont, introduced him as 'the man whose name is on all our lips, whose books are on all our shelves, and whose illustrations are in all our sermons.'[28]

That statement applied to many Primitive Methodist preachers both ministerial and lay.

Primitive Methodist sermons were rarely read. A read sermon was as unpopular as a read prayer. This aversion to reading was probably grounded in the concept of the preacher and the environment in which early Primitive Methodist preaching was done. The preacher was above all a herald proclaiming 'Hark! The gospel news is sounding.' The early Primitive Methodist chapels in the words of Hugh Bourne: 'were the coalpit banks, or any other place; and in our conversation way, we preached the gospel to all, good or bad, rough or smooth.'[29] The relationship between religious revivalism and political radicalism was especially close. It is difficult to think of either herald or outdoor preacher reading their message. Certainly hearers would have been unarrested other than by spontaneous, extempore speech. In his lectures to Hartley students, W. Jones Davies, Principal from 1908–13, while admitting that the method of delivery should suit the man, compared the difference between the read and extempore sermon to that which is noticeable between a gramophone and the spoken voice:

> In the instrument, all the notes are accurately reproduced, the tone and the timbre of the voice are there, but there is something lacking that can only be described as 'life'. People are pleased and entertained by the gramophone but seldom moved.[30]

Like the extempore prayer, however, the extempore sermon did not mean lack of preparation. Conscientious preachers wrote out their sermons in full and then condensed them into notes, thus combining the freshness and spontaneity of extemporaneous speech with a clear concept of the content and presentation of their 'message' from its introduction to application.

Preachers

Primitive Methodist 'plans' show four main categories of preachers: ministers, local preachers, auxiliaries and hired local preachers. The last category may be briefly explained before a more detailed consideration of the preceding three.

Hired local preachers or 'Lay Agents' could only be employed by a circuit after approval had been given by the Primitive Methodist General Committee. Such preachers performed all the functions of ministers including administration of the sacraments although for less pay and no security of permanent employment. Graham shows that hired local preachers dated back to the early days of Primitive Methodism when they were regarded, by their own circuits if not by Conference, as the equal of travelling preachers.[31] In 1932, the names of fifty-four lay agents were listed in the *Primitive Methodist Yearly Handbook and Almanack.*[32]

Ministers

In the period 1920–50 most denominations had one or more ministers who were noted preachers and household names. The Anglicans had Hensley Henson, W. R. Inge and Archbishop Temple, while radio and journalism had popularised W. H. Elliott, Pat McCormick and Dick Sheppherd. The Roman Catholics had Ronald Knox. In the Free Churches, the Baptists had Townley Lord, the Congregationalists, Silvester Horne, J.D. Jones and Campbell Morgan and the Presbyterians, James Reid. In the Wesleyan Methodist Church, older ministers such as Scott Lidgett, Dinsdale Young and Luke Wiseman had up-and-coming successors in W. E. Sangster, Donald Soper and Leslie Weatherhead. In contrast, Primitive Methodism, while having many able ministers, had no name of national standing. The only Primitive Methodist minister who achieved widespread recognition outside his own denomination was Arthur Thomas Guttery (1862–1920). Wilkinson states that Guttery was 'keenly aware that few, if any, Primitive Methodist ministers had achieved a national reputation and set himself to breaking that barrier.'[33] The son of a Primitive Methodist manse, Guttery, on acceptance as a candidate for the ministry, had been sent straight into circuit work without any college training. He regarded himself as not only a minister, but also a prophet 'called by God to denounce abuses and stir up a healthy discontent.' To this end, he lectured countrywide in support of the Liberal Party. It was said that Guttery was liable to confuse the pulpit with the platform. Even when a probationer, his father or mother apparently deemed it necessary to remind him that his chief work was to preach the gospel.[34] His hero was W. E. Gladstone and Wilkinson records how, during the 1914–18 War, his father heard Guttery preach about Lloyd George from 2 Samuel 5.10: 'And David went on, and grew great, and the Lord God of hosts was with him.'[35] Presumably, Lloyd George's predilections for extra-marital peccadilloes were conveniently ignored.

During the war, Guttery appears to have become something of a demagogue who manifested an unthinking patriotism couched in outrageous language. Nevertheless, he had outstanding ministries at South Shields, Newcastle-upon-Tyne and at Princes Avenue, Liverpool, where he died in harness aged fifty-eight. Guttery was President of the Primitive Methodist Conference in 1916 and President of the National Free Church Council in 1919. In 1918 he received the honorary degree of DD from the American Wesleyan University, Middletown.

There are probably several reasons why, Guttery apart, Primitive Methodism had no minister of national reputation. Unlike the Anglicans with St Paul's Cathedral and St Martin's-in-the-Fields, the Congregationalists with the City Temple and the Wesleyans with Wesley's Chapel and the Westminster Central Hall, the Primitive Methodists had no prominent London worship centre. A further factor is that Primitive Methodist ministers appear to have published little outside their own denominational journals. To my knowledge, no sermons of even Guttery were ever published in book form. Possibly for these reasons, Primitive Methodist ministers were not invited to preach on broadcast services.

At the local level, the four ministers who 'laboured' in the Lowton Circuit during the period of this book were R. H. MacFarlane (1924–8), J. H. Rollason (1928–33), L. J. Jackson (1933–7) and T. H. Champion (1937–40). I was too young to remember R. H. MacFarlane but I recall J. H. Rollason and L. J. Jackson as able, dedicated men. Although described as 'a Puritan by temperament',[36] L. J. Jackson had a vein of true humour and was a more-than-useful slow bowler at cricket. Although I would only be aged between ten and twelve at the time, I remember going with my father to a service in the Lane Head chapel where Jackson preached on 'The Gentle Hand'.

The minister I knew best was Thomas Henry Champion. A biographical notice states that when a student at Hartley College 'he was invariably at the head of the Examination list for his large year of forty-two men. Had the facilities for study at the University only been available in those days, he would have had a distinguished academic career.'[37]

For many years he was secretary to Hartley College. Unfortunately, an illness early in his ministry left him with a slight speech impediment but for the consistent quality of his sermons, he ranks with any preacher I have heard. Champion's sermons were beautifully structured, enhanced by captivating illustrations and based on sound scholarship. In every service he conducted hymns, prayers and lessons were related so that not only the sermon but each element fitted beautifully together to provide an integrated act of worship. As a youth, I attended a course of addresses on the prophecy of Isaiah given by Champion at the Bridge Street week-night service. The addresses were based on the famous commentary on Isaiah by Sir George Adam Smith. I vividly recall Champion expounding the fortieth chapter of the prophecy and its final verse:

> But they that wait upon the Lord shall renew their strength; they shall mount up with wings as eagles; they shall run and not be weary; and they shall walk and not faint.

In his exposition, he referred to Smith's comment:

> Soaring, running, walking – and is not the next stage, a cynic might ask, standing still?
>
> On the contrary, it is a natural and true climax, rising from the easier to the more difficult, from the ideal to the real, from dream to duty, from what can only be the rare occasions of life to what must be life's usual and abiding experience.[38]

Champion never knew that that week-evening address given to fewer than twenty worshippers would have a life-long influence on one of his hearers. For me, it reinforced the lesson of the familiar prayer of Sir Francis Drake that I learned at school:

> O Lord God, when Thou givest to Thy servants to endeavour any great matter, grant us to know that it is not the beginning, but the continuing of the same unto the end, until it be thoroughly finished which yieldeth the true glory.[39]

But it did more. It opened my mind to how sound scholarship and exegesis could make the Bible come alive.

Champion preached not only by precept but also by example. He had two sons, both of whom had distinguished themselves at Manchester Grammar School. By 1938, the boys were probably in their middle or late twenties. War seemed inevitable and one Thursday evening, the younger, a convinced pacifist, committed suicide at the home of his fiancée. Champion was not a young man, Lowton being his last Circuit before superannuation, and the shock must have been immense. Nevertheless, he wished to preach as usual on the Sunday and had to be overruled by the Circuit Steward. He was, however, present with his wife and other son at both the Bridge Street morning and evening services. On the Monday preceding his son's funeral on the Tuesday, he took the funeral of a member. Afterwards, he continued his work without interruption. I understand he told the Circuit Steward that when faced by personal sorrow, a minister must show by example that faith is no empty thing. His example certainly influenced me to covet not only his outward bravery but also his inner faith.

Local Preachers

Ritson points out that the pioneers of Primitive Methodism were all local preachers and that nearly every circuit had its local preacher of unusual character and distinction.[40] This was true of the Lowton Circuit. One early local preacher was James

Eckersley, described as 'a man very well versed in Scripture, and who at times could pray and preach as one inspired ... Nevertheless he was erratic and highly eccentric, his speeches occasionally bordering on the most startling themes.'[41] Once, describing the glories of heaven, he said:

> There would be mountains o dumplins an rivers o broth, and th women would have a rare time on't as there would bi no dolly tubs nur washin beillers waiten fur um on a Monday mornin.

On another occasion, he said he would like to see all his neighbours, and all that he had known to be saved, and if he had the power, he would 'slek hell-fire eaut'.

He was apparently a great favourite with the boys who attended one of the chapels on account of his quaint sayings but principally because his services were short. When seeing him walking in the direction of the chapel, one of the lads would ask him: 'Are yo pretcher, Jemmy?' His invariable answer was 'Aye, an al not keep you lung if yo'll promise bi good lads.'

True to his side of the bargain, he would suddenly end the service about half an hour before the usual time and exclaim, 'Ah con see th'lads are getten tyart, so al gie oer, and let um go whom to their dumplins.'

One dark Sunday night, some young men attempted to frighten him when he was returning home from a preaching appointment across some lonely fields. They hid in the hedges and, as Eckersley approached, he was met by a weird apparition enveloped in a white sheet. The old man never changed his pace but on passing the ghost, quietly observed:

> If thert divol thou cawn't hurt me, and if thert human, God al not let thi touch me.[42]

The publication of the *Local Preachers Manual* by James Travis and Henry Yooll, both Primitive Methodist ministers, was indicative of the need to improve lay preacher training. In 1904, the oversight of such training became the responsibility of the

Primitive Methodist Local Preachers' Central Training Council. District and Circuit Training Committees were also established and Connexional examinations in Theology, Homiletics, Biblical Introduction, Connexional Polity, Christian Evidences and English Evidences and English Grammar were inaugurated. These examinations, however, were never made compulsory and candidates for the Plan could opt to be examined by their own circuits. Milburn points out that 'the same held true of other Methodist Connexions, none of which before Methodist Union felt able to enforce on volunteer local preachers a compulsory and uniform system of discipline, training and examination let alone a programme of continued study and development.'[43] The same writer shows that in 1913–14, only sixty-seven out of 1,477 Wesleyan preachers 'on-trial' had taken the examinations set in that year. In 1914, 170 candidates sat for the equivalent examinations set by the Primitive Methodist Connexion.

The improvement in training seems to have coincided with a shift in the occupations from which local preachers were recruited. Field observes that: 'By the early years of this century [twentieth] the social gap between Wesleyan and Primitive Methodist local preachers was narrowing considerably ... and there was a significant shift in favour of recruitment from non-manual backgrounds.' He also states that after Union, 'there is no evidence to suggest that Primitive Methodism was more working class in its orientation than the other two.'[44] These conclusions are supported by a social analysis of the seven fully accredited local preachers whose names appear on the Lowton Circuit Plan in my possession. Details of these preachers in their order of seniority on the Plan are shown in TABLE 5. Only the two farmers had manual occupations but by training and outlook, these were atypical in that one had a high position in the National Farmers' Union and the other had studied agriculture on a full-time basis. All of them resided on the Lowton-Golborne side of the Circuit. All either owned their own home or were in a position to do so.

Robert Barrow was a powerful and dramatic preacher who,

Name	Occupation	Education	Other Activities	Leisure Activities	Possessions
Robert Barrow	Wholesale fruit and potato merchant	Elementary and night school	Justice of the Peace, County Councillor (Labour), Urban Councillor Guardian, Hospital Boards etc.	Cricket	Own business, house, car, telephone
James Edwin Bridge	Tenant farmer	Elementary	Justice of the Peace, Chairman – Lancashire National Farmers' Union	Local historian, poet, painter	Built own house on farm to allow son to occupy farm house. Car, telephone
John Eckersley	Insurance agent	Elementary and night school	Circuit Steward	Cricket, Rugby League	Own house
Joseph Dean	Railway clerk	Elementary and night school	–	Music – organised choirs and orchestras	Own house
Frank Johnson	Headteacher (Methodist School, Withnell)	Grammar School, Teacher Training College	Later became Justice of the Peace	?	Believed to have been living in a school house. Telephone
James Bridge	Farm manager (son of James E. Bridge above)	Grammar School (Higher School Certificate). Full-time attendance at Lancs County Agricultural College, Sutton	–	Golf, football	Lived in farm house. Telephone
Benjamin Holden	Worked in the Leigh Education Office	Unknown. Probably Elementry and night school	Member of Leigh Board of Guardians	Wrote a short history of Methodism in Leigh. Singing	Own house

TABLE 5: SOCIAL ANALYSIS OF ACCREDITED LOCAL PREACHERS, LOWTON CIRCUIT, *C.* 1939

because of his civic connections, was much in demand for special services throughout Lancashire. He had served in the 1914–18 War, rapidly attaining the rank of Sergeant. Mainly because it added a new word to my vocabulary, I recall the subject but not the substance of one of his sermons on 'camouflage'. Had he so wished, Barrow could easily have secured nomination as a Parliamentary candidate. His son later became a local preacher.

James Edwin Bridge put a high premium on the education of his children. Of his four sons, three became farmers, one a graduate teacher and one a Congregational minister. His two daughters became teachers, one after graduating from Oxford. He was a somewhat stern man. Once, when preaching in the Lane Head chapel, he interrupted his sermon to rebuke three or four teenagers who were misbehaving in the gallery and commanded them to come down and sit in the front pew.[45]

James Eckersley was related to the James Eckersley mentioned earlier. He had candidated for the Primitive Methodist ministry and been rejected on health grounds. He nevertheless rode his bicycle in all weathers as an insurance agent. He was a scholarly preacher who, over the years, amassed a fine library not inferior to some ministers and superior to many.

Joseph Dean had also served in the 1914–18 War. He was a fluent preacher and, as shown in TABLE 5, was much in demand to conduct Services of Song and arrange musical events.

Frank Johnson was a product of the Edge Green church. After qualifying as a teacher, he moved away from Golborne and only preached occasionally in the Circuit.

James Bridge was the son of James Edwin Bridge and the son-in-law of Robert Barrow. After grammar school, he could have gone to university but, due to his father's age and indisposition, it became necessary for him to manage the farm. He had an attractive personality and was frequently asked to take harvest festival services.

Benjamin Holden spent most of his life in the Leigh Primitive Methodist Circuit where, for a time, he was Circuit Steward. He was only associated with the Lowton Circuit and the Lane Head chapel in the latter part of his life. He was the only one of the seven whom I cannot recall hearing preach.

Whether the seven local preachers in the Lowton Circuit were a fair sample of the Connexion as a whole, I do not know. All seven men were very acceptable preachers who appealed not only to the heart but also the intellect. They were truly men who preached not because they had to say something but because they had something to say.

Auxiliaries

Each of the seven churches in the Lowton Circuit had two services so that every Sunday, fourteen preachers were required. Three services were normally taken by the minister, leaving eleven to be staffed either by the Circuit local preachers or 'auxiliaries', or helpers. Apart from the designation 'Supply', which meant that the local society was responsible for finding a preacher, the Lowton Plan before me lists the names of sixty-eight auxiliaries, not all of whom were taking appointments in the Circuit in that quarter. These sixty-eight helpers could be categorised as follows:

Visiting ministers (including a student from Hartley Victoria College)	4
Accredited local preachers from other circuits	40
Preachers from non-Methodist churches	3
Local auxiliaries	7
Not known	14
	68

Preachers from other circuits often gave a whole Sunday, taking a morning or afternoon service and being entertained to lunch and/or tea ('getting their feet under someone else's mahogany') before proceeding to an evening appointment. Such a preacher might be away from home for over twelve hours. Not for nothing did one of the most memorable vestry prayers I have ever heard include the petition, 'Lord, remember the local preachers' wives.' When I think about some of these visiting preachers, I am reminded of the incident related by the famous Congregational preacher J. H. Jowett. On holiday, Jowett attended a country Primitive Methodist chapel. The preacher was a farm labourer and the sermon was halting and even crude. Yet the preacher said something that impressed itself indelibly on Jowett's memory. 'Why?' asked the preacher, 'have I walked ten miles here and why will I walk ten miles home again to preach to you? Because', he stated, '*I cannot eat the Bread of Life alone.*' I am sure that many of our visiting preachers were similarly motivated. One auxiliary, after preaching at the Bridge Street morning service, was taken to lunch at the home of a member. It was a hot day and it was suggested that the preacher might like to take off his coat. He demurred. Later, the real reason for his reluctance emerged. His coat hid the fact that under it he was wearing nothing but a shirt front because he had no shirt.

Local auxiliaries were men or women resident in the Circuit who had been approved to take services but were not candidates for the Plan. Five of the seven local auxiliaries were connected with the Ashton chapel. In general, they tended to be more fundamentalist than the accredited local preachers and their sermons were less structured. Some of these preachers were regarded as 'characters'. One often began his sermon with the words: 'As I said t' missus in bed last night.' Congregations began to anticipate the latest nocturnal discussion with interest. On one occasion, the same preacher related how he had been asked if he really believed that the whale (or great fish) swallowed Jonah. 'Believe it!' he retorted. 'Of course I believe it. If it's in t'Bible I'd believe it if it said that Jonah swallowed t'whale!'

Whether by minister, local preacher or auxiliary, the sermon was always given an attentive hearing. It is not strange that I can recall details of sermons heard when only nine or ten years old. One reason for such recollections is that in my home we had 'roast preacher' for Sunday lunch, tea and supper and the day's sermons were always rigorously analysed, criticised and, on occasion, eulogised. This habit of critical listening has remained with me all my life. One is reminded of the man who nostalgically remarked: 'They were great preachers in those days,' to which his companion retorted: 'And there were greater hearers, too.' The two things were not unrelated. I knew a lady who always took a pad and pencil to chapel so that she could note down anything in the sermon that impressed her. In the following week she would refer to her pad and think about the previous Sunday's sermons.

Service books

The first Primitive Methodist Service Book was a book of *Forms for the sacraments and occasional services* 'drawn by the Order of the Primitive Methodist Conference assembled at Newcastle-on-Tyne June 1859.' This book was sanctioned by the Conference held at Tunstall in June 1860. A later book entitled *Order of Administration of Baptism and Other Services for the Use of Primitive Methodists* was published about 1895. A list of the services in the above books and a comparison with the Wesleyan and the 1936 *Methodist Book of Offices* is given in TABLE 6.

It is of interest that the order for 'Maternal Thanksgiving after Childbirth' was not included in any other Methodist service book until the 1936 *Book of Offices*. This service was ultimately derived from the Jewish rite of the Purification (Leviticus 12, Luke 21.22), unlike the corresponding rite in the *Book of Common Prayer*, that in the 1860 *Primitive Methodist Book* consisted of a single prayer which began:

> Almighty God, our Heavenly Father, Thou hast taught us that as man is doomed to a life of toilsome labour, the sorrows of women are greatly multiplied, as a penalty for the original transgression. To these sentences, we bow with becoming contrition and resignation.[46]

The rubric stated that the service was one of 'frequent occurrence' but in the period 1920–40, it was rarely used by Primitive Methodists. This was not the case with the Anglicans. I recall my mother being told by one of our egg customers that her daughter had given birth. The customer went on to say that her daughter had been told that until she had been 'churched', she must not visit her mother's home. I was, of course, too young to understand the ban. I was reminded of the incident when reading that although the Puritans approved the service as a thanksgiving for safe delivery from childbirth, they questioned:

> Whither wake and superstitious womë may not be occasioned to thinke this Service rather a Purification (which were Jewish) than Thankes-giving … as if women were by childbirth uncleane, and therefore unfit to go about their business until they be purified.[47]

The publication of the two service books was probably an attempt to bring some order into the specified forms of worship. The title page of the 1860 book actually quotes 1 Corinthians 14.60: 'Let all things be done decently and in order.'

The books were also intended only for ministerial use. The 1860 book states that the 'Forms' were 'for the use of such Primitive Methodist Ministers as may require them.' Apart from the vows in the marriage service, none of the services required any congregational participation or response. I do not recall these orders of service being used by any Lowton Circuit minister other than T. H. Champion. Probably this was because of the dislike of 'read' prayers mentioned earlier in this chapter. Writing of non-Wesleyan service books, Bowmer observes:

> On the whole, these non-Wesleyan liturgies are not well rubricated. Either everyone knew by tradition what to do, and when; or there were no hard and fast rules about doing it. For example, it is impossible to gather from the printed services whether communicants sat in their pews to receive the elements or whether they came to the rail. Evidently, unwritten laws operated here. The Primitive Methodist book is the best rubricated of them all for its services. It is also nearest to the Book of Common Prayer and therefore to the Wesleyan … However, it is probably because the PM order [of the Communion Service] was

Primirtivw Methdist Service Book, 1860	Primitive Methodist Service Book, *c.* 1900–5	Wesleyan Service Book	Methodist Book of Offices 1936
Baptism	Baptism of Infants	The Ministration of Baptism to Infants	Baptism of Infants
Matrimony	The Solemnisation of Matrimony	The Form of the Solemnisation of Matrimony	Solemnisation of Matrimony
Maternal Thanksgiving	Maternal Thanksgiving after Childbirth		Thanksgiving of Mothers
Renewing our Covenant with God	Covenant Service	Directions for Covenanting with God Alternative Service	For Such as Would Enter into or Renew Their Covenant with God
The Lord's Supper	The Order for the Administrtion of the Lord's Supper	Order for the Administration of the Lord's Supper, or the Holy Communion	The Lord's Supper; or the Holy Communion
The Burial of the Dead	The Order for the Burial of the Dead	The Order for the Burial of the Dead	Burial of the Dead Burial of a Child
	Ministration of Baptism to Such as are of Riper Years	The Ministration of Baptism to Such as are of Riper Years	Baptism of Such as are of Riper Years
			Morning Prayer Collects, Epistles and Gospels Alternative Service for the Holy Communion
		Form for the Public Recognition of New Members Form of Ordination	Public Reception of New Members Ordination of Candidates for the Ministry Ordination of Deaconesses Public Recognition of Local Preachers Dedication of Sunday School Teachers

TABLE 6: COMPARISON OF CONTENTS OF PRIMITIVE METHODIST WITH WESLEYAN AND METHODIST SERVICE BOOKS

so near to the Book of Common Prayer that it was so little used, and, in any case, all the non-Wesleyans preferred the freer mode of celebration.[48]

Sacraments

As with all Protestant Churches, except the Quakers, Primitive Methodists recognised only two sacraments as being of divine institution, namely Baptism and the Lord's Supper. Wesleyan Methodism restricted sacramental administration to ministers. In the Primitive and United Methodist Churches, lay administration was not only permitted but was a matter of principle deriving from the doctrine of the priesthood of all believers. As Bowmer states, however, even in Wesleyan Methodism 'there was no doctrinal reason' why lay persons should not officiate and that Wesleyan practice was a matter of Church Order, rather than one of Ministerial Orders.[49] The Congregationalist J. S. Whale put the matter succinctly by quoting Martin Luther: 'All Christians are priests, true; but they are not all parsons.'[50] The 1932 Deed of Union affirmed the doctrine of the priesthood of all believers in the statements that in the newly United Church, there is 'no priesthood differing in kind from that which is common to the Lord's people …' and that 'no priesthood exists which belongs exclusively to a particular order or class of men.' A Report adopted by the 1947 Methodist Conference recommended that the common policy should be 'the general usage of administration by ministers, but with provision for lay administration where it is needed or required.'[51]

In my experience, little attempt was made by Primitive Methodism at the local level to provide any instruction in the doctrinal basis of the sacraments. In consequence, there was often little understanding of their significance by most lay people. In some cases, as with the example of 'churching' given earlier, this could easily degenerate into something little removed from superstition. As a small boy, I was taught that a baptismal service was one at which 'a baby is given a name'. In some cases there was the fear dating back to Irenaeus (*d.* AD 202) and Augustine (354–430) that an unbaptised infant would be excluded from heaven.

In general, Primitive Methodist attitudes to the sacraments followed the teaching of Calvin who placed the sacraments in the same category as prayer, the study of the Scriptures and preaching. As Davies shows, the Puritans inherited the Calvinistic position and the sacraments, 'since they were dramatic representations of the Word', were necessarily subordinate to the gospel.[52] Some Puritans such as Thomas Goodwin had a 'high' view of the sacraments and regarded them as the 'seals' of the Word. Others, however, believed that in Puritan worship the sermon surpassed not only the prayers and praises but also the sacraments. This was almost certainly the predominant Primitive Methodist view.

Baptism

The service in the 1895 Primitive Methodist *Order of Administration* was very similar to that in the Wesleyan *Order of Administration of the Sacraments and Other Services* first issued in 1835, which underwent many variations until the publication in 1882 of the *Book of Public Prayers and Services*, which remained in use until 1932. An interesting deviation is that the Primitive Methodists seemed reluctant to use the term 'Sacrament' and substituted the word 'Ordinance'. Both services differed in several ways from the corresponding service in the *Book of Common Prayer*.

Doctrinally, the *Book of Common Prayer* emphasised the regeneration of the infant and removal of the guilt of original sin. The Methodist services assumed that the child was already Christ's. The rubric to the Primitive Methodist service stated that:

> Parents bringing their child for Baptism should be reminded that ... in this Ordinance they dedicate their offspring to the Lord and acknowledge their obligation to return them in the love and fear of His Name.[53]

It can, of course, be objected that Baptism is not merely a Dedication service. At a Dedication service, the parents declare what they will do. At a Baptismal service, it is Christ who, through his representative, the minister, takes the child in his arms and declares what he has done and will do for the child.

The *Book of Common Prayer* required the attendance of either two godfathers and one godmother or two godmothers and one godfather according to whether the child was male or female. The Godparents made promises on behalf of the child and were exhorted regarding their responsibility to see that the promises were kept. The Methodist services required no godparents and the parents made no promises. When, as an attender at a Church of England School, I learned my Catechism, I asked my father who were the godparents who at my baptism had given me the name wherein I was made a member of Christ, the child of God, and an inheritor of the kingdom of heaven. The answer was short: 'You don't need godparents.'

In both the *Book of Common Prayer* and the Methodist services, identical wording was used to declare that the child had been received into the 'congregation of Christ's flock'. In the Anglican service, this was signified by the sign of the Cross made by the priest on the child's forehead. Puritans objected to this sign on the ground that what is not expressly sanctioned in Scripture should be forbidden. In both Methodist services, the minister was instructed to 'sprinkle' the child with water.

Finally, in the *Book of Common Prayer*, Baptism was the first part of the one act of Christian initiation that should culminate in Confirmation as soon as the child could 'say the Creed, the Lord's Prayer and the Ten Commandments in the vulgar tongue.' The Methodist services were complete in themselves although both stated that 'if deemed expedient', ministers might exhort and encourage the parents of the newly baptised child and all others present in the diligent discharge of their duties. It is very doubtful if many ministers or local preachers knew anything of the three-fold Puritan objections to Confirmation: that it was, in effect, a third sacrament; that the grace received in Baptism was sealed by the Lord's Supper, which made Confirmation superfluous and that the Bishop's laying on of hands was an unapostolic practice by a man who claimed to be in the apostolic succession.

I can never remember the *Primitive Methodist Service Book* being used. Whether conducted by minister or layman, the Baptismal services I witnessed were shorter and even less formal. We usually began by singing Phillip Doddridge's baptismal hymn:

> See Israel's gentle Shepherd stand
> With all engaging charms;
> Hark, how he calls the tender lambs
> And folds them in his arms.[54]

There would follow a brief Scripture reading, normally Mark 10.13–16, the naming of the child and the baptism. The service would end with a short extempore prayer and the Grace. Afterwards the particulars would be recorded in the chapel's Baptismal Register and a Certificate of Baptism given to the parents.

Doubtless many parents who brought their children for baptism did so because it was a recognised rite of passage or even from superstition. For most it was a service of dedication and an earnest of their desire that the child should be 'instructed and trained in the doctrines, privileges and duties of the Christian religion.' It might also indicate that they wished the child to be received into the Primitive Methodist rather than the Anglican 'congregation of Christ's flock' and be brought up 'Chapel' rather than 'Church'. From the standpoint of the local congregation, baptism meant that the child had become not only Christ's but 'one of ours' who, in due course, would attend Sunday school and, hopefully, on the basis of a profession of faith and evidence of a consistent life, be eventually received into full membership.

Baptism was open to all. Holland draws attention to 'the bold and imaginative claim' made by Hugh Bourne for the function of the Church. In his booklet *A Treatise on Baptism, in Twelve Conversations with Five Original Hymns* published in 1832, Bourne observes that it is 'the duty both of natural and guardian parents to bring [their child] on [to] inward baptism. He then affirms that every infant may be baptised even if the parents lack faith since:

> The whole Church of Christ upon Earth, are guardian parents to all infants. Their united prayers are sounding before God, day and night; and all the infants upon the Earth, have part in their prayers, and in the operation and effect of their united prayers.

Holland shows how, as time passed, Bourne's influence on Baptism waned. Baptism emerged as 'a reception into the new covenant of the children of Christians who dedicate their child to God with the prayer that he will give the Holy Spirit to the infant that he may be born again.' Bourne's fine vision of the Church as the 'guardian parents of all infants' was lost.[55]

The Lord's Supper

The Order for the Administration of the Lord's Supper or Holy Communion appears first in the eight services contained in the *Wesleyan Order of Administration of the Sacraments and Other Services.* In the *Primitive Methodist Order of Administration of Baptism and Other Services*, the Lord's Supper is in the penultimate place of six services, precedence being given to the two services for baptism, marriage, maternal thanksgiving for childbirth and the burial of the dead. This placing is probably indicative of the lesser importance placed on the service by the Primitive Methodists than their Wesleyan contemporaries. With some minor amendments, the Wesleyan service followed the *Book of Common Prayer.* As shown in the comparison of the three services in TABLE 6, the Primitive Methodist service differed from the other two in several respects. It was much shorter. Like the Wesleyan service it would follow the normal service although in many Wesleyan churches, Holy Communion was often incorporated into the preaching service. The *Book of Common Prayer* and Wesleyan Service Book assumed that communicants would have service books that would enable them both to make the prescribed responses and kneel or stand as instructed. The Primitive

Methodist Service Book was for ministerial use only so that there was no communicant participation.

The title of the Primitive Methodist service was simply 'The Lord's Supper'. Until my late teens this and 'The Sacrament' were the only names I associated with the service. Davies states that the Puritan preference for 'The Lord's Supper' rather than 'The Communion' or 'Eucharist' is significant. It is 'yet another indication of the Puritan loyalty to the Word of God.'[56]

The omission from the prayer 'for the whole estate of Christ's Church militant here on earth' of the references to 'Christian Kings, Princes and Governors', the reigning sovereign and 'all that are put in authority under him' exemplifies Primitive Methodist radicalism and its dislike of the Establishment. Similarly, the omission of the Absolution after the Prayer of Confession is indicative of a desire to avoid anything that might be construed as 'priestly' or at variance with the priesthood of all believers. Finally, the changing of the petition in the Prayer of Consecration 'that we may be partakers of His most precious Body and Blood' to 'that we may become more fully one with Him in spiritual life and fellowship' reflects the view of the Swiss religious reformer Ulrich Zwingli (1484–1531) who regarded the Lord's Supper as a memorial of Christ's death. To Zwingli, the Supper was both a commemorative rite and an act of renewed union with Christ, the bread and wine being symbols of the broken body and shed blood and seals of our renewed union with Christ who is spiritually present at the Supper through faith. Thus as Jones-Davies stated in a lecture to the students of Hartley College:

> It is the experience of the believer that Christ is present in this ordinance in a peculiar sense; it is a special means by which he lays hold of Christ. At the same time, while it is this, it is not, as the Sacerdotalists assert, the one supreme channel of grace … and such that no other means is comparable to it. Such a view is unscriptural. The Scriptures put the 'Word of God' in the front as the

> chief means of salvation and channel of grace ... But while it is only one among other means of grace, it is a means most nourishing and helpful to the soul, and ought not to be neglected; and those who do so suffer much spiritual loss. [57]

There were several facets of my early experience of Primitive Methodist administration of the Lord's Supper that I can clearly recall. It was only celebrated once each quarter after the close of the normal preaching service and was often even less formal than the order suggested in the *Primitive Methodist Service Book*. The service was normally taken by the Circuit minister but I can recall several occasions when the celebrant was a local preacher. Every chapel in the Lowton Circuit had individual communion glasses. Before the service, these would be filled with unfermented wine and the bread cut into small squares. After a prayer of consecration, the celebrant would hand the elements to the Stewards who would distribute them to the communicants who sat in their pews. Unlike the Wesleyans, we did not kneel at the communion rail and receive the bread and wine directly from the minister. It was held that sitting was probably the posture in which the elements were received by the disciples at the Last Supper. Kneeling was rejected by the Puritans since they feared that this might, in time, revive the doctrine of transubstantiation or the conversion of the bread and wine into the actual Body and Blood of Christ. The service was open to all. Bowmer points out that in early Primitive Methodism admission to the sacrament was carefully controlled.[58] As late as 1860, Primitive Methodist Consolidated Minutes stated that:

> Each member must show his [class] ticket to the appointed doorkeeper ... and no person belonging to any other community must be admitted without a note of admission received from the person authorised to give notes.

Later, this exclusiveness was abandoned. I was accustomed to hearing the preacher when announcing the service to invite 'all who love the Lord Jesus Christ' to stay and participate. The Lord's Supper was administered to children. It was given to me at a very early age long before I had even a rudimentary understanding of the rite. Whether it was administered to children generally or only to those of church members I do not know. I may not have understood the sacrament but I always had a sense of participating in something holy and mysterious. The Primitive Methodist Lord's Supper was essentially a simple service. Apart from the bread and wine, it had no additional symbolism. There was no recognition of the minister as Christ's representative receiving his guests at the table or the bringing to the table of the bread and wine as symbols of the products of human labour and the means of sustenance. There was no fraction or breaking of the bread. Yet I am sure that, for many worshippers, it was the very simplicity of the service that made it a means of grace, so that in the words of the most used Communion hymn, they could declare with sincerity:

> Here, O my Lord, I see Thee face to face;
> Here would I touch and handle things unseen.
> Here grasp with firmer hand the eternal grace
> And all my weariness upon Thee lean.[59]

9

Church and Chapel

My father had a strong antipathy to the Church of England which, as a boy, I found difficult to understand. Although I uncritically accepted the general Primitive Methodist view that Anglicans were poor at preaching, praying and praising, my youthful relations with them were generally cordial. As a small boy I passed the Lowton St Luke's Rectory each morning on my way to school. The Rector, Francis Smith, would often be leaning over his gate waiting for the postman. He always wished me a cheerful 'Good morning!' and sometimes gave me a sweet.

The Rector and his wife once paid a pastoral visit to our farm. My mother, who had Anglican antecedents, was flattered by the visit. She brought out her best china and made tea. The visit began pleasantly. Mrs Smith had been a missionary in Africa and promised that next time she came she would tell me about the lions and tigers. Sadly, there was no next time. Father unnecessarily initiated an argument about disestablishment that became heated and the visit ended acrimoniously.

In my early teens I often spoke to J. H. Preston who had succeeded Smith as Rector. I was struggling with Latin and Preston offered to help. Unknown to my father, I visited the Rectory on several occasions and Preston gave generously of his time in correcting my translations. My visits were, however, observed. A chapel member informed father who admonished me for, in effect, fraternising with the 'enemy' and accused Preston of attempting to proselytise. I still recall my embarrassment at having to tell Preston – a good man – that I had been forbidden to accept further help and kindness.

My father's prejudice can be explained if not defended. It

stemmed from two factors; history and politics. My father was steeped in Primitive Methodist history. Some early Primitive Methodist preachers suffered much persecution from mobs often incited by the local clergy. The last recorded persecutions took place in the 1850s, but in the 1930s father referred to them as if they had occurred in the previous week.

For a self-taught man, Father had also an excellent grasp of the history of dissent. His heroes were Cromwell, Hampton, Pym and the estimated 2,000 clergy who, for non-compliance with the 1662 Act of Uniformity, were forced to resign their livings. He was noticeably reticent about the earlier expulsion of Anglican clergy under the Commonwealth. As a boy I was more interested in the people than the politics. I found rumbustious Royalists such as Prince Rupert more attractive than the prim Puritans. As I more fully understood the Parliamentarian contributions to democracy, realism replaced romanticism, but I still have sympathy with Sellar's view that the Cavaliers were 'Wrong but Wromantic' and the Roundheads 'Right but Repulsive'.[1]

Father had also experienced the Victorian and Edwardian period which was obsessed with church-chapel confrontations arising from the six grievances listed in a petition presented to the House of Commons in 1833. The first grievance, 'the contempt and persecution experienced from Episcopal dignitaries' was not amenable to legislation. The other five were: (i) exclusion of dissenters from the universities of Oxford, Cambridge and Durham; (ii) church rates and other dues; (iii) the legal requirement of a Certificate of Baptism; (iv) the lack of right of burial according to Dissenting forms and (v) the compulsion to be married by a clergyman using the *Prayer Book* service.

By the end of the nineteenth century all these disabilities had been legally remedied not, however, without fierce opposition from some bishops, particularly Christopher Wordsworth,[2] and many incumbents.

Father often quoted an example of such clerical intransigence which has been recorded by Ridyard.[3] Gladstone's 1880 Government enacted the Burials Law Amendment Act 1880 which gave

Nonconformists the right to be buried by their own ministers according to their own rites in parish graveyards providing prior notice had been given to the incumbent. Ridyard relates that in November 1880 the death occurred of Edwin Boydell, son of Simon Boydell, superintendent of the Lowton Independent Methodist Sunday school. The father owned a grave in the Lowton St Mary's churchyard and, as required by the Burials Act, handed written notice to the Vicar of his intention to bury his son and that the service would be conducted by the James Eckersley mentioned in the previous chapter. The Vicar, however, objected to the interment on three grounds: that the grave had been forfeited by not having a headstone placed upon it within a prescribed time; that a new grave would have to be purchased and that, as a non-parishioner, Boydell was trying to uphold a groundless right. These objections were confirmed in writing as follows:

> J. W. S. SIMPSON, MA, Vicar of St Mary's Church, Lowton, do hereby give you notice that I object to the interment of your son, Edwin Boydell, taking place in St Mary's Churchyard, Lowton, excepting according to the rites of the Church Of England, any other manner of interment in this case, being contrary to Section G of the Burial Laws Amendment Act of 1880.

Boydell replied that he had arranged with Mr Eckersley to officiate, adding that he (Boydell) had been advised that such an interment was allowed by the Burials Act.

Notwithstanding the Vicar's objection, the funeral was arranged for four o'clock on the afternoon of 11 November. On the appointed day there were no signs of a grave being dug and padlocked gates excluded the public from the churchyard. At three o'clock the cortège left for a service in the Independent Methodist chapel, the coffin being carried by four bearers. Meanwhile, a crowd of several hundred had assembled near the church gates. As the burial time approached, the onlookers were augmented by others from the surrounding area, including the Leigh Congregational and Primitive Methodist ministers. When the funeral arrived at the churchyard the mourners found the gates locked and the coffin had to be rested on four chairs. Eventually the Vicar appeared at the gate and informed Mr Boydell that 'the new Act did not allow the burial of non-parishioners.' At this point the Congregational and Primitive Methodist ministers addressed the Vicar, who replied that he would speak only to Mr Boydell. This remark drew the retort 'loudly applauded by the onlookers', that the Vicar was 'pitted against the Nonconformists of England'. The Vicar then conferred with his warden and announced that the gates would be opened at five o'clock and that, in the interim, a grave would be dug. Meanwhile, the coffin was taken back into the chapel. In the chapel schoolroom the Congregational minister addressed a large crowd advising moderation since it was known that men were present with tools and appliances to smash the churchyard gates. At five o'clock the gates were opened, the coffin brought from the chapel and the burial took place with the help of oil lamps, Mr Eckersley officiating.

On the following Monday night a deputation from Leigh attended a meeting of the Manchester and District Liberation Society which passed the following resolution, a copy of which was sent to Simon Boydell:

> This Committee expresses its approval of the firm manner in which Mr Simon Boydell of Pennington, has asserted his right to bury his son with Nonconformist Services, in the Parish Churchyard of St Mary's, Lowton, in which he possessed a grave; and thanks him and his friends for having vindicated his claim in face of the hostility of the Vicar of the Parish.[4]

The incident received wide press coverage. The *Manchester Guardian* stated: 'Every occurrence like this at Lowton, places a new weapon in the hands of the Liberation Society.' The *Manchester Examiner and Times* commented: 'It passes understanding why clergymen should insist, at the cost of discord and disorder, in thrusting the liturgy of the church upon people who object to it on conscientious grounds.'[5]

Similar cases, some of which were reported in the *Primitive Methodist Magazine*, provided Nonconformists with a new grievance and it was not until the enactment of the Burial Grounds Act 1900 that residual matters such as consecration of separate cemetery areas and the reservation of chapels for one church ceased to be compulsory. The 1900 Act also provided that the clergy and ministers were only entitled to fees for services actually performed.

My father's prejudice must, therefore, be appraised in the light of the resentment which he shared with many other Nonconformists at Anglican privilege and patronage. Three issues in particular coloured Primitive Methodist attitudes to the Church of England: disestablishment, education and tithes.

Disestablishment

Nonconformist resentment of Anglican privilege led Edward Miall (1809–91), a Congregational minister and MP for Rochdale (1852–7) and Bradford (1869–74), to found the Anti-Church Association. In 1853 the Association, founded in 1844, was renamed the Society for the Liberation of Religion from State Patronage and Control or, more shortly, the Liberation Society. Through his paper, *The Nonconformist*, Miall ensured that the demand for disestablishment as expressed in the slogan 'A free Church in a free State' was kept constantly before the public. Such a demand could, however, be met only through political action and for the achievement of their aims Primitive Methodists along with Free Churches looked to the Liberal Party.

My father was a life-long advocate of disestablishment. When, in 1932, he was studying 'Nonconformity' for the Primitive Methodist Sunday School Teachers' Diploma, the textbook was *Nonconformity, Its Origin and Progress* by W. B. Selbie. I have kept the book. I note that father had underlined a quotation from John Bright: 'The past and present state alliance with religion is hostile to religious liberty, preventing all growth and nearly destroying all vitality in religion itself.'[6]

Father was a life-long Liberal. To him, and many other Primitive Methodists, the Church of England was 'the Tory Party at prayer'. When there was no Liberal candidate, he voted Labour, particularly since his candidate for local council elections was Robert Barrow, who was not only a local preacher but had been father's best man on his marriage to my mother. Along with his sister, Sarah Jane, father shared what an 1890 correspondent of *The Times* called 'the fascination amounting to fetishism of the great name and personality of Gladstone.'[7] Bebington observes that from 1860, when Gladstone was successively responsible for parliamentary reform, the abolition of compulsory church rates and the disestablishment of the Church of England in Ireland, Nonconformist respect 'ripened into veneration'.[8] Whether Gladstone, a high Anglican, wholly reciprocated this respect is questionable. Although he kept the Liberation Society with its strident demands at arms length, he was careful to cultivate good personal relations with the Nonconformist churches to which many of the lower and middle classes belonged. Free Church esteem for Gladstone certainly helped the Liberal Party. Koss states that in the mining constituencies Primitive Methodism 'yielded high returns for Liberalism much as it did later on for Labour.'[9] In the homes of both my father and his sister, large framed prints of Gladstone glowered from the walls. Copies of Morley's famous *Life* were in both their bookcases. A small Gladstone bust adorned my aunt's parlour mantelpiece and I was told from an early age that 'Gladstone was a good man who said his prayers.'

Father's Liberalism was also evidenced by his daily newspaper. Founded by Charles Dickens in 1846, the *Daily News* was, from 1869, the recognised Liberal Party organ. In 1930, the *Daily News* amalgamated with the *Daily Chronicle* and became the *News Chronicle*.

My father also had considerable regard for Lloyd George who, as a Baptist married to a Calvinistic Methodist, was himself a Nonconformist. Although Lloyd George was a prominent Parliamentary spokesman on Nonconformist issues, father's esteem derived more from such social legislation as the Old Age Pensions Act (1908) and the National Insurance Act 1911. There was also Lloyd George's wartime leadership.

Addison shows that, by 1912, 'lengthy and frequent parliamentary discussion on ecclesiastical topics was already receding into the dim and distant past.' Disestablishment had, from a political standpoint, become a dead issue:

> The domestic issues of the hour had, without doubt, their repercussions on the relative position of the National Church and Nonconformity; Lloyd George's Liberal Socialism assisted the drift of respectable middle class Nonconformists to the Conservative allegiance, while, as the second stage of Socialist propaganda got under way, the sons and daughters of the Trade Unionist local preacher forsook the chapel to follow, uninhibited, the crusade for economic, not religious equality, for social, not personal, salvation.[10]

After 1906, the Primitive Methodists were in the van of the transfer of working-class Nonconformity from the Liberal to the Labour Party and, following the 1914–18 War, this process accelerated. An age of toleration had arrived. Nevertheless, with individuals such as my father, who were, in a sense, survivors from the Gladstonian age, and in organisations, especially the Liberation Society, which lingered on well into the twentieth century, opposition to Anglican privilege remained.

In addition to disestablishment, education and tithes remained contentious church-chapel issues.

Education

Primitive Methodist day schools

Elementary education in England originated in voluntary provision, first, Sunday and dame schools and, secondly, the pioneering work of the Anglican National Society for the Education of the Poor in the Principles of the Church of England (1811) and the Nonconformist British and Foreign School Society (1814).[11] Roman Catholics and Wesleyans were also active in school provision. By 1870 the respective statistics were: [12]

	No. of schools	Average attendance
Church of England	6,382	844,334
Roman Catholic	850	66,066
British and Wesleyan	1,549	241,989

In 1837 the first Report of the Wesleyan Education Committee, which became a permanent body in 1838, advocated, on the principle 'all education should be centred on religion', that the denomination should have 'a comprehensive and extended scheme for infant schools, day and Sunday schools.' The Wesleyan Conference of 1843 set a target of 700 new day schools within the next seven years and, in 1847, the Wesleyan Education Committee stated that: 'No chapel will be complete in all the great practical objects that are or ought to be intended, unless there be found in immediate connection with it an efficient day school.' It was not until 1870 that the Wesleyans could report 743 efficient day schools. [13]

A strong motivation for the establishment of Nonconformist day schools was the recognition that the child taught in an Anglican day school was also likely to attend the Anglican Sunday school and church.

Although the predominantly working-class Primitive Methodists could not normally raise funds for the building and maintenance of schools, they were not inactive even though, in 1860, the Yarmouth Conference had declared that day schools were a local and not Connexional responsibility. [14]

Numbers relating to Primitive Methodist day schools are difficult to ascertain since, in official statistics, they are often subsumed under Wesleyan schools. There were, however, a significant number. Russell mentions the 'opening in 1867 of a Primitive Methodist school in Garibaldi Street, Grimsby.' [15] The school cost £600, had 212 pupils and remained open for nearly thirty years. He also mentions Primitive Methodist schools built at Scotter (1881), Louth (1867) and Horncastle (1877). The latter appears to have been in competition with British and Wesleyan schools since, in a report of the impending closure of the former, the *Stamford Mercury* observed:

> The first blow to its prosperity was the founding of a day school by the Wesleyans. The Primitive Methodists also have now their elementary School, so it is not surprising that the crisis should have come.[16]

Conversely, in 1846–7 Wesleyans and Primitives joined forces to provide a school at East Stockwith in opposition to a Church of England school erected in the same year. Here the *Mercury* stated:

> all the poor Wesleyans and Primitive Methodists require is to be allowed to send their children to the school of their choice on the Sabbath day and not be compelled by threats to send them to the church school.[17]

McKeon provides the following sample of Primitive Methodist day schools from 1819–1932:[18]

Name	**District/Station**	**Date of foundation**
Chasewater Chapel Redruth	Bristol	1831
Lees Infant School	Oldham	1834
Wolverhampton Infant	Tunstall	1835
Tunstall Calver St.	Tunstall	1843
Boylestone Free PM School Derby	Nottingham	1844
Wooton Bassett Mixed & Infant	Brinkworth	1847
Spelisbury, Poole	Brinkworth	1852
Wolsingham, Crook	Sunderland	1852
Bolton Industrial PM School	Manchester	1852
Great Yarmouth	Norwich	1854–9

Clay Cross	Nottingham	1855
Hadnall	Tunstall	1856
Bilston	Tunstall	1861
Knighton	Tunstall	1862
Thetford	Norwich	1862
Weston Luton, Driffield	Hull	1862
Lindslade, Leighton Buzzard	London	1862
Hockham		1866
Murrow, Wisbech	Norwich	1866
Northumberland Terrace, Everton	Manchester	1866
Burringham	Scotter / Hull	1867
Holderness Road	Hull	1867
Adfontin, Leintwardine	Tunstall	1868
Hexthorpe Villa		1868
Great Horton, Bradford	Leeds	1869
Haslingden	Manchester	1869
Hullavington		1870
Middleton, Teesdale	Sunderland	1870–9
Grimsby	Hull	1880
Grassmoor Day School, Clay Cross	Nottingham	1896
Nottingham PM	Nottingham	1912–14

Unclassified or undated in sample

Swerford

St Peter St Cambridge

Ellesmere Port PM Day School

High Town, Luton

Penton St, Cambridge

McKeon's list is, as he states, only a 'sample'. It omits the Lincolnshire schools mentioned by Russell, Primitive Methodist schools in Bilston and Willenhall, Staffordshire [19] and schools known to the writer at Banks (Southport) and Helmshore (Lancashire).

National conflicts (1902–32)

My mother wished to name me *Joseph* Kenneth. Father, however, overruled her and insisted that I should be *Clifford* Kenneth after one of his Nonconformist heroes, Dr John Clifford. Clifford, born in 1836, died on 20 November 1923. Only many years later did I discover that both our birthdays fell on 16 October.

Clifford who, from 1858–1915 was minister of Westbourne Park Baptist chapel, first achieved national notoriety by his criticism of the Boer War but it was his role as leader of the Nonconformists' opposition to the Balfour Education Act of 1902 that caused him to be variously described as 'the new Knox', 'the new Bunyan' and 'the uncrowned king of Nonconformity'. This opposition must, however, be placed in context.

Foster's 1870 Elementary Education Act aimed to provide 'sufficient, efficient and suitable elementary schools throughout the Kingdom' and to 'fill up the gaps' in the existing voluntary provision. Essentially, the country was to be divided into several thousand school districts. Voluntary bodies were allowed a period of six months for making good local deficiencies with the help of 50 per cent building grants. After this six months had elapsed, School Boards elected by local ratepayers would be established in areas where elementary education was deemed by the Education Department to be insufficient, inefficient or unsuitable. School Boards could establish their own undenominational schools.

Two important amendments in the course of the Bill related to rate-aid and conscience. The initial proposal to extend rate-aid to denominational schools was withdrawn due to bitter Nonconformist opposition. As enacted, Board schools were to be financially supported by central grants, parental fees (maximum 9d per week) and rate-aid. Denominational schools were expected to meet expenditure from central grants, parental fees (no maximum) and church subscriptions, rate-aid being specifically denied them. Where, formerly, Government aid was given only to schools providing religious instruction, the Act declared that henceforth funds would be provided in respect of secular education.

Two conscience clauses were also extensions of the secular principle. The first, the Cowper Temple clause, related only to School Boards. This gave Boards discretion to choose between wholly secular or undenominational religious instruction defined as 'catechisms or religious formularies distinctive of any particular denomination.' The second, a timetable clause, related to both Board and denominational schools and gave parents the right to withdraw children from religious worship or instruction. To facilitate such withdrawal, schools were required to timetable religious teaching at either the beginning or end of the school day.

Nonconformists, along with secularists and some Anglicans who had supported the Liberals, were deeply critical of the Act, denouncing capitation grants to denominational schools as an infringement of the right of conscience and an obstacle to creating a national education system. Cruickshank states that of all Nonconformists, Methodists had the best cause for satisfaction: 'In the future, their own schools would benefit from increased grants while the new board schools would run on undenominational lines.'[20]

There were, however, longer-term implications for both Anglicans and Nonconformists. Rate-aid enabled the Boards to build large, well-equipped schools and attract energetic and ambitious teachers to whom they paid relatively high salaries. Denominational schools were difficult to maintain and could only pay lower salaries so that teachers, often trained in denominational colleges, left for better salaries and prospects in the Board schools.

A pamphlet issued by the National Education Association (NEA), founded in 1889 'to promote a system of national education which shall be efficient, progressive, unsectarian and under popular control', quoted an Anglican complaint: 'At present the School Boards with practically unlimited resources at command have undue advantage in staffing their schools.'

'Give us cheap teachers,' was the constant cry of the voluntary school managers.[21] A Wesleyan witness to the Cross Commission

(1886–9) declared that day schools were 'a dead weight on the circuits and injured all the Connexional funds.' [22] In 1891 the Wesleyan Education Committee finally abandoned the expansion of day schools and declared unequivocally that 'the primary objective of Methodist policy is the establishment of school boards everywhere ... and the placing of a Christian unsectarian school within a reasonable distance of every family especially in rural districts.' McKeon also observes: 'To the poor communities of Primitive Methodists, schools were ten times as costly as chapels to maintain. A denomination with limited financial resources could not meet both the costs of elementary education and improved ministerial training.'[23] As early as 1867, the *Primitive Methodist Magazine* observed: 'The Connexion is in no degree dependent on them [day schools] for the accomplishment of its specific work.' [24]

After 1870 Nonconformist suspicion of every move to strengthen Anglican provision of elementary education found expression in the establishment in 1896 of the Northern Counties Education Board to:

1 Defend the existing Board School System in England and Wales against the attacks of ecclesiastical parties.
2 Demand that all elementary schools receiving Government grants or local rates shall be brought under popular control.
3 Secure throughout England and Wales a Universal Board School system such as already exists in Scotland. [25]

The following year (1897) the Primitive Methodist Conference appointed a Connexional Education Committee to:

> watch the interests of the Connexion as they are affected by the different phases of the education question and take any action they may deem desirable. [26]

A manifesto issued by the Committee in 1900 identified three educational grievances which the Primitive Methodists shared with most but not all other Nonconformists. [27]

First, out of 5,000 places in the UK where Primitive Methodists held religious services, at least 3,000 were in rural districts, in practically the whole of which there were no schools save those under Anglican management. In 1,976 preaching places from which information had been obtained, 1,124 had only Anglican schools. Primitive Methodist parents had, therefore, often no alternative to sending their children to schools where Anglican religious instruction was given and pressure often applied for children to attend the parish church and Sunday school.

My father often referred to a curate who in one village school asked the children how many attended the Nonconformist Sunday school. When a number raised their hands, the curate remarked: 'I am sorry there are so many children who are not going to heaven' and went on to say that Jesus never went to chapel and that chapels were not mentioned in the Bible.

In practice, the 'conscience clause' in the 1870 Act provided little protection against such indoctrination since few parents were willing to subject their children to the stigma of withdrawal. Speaking to the first Free Church Congress, Sir Robert Perks drew a pathetic picture of a child 'shivering outside a school house on a winter's day, waiting to get in and get warm and having the finger of scorn pointed at it because it took advantage of the conscience clause.'[28]

Secondly, the manifesto referred to the difficulties experienced by young Primitive Methodists in securing pupil-teacher posts and, afterwards, admission to training colleges. From the limited number of circuits that had reported:

> there have been fourteen cases of young people who have been compelled to join the Episcopal Church in order to become pupil teachers; seven pupil teachers have been compelled to join the same church in order to enter a teacher training college and, most painful of all, twelve members of the Primitive Methodist Church have been required to become Wesleyan Methodists in order to enter a Wesleyan Training College.[29]

The third grievance was that:

> not only are Nonconformists not allowed to be masters in schools under clerical management but those who are appointed to such positions are often required in addition to their proper duties to teach in the Church Sunday School, to play the organ at the church services and to render other assistance to the Vicar.

To remedy these grievances the 1901 Primitive Methodist Conference confirmed its strong conviction that:

> All schools which receive public money shall be under public control.
>
> ... All forms of education – primary, secondary and technical – be placed under the management of the authority popularly elected for educational purposes only, and whose duties shall be presented by Parliament.
>
> ... It also calls for the setting up of a sufficient number of Training Colleges, free from all sectarian tests, to meet the educational needs of the country.[30]

In 1902 Balfour's Education Act replaced School Boards with Local Education Authorities. The new LEAs controlled all secular but not denominational education in 'non-provided' schools as voluntary schools became known; Board schools became 'provided' schools. Thus, for the first time, rate-aid was given to 'non-provided' Anglican, Roman Catholic and Nonconformist schools.

Since the overwhelming number of schools were Anglican, the favourable treatment given by the Act was the spark that ignited the Nonconformist opposition led by Clifford. In addition to the Northern League, Clifford was supported by a majority of the National Council of the Evangelical Free Churches, the Labour Party and the TUC. Most importantly, as Koss states, the Act transformed 'seemingly overnight – the Nonconformist commitment to Liberalism from a vague sentiment into an active electoral alliance.'[31]

The Primitive Methodists were at the forefront of this opposition. The 1902 Conference met as the Education Bill reached its Committee stage in the Commons. After setting forth in detail the reasons 'for expressing its intense dissatisfaction with the measure' Conference declared:

> Because the Bill proposes to accentuate existing disabilities from which, both as citizens and Free churchmen, Primitive Methodists suffer; and because it threatens to impose new and scandalous injustices on millions of the loyal subjects of the King, this Conference resolves to vehemently and persistently oppose it; and calls upon all our people to resist this retrograde and disastrous movement with all possible power and at every possible stage, and to the utmost extremity.[32]

Free church rallies against the Act were organised throughout the UK. Clifford was indefatigable in addressing packed meetings and large protest meetings. His rallying cry 'Rome on the Rates' referred to growing evidence of Romanish practices in the Anglican Church as well as grants to Roman Catholic schools.

Apart from such demonstrations, the support of the Liberal Party in Parliament and the lobbying of ministers, the opponents of the Act had another weapon; passive resistance. Even before the Bill's first reading, George, a Baptist and MP for North West Norfolk, had suggested in a little known woman's magazine, *The Light of Home*, that Free Churchmen should refuse payment of any school rate applied to helping denominational schools or paying for religious instruction. In April 1902, Robertson Nicoll, Editor of the *British Weekly*, urged the Free Church Council to give the lead in rate refusal. Largely due to the moderating influence of the Revd John Scott Lidgett, an eminent Wesleyan minister and leader of the London School Board, the Free Church Council was not unanimous in supporting passive resistance in the form of refusing to pay that portion of the local rate that applied to education. As Lidgett stated:

> During the autumn of 1902 I was busily engaged upon the subject (Educational controversy) and particularly in a successful endeavour to keep the National Free Church Council from identifying itself with the Passive Resistance Movement.[33]

In December 1902 the Free Church Council declared that, while it could not officially organise a Passive Resistance Movement, a Special Resistance Committee should be established not as a sub-committee of the Council, but operating separately.[34]

Many Wesleyans appreciated the support given by the Act to their 450 schools. The Wesleyan Conferences of 1902 and 1903, while expressing sympathy for passive resisters, refrained from endorsing their actions. The Primitive Methodists were more forthright. Their 1903 Conference conceded that 'Passive resistance is a matter to be decided by each individual in his own conscience' but affirmed:

> that in our opinion such a policy is forced upon us by the failure of the government to recognise the principle of religious liberty, and any members who pursue this line of action as in their opinion the only practical way of compelling the amendment or repeal of the Act are entitled to our moral support.[35]

The Education Committee was also recommended to set up a fund to support 'those of our poorer members against whom distraints are issued because of their determination not to pay that portion of the Education Rate which is used for Sectarian purposes.'

Usually a Council refused to accept a rate payment from which the education element had been deducted. Passive resisters were summonsed to appear before the Magistrates' Court, itself an ordeal for otherwise respectable persons. Resisters were given the opportunity to pay the full rate plus the cost of the summons. On refusal, a warrant was issued for the distraint of the resister's goods to the value of the total amount due. Later the goods seized were usually sold at public auction. If there were no goods or the bailiffs could not obtain them, the Council could ask for the Resister to be committed to prison.

The progress of passive resistance can be followed in the pages of the Primitive Methodist *Aldersgate Magazine* and Conference Minutes. Early in 1904 it was reported that 'more than 20,000 passive resisters had appeared in court … and the goods of many of them had been sold, whilst quite a number have suffered imprisonment including one lady.' [36]

Later, it was reported that, in September, the number of summonses for what was termed 'the priest's rate' had risen to 27,890 and that, in the same month, two prominent Nonconformist ministers, H. B. Mayer and J. H. Jowett, had stood in the police court. [37] In December, the number of reported summonses was 35,000 and that 'two or three of our ministers have been in prison.' [38] One of these was the Connexional Sunday School Secretary, S. S. Henshaw, who related his experience of three days of imprisonment in Armley Gaol, Leeds, in the January 1905 issues of the *Aldersgate Magazine*. [39]

Later it was reported that more than 50,000 summonses had been issued and 150 imprisonments. Of the latter, sixty-one had been ministers. One resister had been imprisoned four times; seven three times and one twice. [40] Munson relates that, by November 1906, 189 Nonconformists had been imprisoned for having no goods to be distrained; of this total, 118 were imprisoned once; 46 twice; fourteen three times and two seven times. A survey in March of the same year showed that Primitive Methodists provided 54, Baptists 42, Congregationalists 37, Wesleyans sixteen and the balance from smaller denominations. [41]

The main hope of amending the law, however, was through a change of government. Sometime in 1904 a deputation from the Free Church Council met the Liberal Party leaders and were assured by Asquith and Herbert Gladstone that, if the Liberals were returned at the next election, they would take steps to 'accomplish a fair and just settlement of the education question.' The result was that the Council virtually committed itself to work for a Liberal victory. A Free Church Council Election Fund Appeal for £50,000 was launched, to which the Primitive Methodist benefactor, W. P. Hartley, promised £5,000.[42] When a General Election in January 1906 was announced, militant Nonconformity directed its energies to securing return of the Liberals. The *Aldersgate Magazine* urged every Primitive Methodist to 'do his uttermost to gain supporters for the Liberal candidates. Ministers should have no night appointments for the month of January.'[43] Hartley College, where A. S. Peake had become a resister, postponed examinations to allow students to work for the Liberal cause.[44] This Nonconformist support was evident not only in the sweeping Liberal victory and the return of 399 Liberal and 29 Labour MPs against 156 Tories, but also in the large number of Nonconformists elected to the Commons.

When the new Parliament assembled in February there was every indication that the Government intended to respond quickly to the Nonconformist desire for a drastic revision to the 1902 Education Act. A Bill, prepared by Augustine Birrell who described himself as 'a Nonconformist born and bred',[45] was introduced in April. Of the deputations who waited on Birrell concerning the Bill he professed to have been most influenced by that of the Primitive Methodists who informed him that, although they had 200,000 communicants and chapels in 4,000 villages, only in 850 of the latter was there any school other than an Anglican.[46] Clifford and the more militant Nonconformists, however, objected to Clause IV which permitted denominational teaching in schools if a certain percentage of parents in an area favoured it. Birrell, in fact, could only satisfy Clifford, who would tolerate 'no statutory foothold for sectarian privilege in the State school system', at the cost of alienating the Anglicans and Roman Catholics.[47]

The Bill passed its third reading in the Commons in July by a vote of 369 to 177. It was then greatly amended in the Lords to the point where it no longer resembled Birrell's original draft. Finally, it was dropped by the Government in December 1906 and attention was directed to the constitutional role of the Lords. Further Education Bills introduced in 1907 and 1908 by Mackenna, who had replaced Birrell at the Board of Education, also failed. Nonconformists showed little enthusiasm for either since the proposed measures were less favourable than Birrell's initial Bill.

In 1908 the final attempt to abolish the dual system was foiled by the united opposition of Anglicans and Roman Catholics who, in turn, threatened a campaign of passive resistance.

Primitive Methodist disappointment at the failure to secure Nonconformist educational aims was expressed in the *Aldersgate Magazines* for 1908 and 1909:

> We are faced by the conviction that once more we have been betrayed – by a Liberal Government; by a minister of that Government who is a Nonconformist (Mr Runciman) and by the Nonconformist members of Parliament.[48]

> On the education question, it is difficult to write with any degree of hope ... It is three years since the Nonconformists returned this Government to power pledged to settle the Education question first. Not one Nonconformist grievance has been removed or even lessened. Nonconformists are not alone in thinking that for this the chief responsibility lies not with the House of Lords but the Government itself.[49]

The latter sentence was near the truth. When the Government withdrew the Education Bill of 1906, Campbell Bannerman decided that the Education Bill was not a big enough issue for him to recommend dissolution.[50]

As the provisions of the 1902 Education Act remained in force, militant Nonconformists continued the policy of passive resistance by non-payment of rates. In 1909 the Connexional Education Committee reported that 'over 30 members suffered imprisonment rather than pay rates for clerical schools.'[51] Even in the War year of 1915 Conference was reminded that 'many of our people are still passive resisters and several of them are periodically hauled to prison because of their objection to a sectarian educational rate.'[52]

In April 1918 the Connexional Education Committee gave hearty support to the main proposals of H. A. L. Fisher's Education Bill, but expressed 'deep regret' that the new Bill had not been used to 'remedy those unjust sectarian grievances which were created by the Act of 1902.' The Committee, however, learned 'with some interest that there is a possibility of a settlement of these grievances being reached by consent.'[53] In 1923, however, it was reported that none of three schemes, submitted to a Committee on dual control charged with reaching common agreement on a uniform educational system, had been successful.[54] In 1929, while endorsing 'with some modification' a joint proposal of the National Free Church Council and the Federal Council of the Free Churches 'which were in the nature of a compromise', the Primitive Methodist Educational Committee continued to reaffirm the principles of (1) no right of entry, (2) no tests for teachers and (3) that no building grants should be made from national funds to non-provided schools.[55]

Between 1914 and 1932 an increasing number of LEAs adopted agreed syllabuses of religious instruction. This, to a limited extent, appeased the Primitive Methodists. The last report of the Connexional Education Committee in 1932 noted that 58 per cent of the 317 Local Education Areas in England and Wales representing 73 per cent of the school population were using an agreed syllabus of religious instruction.[56]

National conflicts – an appraisal

My father, as stated earlier, was proud of the Primitive Methodist opposition to the 1902 Act and venerated Dr Clifford. The Nonconformists had real educational grievances that needed to be remedied, such as the situation in many rural areas where only an Anglican day school was available and sectarian tests for teachers and pupil teachers. In retrospect, it is hard to avoid the conclusion that Primitive Methodist opposition and that of a wider Nonconformity to the 1902 Act was misplaced. As Cruickshank states: 'It is hard to forgive the fanatical extremists on both sides who had degraded national education to a miserable quarrel between Church and Chapel.' [57] This fanaticism blinded such extremists to the virtues of an Act which Ensor claims 'ranks for England and Wales among the two or three greatest constructive measures of the twentieth century.' [58]

The 1902 Act greatly simplified administration. It replaced nearly 3,000 School Boards by 328 Local Education Authorities empowered to co-ordinate elementary and secondary education and, by the award of scholarships to promising elementary pupils, provided 'a ladder from the elementary school to the university.' It ensured that the schools of all denominations had a place in the national education system and raised the standard of education provided for their pupils. Salaries of teachers in non-provided schools rapidly improved. The pupil teacher system was changed and the number of teacher training colleges substantially increased. As Curtis observes: 'The Balfour Morant Act did not go so far as to create a national system of education, but it laid the foundation on which others would be able to build.' [59]

Clifford, the Primitive Methodists and their Anglican adversaries also lost sight of three other things: the child, parental attitudes and the effect of their squabbles on neutral observers.

As Rogers observes: 'In all their debates on the Bill, in or out of Parliament, in the sermons preached about it, and the pamphlets in their thousands little was heard of the child. He or she was a mere pawn – it was the system that mattered.' [60]

Simon mentions that: 'In the many meetings on the Education Bill children were seldom mentioned' [61] and quotes from an article in *Justice* – the organ of the Social Democratic Foundation:

> Dr Clifford, the stern, unrelenting High Priest of dogmatic Nonconformity, can declaim for hours and hardly mention the children.

Most parents, apart from those closely associated with either church or chapel, were indifferent to the controversy. In 1902 the words of Gathorne Hardy respecting the 1870 Education Act were still relevant:

> I venture to assert with great respect to those who are agitating the religious difficulty, that the difficulty is one which has gone down from London into the country and would never have struck the minds of the people unless they had been told by those having authority over them that they ought to raise the question.[62]

Further, the squabbles between church and chapel only served to provide ammunition to those who advocated the complete secularisation of education. In 1907, for example, a speaker at the Trades Union Congress, stated that as the various denominations could agree upon nothing themselves, the TUC had the right to say, 'Keep your quarrels out of our schools.'[63]

The most important result of the Liberal failure to abolish the dual system of education was the end of political nonconformity as a separate force within the Labour Party.

So far as Primitive Methodism was concerned, there was already a movement, especially in mining areas, from Liberalism to Labour. After 1906, in Primitive Methodism, this movement became more widespread and gathered pace.

A personal experience

In view of my father's hostility to all things Anglican it was ironical that, for reasons of distance, my formal education had to begin at the Lowton St Luke's Church of England school. The Lowton Parish schools originated in 1751 when Peter Lees of Lymm donated land and funds for the maintenance of a schoolmaster and the education of up to six poor children in Latin, English, Writing and Accounts.[64] In 1855 'Mary Leigh of Hale, spinster, presented the Rector and Churchwardens of the St Luke's Parish with a school house and a school built at her own expense for the education of children or adults for the labouring, manufacturing and other poorer classes.'[65]

My early schooling was generally happy. I could read and write before I actually started school aged five in 1928 and was bored by having to enunciate words phonetically that I could immediately recognise, and form letters that I was already able to write. With other pupils, I cheerfully chanted multiplication tables, used cowrie shells for counting, imbibed parts of my catechism and a patriotism that I have never lost. Along with Anglican hymns such as John Keble's 'New Every Morning is the Love' and happy rhymes:

Come little leaves said the wind one day
Come to the meadows with me and play.
Put on your dresses of red and gold
For summer is gone, and the wind blows cold.

I learned a song, each verse of which ended with the refrain 'Ready to fight and ready to die for England', something that a decade later some of us were actually required to do.

I was never conscious of any Anglican / Nonconformist antipathy except on one occasion when the school was visited by the then Bishop of Liverpool, Albert Augustine David[66] and I, innocently, stepped out of line. I recall this seemingly venerable gentleman entering my class accompanied by a retinue including the headmaster, Mr Wood, and some school managers. After we had sung a hymn, the Bishop asked if any pupil could recite a verse of Scripture. There was an uncomfortable silence in which there were no volunteers. Eventually, I put up my hand and was called to the front of the class. I recited not a verse but the whole Parable of the Good Samaritan. I was the hero of the hour. The headmaster and managers beamed. The Bishop placed his arm affectionately around me. 'You're a very clever boy', he said. 'You do go to church on Sundays?' A simple affirmative and all would have been well. Unfortunately, I had not learned that it is possible to ruin a case by saying too much and gave a precise answer: 'No,' I replied, '*I go to chapel!*' Even at that tender age, I was immediately conscious of having made a *faux pas*. The atmosphere discernibly cooled. The approving smiles disappeared from the faces of the head teacher and managers. The Bishop made some conciliatory remark. I returned to my place, no longer hero but heretic.

I liked the school and my teachers, some of whom I still vividly recall, such as Miss Sowerbutts, the head teacher of the infant school; Miss Unsworth, who was hard of hearing and had one of the first hearing aids – a cumbersome contraption, the size of a radio, which she placed on the desk. I also have happy memories of Mrs Aspinall and Mrs Shaw. Unfortunately, my father was opposed to my attending. At about eight or nine, when able to walk the considerably greater distance, I was taken away and transferred to a council school. It may be a harsh judgement, but the main factor in this decision was probably consistency to my father's Nonconformist principles rather than any consideration of my preferences.

Tithes

Space does not permit of any detailed treatment of tithes, which were a further factor in the hostility which my father, along with many other Primitive Methodists, harboured towards the Church of England.

Tithes, 'a tenth part of the increase yearly arising from the profits of lands, stocks upon lands and the industry of parishioners', [67] date back to Old Testament times (see Genesis 14.20) and were originally voluntary gifts of wood, corn or other farm produce. From about the mid-tenth century, however, canon law made the payment of tithes a legal obligation. Payment of tithes was bitterly resented as unfair and, in times of depression, a crippling imposition on their profits. Secondly, it was unjust that they should be compelled to contribute to the provision and maintenance of a parish priest whose church they never attended.

The Tithe Commutation Act 1836 commuted all the tithes of England and Wales into a tithe-rent charge. Valuers were appointed to apportion the sums to be paid in lieu of actual tithes on crops and each benefice had its tithe map and schedule showing the amounts of tithe-rent charge applicable to each field. Prior to purchase by my father, Boundary Farm had been owned by Leadbetters Charities. From the Tithe Map for the Parish of Lowton, I see that, in Lowton, the Charity owned a total of eleven properties subject to tithe, covering over ten acres. The total tithe rent charge was thirteen shillings and fourpence.

Between 1885 and 1891 there was considerable Nonconformist opposition to tithes, particularly in Wales where David Lloyd George was then Secretary to the South Caernarvonshire Anti-Tithe League. The League organised refusals to pay the tithe-rent charge and demonstrations of solidarity for defaulters whose goods were seized. At first peaceful, these demonstrations later became violent and, on occasion, bailiffs, auctioneers and agents had to be given police and even army protection. These protests led to the enactment of the Tithe-Rent Charge Redemption and Recovery Act 1891, which transferred the obligation to pay tithe from tenant farmer to his landowner. Roper suggests that one reason for this measure was the belief that, while tenant farmers might be Nonconformists, landowners were usually Anglicans who could be expected to pay the charge without protest.[68] The landowners, however, recovered the charge by increasing the rents of their tenants.

After the First World War, several Tithe Acts were enacted culminating in the Tithe Act 1925, which placed responsibility for the collection of tithes under the auspices of the Queen Anne's Bounty which had been founded in 1703 to augment small stipends, build parsonage houses and generally give grants for ecclesiastical purposes. Working through fifteen regional committees, the Bounty thus became virtually the Tithes Department of the Church of England.

This legislation abolished direct dealings between incumbents and their tithe-paying parishioners. The most important consequence, however was that:

> The 'tithe war' soon broke out in real earnest as the

> Bounty got to work and brought all the resources of an efficient centralised bureaucracy to bear upon matters which the individual clergy when they had full charge of them had often let slide.[69]

Faced by this development, many Nonconformist farmers resorted to the now familiar weapon of passive resistance. My father told of a Primitive Methodist farmer in a neighbouring circuit who refused to pay a small tithe charge of about five shillings. He was taken to Court by the Queen Anne's Bounty and an Order was made for the distraint of his goods to the value of the amount owing, plus costs. In due course, he was visited by two bailiffs who courteously suggested that the debt might be settled by the seizure of a quantity of eggs and a cockerel. The eggs presented no problem and the bailiffs were then invited to select a cock from several strutting in the farmyard. They made their choice and asked the farmer if he could catch it for them. He refused. He had offered them a bird, it was up to them to catch it themselves. Catching a cockerel in the open air is not easy. The bailiffs chased the bird, which easily avoided capture. At last the cock was caught but not before one of the bailiffs had slipped and become covered with the mud of the farmyard. Frustrated and exasperated, they had asked the farmer if he would wring the cock's neck so they could take it away. Again, he refused – his agreement was to provide a bird not to kill it. The last he saw of the two disgruntled bailiffs was their departure from his farm, one dirty and begrimed, the other with a struggling, squawking cock under his arm.

Eventually the grievance was resolved by the passing of the Tithe Act 1936. This Act provided that the rent charge previously payable to the Church, the Ecclesiastical Commissioners, Queen Anne's Bounty and some lay owners should be replaced by 'redemption annuities' payable to the Crown and the issue of government stock to the tithe owners. Thus, for the first time in its long history, tithe was divorced from the Church of England. The annuities ceased to be payable in 1996 when, with a few minor exceptions, all tithes were abolished. It was estimated that the Act of 1936 resulted in a capital loss to the Church of England of £17,750,000.[70] In 1948 the Queen Anne's Bounty and the Ecclesiastical Commissioners were united as the Church Commissioners.

Notes to the Text

Introduction

1 Moberg, D. O., 'The Life Cycle of a Church' in *The Church as a Social Institution*, Prentice Hall 1962, pp. 118–25. Moberg's five stages are (1) incipient organisation; (2) formal organisation; (3) maximum efficiency; (4) the institutional stage and (5) disintegration.

2 Turner, J. M., *The People's Church*, Fourth Chapel Aid Lecture, Englesea Brook 1994, p. 1.

3 Wilson, B. R., *The Social Dimensions of Sectarianism*, Oxford 1990, Introduction pp. 9, 16.

4 Gosse, Edmund, *Father and Son*, Oxford University Press 1974, Preface p. 3.

5 *Iolanthe*, first performed 1882.

Chapter 1: Precedents, Pioneers and Polity

1 See Petty, J., *History of the Primitive Methodist Connexion to the Conferences of 1860*, R. Davies Conference Offices 1864.
Kendall, H. B., *The Origin and History of the Primitive Methodist Church*, Robert Bryant.
Ritson, J., *The Romance of Primitive Methodism*, E. Dalton 1909.
Barber, B. A., *A Methodist Pageant*, Holborn Publishing House 1932.
Werner, J. S., *The Primitive Methodist Connexion*, University of Wisconsin Press 1984.
Also the *Bourne Papers*, Methodist Archives, John Rylands Library Manchester and *Lives* of Bourne and Clowes.
At the time of writing a book by Milburn, G. is in preparation for the Epworth Press *Understanding Methodism* series.

2 Davies, R. E., *Methodism*, Pelican 1965, p. 65.

3 Wesley, J., *Journal*, 31 March 1739.

4 Quoted in Townsend, Workman and Eayrs, *A New History of Methodism*, Hodder and Stoughton, Vol. I, p. 283.
5 Green, J. R., *A Short History of the English People*, Everyman Edition, J. M. Dent 1915, Ch. 10, p. 696.
6 Eayrs, as 4 above, Vol. I, pp. 488–9.
7 These were John and Charles Wesley, Thomas Coke and James Creighton.
8 Currie, R., *Methodism Divided*, Faber and Faber 1968.
9 Much of this information is taken from Wilkinson, J. T., *Hugh Bourne*, Epworth Press 1962, Ch. 1, pp. 13–28.
10 Bourne MSS, Quoted in Wilkinson, as 9 above, Ch. 1, p. 27.
11 Dolan, J., *Peter's People*, Independent Methodist Churches 1996, p. 6.
12 Quoted in Dolan, as 11 above, p. 8.
13 As 11 above.
14 Werner, J. S., *The Primitive Methodist Connexion*, University of Wisconsin Press 1984, Ch. 2, p. 47.
15 Kendall, H. B., *The Origin and History of the Primitive Methodist Church*, Robert Bryant, Vol. I, Ch. 1, pp. 59–61.
16 Minutes 1807 in *Methodist Magazine*, 1807, p. 432.
17 Bowmer, J. C., *Pastors and People*, Epworth Press 1975, Part 2, Ch. 1, pp. 82–3.
18 Minutes 1803, p. 184.
19 Ashworth, J., *The Life of the Venerable Hugh Bourne*, Joseph Toulson 1888, Ch. 6, p. 59.
20 Wilkinson, *Hugh Bourne*, as 9 above, Ch. 5, p. 76.
21 Wilkinson, *Hugh Bourne*, as 9 above, Ch. 3, p. 42.
22 Walford, J., *The Memoirs of the Life and Labours of the Late Venerable Hugh Bourne*, Vol. I, 1855, pp. 105–10.
23 Quoted in Petty, J., *History of the Primitive Methodist Connexion to the Conference of 1860*, R. Davies Conference Offices 1864, Ch. 2, p. 24.
24 Quoted in Kendall, as 16 above, Vol. I, Ch. 4, pp. 101–2.
25 Bourne, H., *Autobiography*, 'A' Text, p. 227.
26 Quoted in Wilkinson, J. T. *William Clowes (1780–1851)*, Epworth Press 1951, Ch. 2, p. 30.

27 See Wilkinson, *Hugh Bourne*, as 9 above, Ch. 6, p. 88.
28 As 9 above, pp. 30–31.
29 Bourne, H., *Journal*, Thursday, 30 May 1811.
30 Kendall, as 15 above, Vol. I, Ch. 5, p. 111.
31 Taken from Kendall, as 15 above, Vol. I, Ch. 5, p. 112.
32 An illustration of this plan is in Kendall, as 15 above, Vol. I, Ch. 5, p. 115.
33 Bourne, H., *Journal*, 13 February 1812.
34 On his tombstone in Tarvin Churchyard, the name is spelt 'Crawford'.
35 Petty, J., *History of the Primitive Methodist Connexion to the Conferences of 1860*, R. Davies Conference Offices 1864, Ch. 3, pp. 36–7.
36 Wilkes, A. and Lovatt, J., *Mow Cop and the Camp Meeting Movement*, Orphans Printing Press 1942, Ch. 6, p. 43.
37 Kendall, H. B., as 15 above, Vol. I, Ch. 1, p. 39.
38 Rack, H. D., *How Primitive was Primitive Methodism?*, Sixth Chapel Aid Lecture, Engelsea Brook 1996.
39 Wilkinson, as 9 above, Ch. 6, p. 89.
40 As 39 above.
41 Petty, as 35 above, Ch. 9, p. 97.
42 As 41 above, Ch. 9, p. 98.
43 Kendall, H. B., as 15 above.

Chapter 2: Expansion 1810–60

1 Clowes, *Journals*, pp. 99–100, quoted in Wilkinson, J.T., *William Clowes (1780–1851)*, Epworth Press 1951, Ch. 2, pp. 31–2.
2 Petty, J., *History of the Primitive Methodist Connexion to the Conference of 1860*, R. Davies Conference Offices 1864, Ch. 5, pp. 48–9.
3 Currie, G. and Hosley, *Churches and Churchgoers*, Oxford 1977, Ch. 6, p. 118.
4 Kendall, H. B., in Townsend, Workman and Eayrs (eds.), *A New History of Methodism*, Hodder and Stoughton 1909, Vol. I, p. 580.

5 Obelkevitch, J., *Religion and Rural Society*, Oxford 1976, Ch. 5, pp. 249–50.
6 Quoted in Watts, M. R., *The Dissenters*, Vol. II, Oxford 1995, Ch. 3, p. 375.
7 *Report of the Census of Religious Worship*, 1851, Table 23.
8 Field, C. D., 'The Social Structure of English Methodism, Eighteenth–Twentieth Centuries', *British Journal of Sociology* Vol. XXVIII, No. 2, June 1977, pp. 199–221.
9 Werner, J. S., *The Primitive Methodist Connexion*, University of Winsconsin Press 1984, Ch. 6, p. 142.
10 Bebbington, D. W., *Evangelicalism in Modern Britain*, Unwin Hyman 1989, Ch, 2, p, 25.
11 *Report of the Census of Religious Worship*, HC 1852–3, pp. CI XIV–CI XV.
12 Inglis, K. S., *Churches and the Working Class in Victorian England*, Routledge and Kegan Paul 1963, Introduction p. 12.
13 Petty, as 2 above, p. 579.
14 Werner, J. S., *The Primitive Methodist Connexion*, University of Winsconsin Press 1984.
15 Primitive Methodist Minutes 1896.
16 Obelkevich, J., *Religion and Rural Society in South Lindsay*, Oxford 1976, Ch. 5, p. 257.
17 Ritson, J., *The Romance of Primitive Methodism*, E. Dalton 1909, Ch. 6, pp. 205–6.
18 Kendall, H. B., *History and Origin of the Primitive Methodist Church*, Vol. I, p. 151.
19 Petty, as 2 above, Ch. 20, p. 572.
20 Ambler, R. W., *Ranters, Revivalists and Reformers*, Hull University Press 1989, Ch. 3, pp. 46–7.
21 Bourne MSS, *Journal*, 7 April 1808.
22 Werner, J. S., *The Primitive Methodist Connexion*, University of Winsconsin Press 1984, Ch. 6, p. 149.
23 *Primitive Methodist Large Hymn Book*, 1824, No. 82.
24 Quoted in Ashworth, J., *Hugh Bourne – A Biography*, J. Toulson 1888, Ch. 14, p. 128.
25 Maslow, A. H. A., 'Theory of Human Motivation', *Psychological Review*, Vol. L, 1943, pp. 370–96.

26 Bebbington, D. W., *Evangelicalism in Modern Britain*, Unwin Hyman 1989, Ch. 2, p. 25.
27 Werner, as 9 above, Ch. 6, p. 154.
28 Telford, J., *The New Methodist Hymn Book Illustrated*, Epworth Press 1934, p. 193.
29 *Hymns and Psalms*, No. 706.
30 Hobsbawm, E. J., *Primitive Rebels*, Manchester University Press 1974, Ch. 8, p. 138.
31 Hempton, D., *Methodism and Politics in British Society 1750–1850*, Hutchinson 1984, Ch. 7, p. 233.
32 Scotland, N., *Methodism and the Revolt of the Field*, Alan Sutton 1981, Ch. 1, p. 32.
33 Kendall, H. B., in *History and Origin of the Primitive Methodist Church*, Ch. 23, pp. 333–4.
34 Graham, Dorothy E., 'Women preachers' in Milburn, G. (ed.), *Workaday Preachers*.
35 Methodist Publishing House 1995, Ch. 8, p. 168.
36 Kendall, M. B., *Handbook of Primitive Methodist Church Principles and Polity*, Holborn Publishing House 1923, Ch. 5, p. 38.
37 Werner, *The Primitive Methodist Connexion*, University of Winsconsin Press 1984, Ch. 6, p. 154.
38 Ritson, J., *The Romance of Primitive Methodism*, E. Dalton 1949, Ch. 6, pp. 205–6.

Chapter 3: Tensions

1 Kendall, H. B., *History and Origin of the Primitive Methodist Church*, Vol. II, Ch. 1, pp. 37–45.
2 Primitive Methodist General Minutes 1854, pp. 24–5, 28.
3 Vickers, J., *History of Independent Methodism*, I. M. Bookroom 1920, Ch. 14, p. 20–22.
4 Vickers, as 3 above, Ch. 14, p. 170–71.
5 Watts, M. R., *The Dissenters*, Oxford 1995, Vol. II, Ch. 3, p. 407.
6 See Semmel, B., *The Methodist Revolution*, Heinemann 1974, Ch. 5, pp. 131–6.

7 Halévy, E. A., *History of the English People in 1815*, Pelican Books 1938, Ch. 1, p. 47.
8 Townsend, A., in *A New History of Methodism*, Hodder & Stoughton 1905, Vol. I, p. 371.
9 Semmel, as 6 above, Ch. 5, pp. 131–6 and Gilbert, A. D., 'Methodism and Political Stability in Early Industrialised England', *Journal of Religious History*, Vol. X, pp. 281–99.
10 Hempton, D., *Methodism and Politics in British Society 1750-1850*, Hutchinson 1984, Conclusion p. 227.
11 Walford, J., *The Memoirs of the Life and Labours of the Late Venerable Hugh Bourne*, 1855, Vol. II, p. 101.
12 Wearmouth, R. F., *Methodism and the Working Class Movements of England 1800-1850*, Epworth Press 1937, Ch. 6, p. 212.
13 Primitive Methodist Minutes 1835, pp. 9–10.
14 Wearmouth, R. F., *Some Working Class Movements of the Nineteenth Century*, Epworth Press 1948, p. 145.
15 Wearmouth, as 12 above, Ch. 6, p. 65.
16 Quoted in Watts, *The Dissenters*, Oxford 1995, Vol. II, Ch. 14, p. 503.
17 Thompson, E. P., *The Making of the Working Class*, Pelican 1968, Ch. 11, p. 438.
18 Hobsbawm, E. J., *Primitive Rebels*, Manchester University Press 1974, Ch. 8, pp. 139–40.
19 As 18 above.
20 As 17 above, Ch. 11, p. 430.
21 Webb, S., *The Story of the Durham Miners 1662–1921*, Fabian Society 1921, p. 28.
22 Scotland, N., *Methodism and the Revolt of the Field*, Ch. 2, p. 36.
23 Watts, M. R., *The Dissenters*, Oxford 1995, Vol. II, Ch. 3, p. 376.
24 Conference MS Journal 1842, quoted in Wilkinson, J. T., *Hugh Bourne*, Epworth Press 1952, Ch. 9, p. 155.
25 See Bedford, F., 'James Bourne 1781–1860 and the Bemersley Book Room', *Wesley Historical Society Proceedings*, Vol. XXX, Ch. 7, pp. 138–50.
26 Wilkinson, J. T., *William Clowes 1780–1851*, Epworth Press, 1951, Appendix B, pp. 95–6.

27 Clowes, S., MSS quoted in Wilkinson, as 26 above, Appendix A, pp. 83–93.
28 As 27 above.
29 Kent, J. S., *Holding the Fort*, Epworth Press 1978, Ch. 2, p. 57.
30 Sheard, M., *The Origin and Early Development of Primitive Methodism in Cheshire and Lancashire 1800–1860*, Unpublished PhD, Manchester 1976, Vol. I, p. 89.
31 Quoted in Wilkinson, as 26 above, Appendix B, pp. 95–6.
32 Primitive Methodist Minutes 1832.
33 Quoted in Baker, F., 'James Bourne (1781–1860) and the Bemersley Book Room', *Wesley Historical Society Proceedings*, 1955, Vol. XXX, p. 177.
34 Wilkinson, as 26 above, Appendix A, p. 91.
35 Hatcher, S. G., *The Origin and Expansion of Primitive Methodism in the Hull Circuit*, Unpublished PhD, Manchester 1993, Vol. II, p. 553.
36 As 26 above, Appendix A, p. 97.
37 Wilkinson, J. T., *Hugh Bourne*, Epworth Press 1952, Ch. 9, p. 144.
38 Brown, L., 'William Clowes in the North of England', *WHS Proceedings*, Vol. XXXVII, pp. 169–72.
39 As 38 above, pp. 171–2.
40 Wilkinson, *Hugh Bourne*, as 37 above, footnote to p. 145.
41 Bourne, *Journal*, 20 September – 29 September 1843.
42 Hatcher, S. G., *The Origin and Expansion of Primitive Methodism in the Hull Circuit*, Vol. II, p. 552.
43 Quoted in Morrell, D. J., *Some Aspects of Revivalism and Charismatic Movements in England 1800–1862*, Unpublished MPhil thesis, Manchester 1987, p. 191.
44 Wilkinson, *Hugh Bourne*, as 37 above, Ch. 11, p. 172.
45 See Wilkinson, *Hugh Bourne*, as 37 above.
46 Kent, J. S., *Holding the Fort*, Epworth Press 1978, Ch. 2, p. 56.
47 Baker F., 'The Bournes and the Primitive Methodist Deed Poll', *Wesley Historical Society Proceedings*, Vol. XXVIII, p. 138.
48 Kent, as 46 above, Ch. 2, p. 57.
49 Sheard, as 30 above, Vol. I, p. 89.

50 Wilkinson, *William Clowes*, as 26 above, Appendix B, p. 97 and Wilkinson, *Hugh Bourne*, as 137 above, Ch. 11, p. 177.
51 Hatcher, S. G., *The Origin and Expansion of Primitive Methodism in the Hull Circuit*, Vol. I, Ch. 2, pp. 88–9.
52 Petty, J., *History of the Primitive Methodist Connexion to the Conferences of 1860*, R. Davies Conference Offices 1864, Ch. 19, pp. 428–9.

Chapter 4: From Sect to Denomination

1 Kendall, H. B., *Handbook of Primitive Methodist Church Principles and Polity*, Holborn, Ch. 4, p. 48.
2 Pope, Liston, *Millhands and Preachers*, Yale University Press 1942, p. 119.
3 Hill, M. A., *A Sociology of Religion*, Heinemann 1973, Ch. 3, p. 65.
4 Primitive Methodist Minutes 1849, p. 400.
5 Primitive Methodist Minutes 1860, p. 38.
6 *Primitive Methodist World*, 17 May 1883.
7 Graham, Dorothy E., *Three Colleges – Eighth Chapel Aid Lecture 1998*, Englesea Brook, Ch. 3, p. 28. This booklet provides a comprehensive account of the three schools.
8 Watts, M. R., *The Dissenters*, Oxford University Press, Ch. 2, p. 223.
9 Kendall, H. B., *The Origin and History of the Primitive Methodist Church*, Edwin Dalton Volume.
10 As 8 above.
11 Wickham, E. R., *Church and People in an Industrial City*, Lutterworth Press 1957, Ch. 4, p. 131–2.
12 Milburn, G., *Unique in Methodism – 100 years of Chapel Aid*, Englesea Brook and the Methodist Chapel Aid Association 1990, p. 2.
13 Primitive Methodist Minutes 1836.
14 Kendall, as 9 above, Vol. II, Ch. 6, p. 457–8.
15 Milburn, as 12 above, p. 8.
16 Milburn, as 12 above, p. 11.
17 Milburn, as 12 above, p. 18.

18 Pope, Liston, *Millhands and Preachers (a study of Gastona)*, Yale University Press 1942, Ch. 7, p. 122.
19 Obelkevich, J., *Religion and Rural Society in South Lindsay 1826–1875*, Ch. 5, p. 253.
20 Barber, B. A., *A Methodist Pageant*, Holborn Publishing House 1932, p. 311.
21 Hatcher, S. G., *The Origin and Expansion of Primitive Methodism in the Hull Circuit 1815–1851*, Unpublished PhD, Manchester, p. 276.
22 See Morrell, D. J., *Some Aspects of Revivalist and Charismatic Movements in England 1800–1862*, Unpublished MPhil thesis, Manchester 1984.
23 Obelkevich, J., *Religion and Rural Society: Smith Lindsey 1825–1875*, Clarendon Press, Oxford 1976, Ch. 5, pp. 238–44.
24 As 23 above, p. 234.
25 *The Primitive Methodist*, 31 July 1902, p. 97.
26 Primitive Methodist Minutes 1820, pp. 4 and 5.
27 As 26 above.
28 Primitive Methodist Consolidated Minutes 1832, p. 22.
29 Primitive Methodist Minutes 1869, p. 73.
30 Primitive Methodist Consolidated Minutes 1849, p. 85.
31 Primitive Methodist Minutes 1862, pp. 35 and 36.
32 Primitive Methodist Minutes 1869, pp. 74–5.
33 Kendall, as 14 above, p. 396.
34 As 32 above.
35 *Primitive Methodist Magazine*, 1860, p. 678.
36 *Primitive Methodist Magazine*, 1855, p. 405.
37 As 36 above, p. 406.
38 Milburn, G., *A School for the Prophets – Chapel Aid Lecture 1981*, p. 6.
39 Brown, K. D., *A Social History of the Nonconformist Ministry in England and Wales 1800–1930*, Clarendon Press 1988, Ch. 4, p. 133.
40 Primitive Methodist Minutes 1855.
41 Primitive Methodist Minutes 1855, p. 25.
42 Brown, as 39 above, Ch. 3, pp. 81–2.

43 *Primitive Methodist*, 23 March 1871.
44 Primitive Methodist Minutes 1865, p. 75.
45 Primitive Methodist Minutes 1865, p. 35.
46 Graham, as 7 above, p. 7.
47 Primitive Methodist Minutes 1865, p. 96.
48 Primitive Methodist Minutes 1866, pp. 4–5.
49 Wilkes, A. and Lovatt, J., *Mow Cop and the Camp Meeting Movement*, Orphans Printing Press 1942, Ch 11, p. 79.
50 *Primitive Methodist Magazine*, 1870, p. 63.
51 Primitive Methodist Minutes 1873, p. 65.
52 Quoted by Bretherton, F. F., *Wesley Historical Society Proceedings*, Vol. XXX, June 1956, p. 118.
53 Kendall, as 9 above, Vol. II, Ch. 9, p. 256.
54 Primitive Methodist Minutes 1876, pp. 79, 93–4.
55 Primitive Methodist Minutes 1880, p. 111.
56 Primitive Methodist Minutes 1871, p. 59.
57 Primitive Methodist Minutes 1876, pp. 93–4.
58 Primitive Methodist Minutes 1881, pp. 88–9.
59 Primitive Methodist Minutes 1886, p. 100.
60 Humphries, A. L., 'Hartley Primitive Methodist College' in Brash, W. B., *The Story of Our Colleges*, 1935, p. 7.
61 Primitive Methodist Minutes 1891, p. 165.
62 Primitive Methodist Minutes 1895, pp. 147 and 176.
63 Primitive Methodist Minutes 1894, p. 165.
64 Primitive Methodist Minutes 1903, p. 202.
65 Primitive Methodist Minutes 1907, p. 179.
66 Peake, A. S., *The life of Sir William Hartley*, Hodder and Stoughton 1926, Ch. 10, pp. 142–3 and 145–6.
67 Peake, as 66 above, pp. 148–50.
68 Peake, as 66 above, p. 151.
69 Pope, as 2 above, Ch. 7, p. 120.
70 Peake, as 66 above, Ch. 10, p. 134.
71 Peake, as 66 above, Ch. 10, p. 135.
72 Lysons, C. K., 'Always a Student', *Methodist Recorder*, 16 Aug 1979.
73 Meecham, H. G., in Wilkinson (ed.), *A. S. Peake*, Epworth Press 1958, p. 19.

74 Peake, as 66 above, p. 141.
75 Lysons, as 72 above, p. 12.
76 Primitive Methodist Minutes 1922, p. 173.
77 Primitive Methodist Minutes 1928, p. 219.
78 Primitive Methodist Minutes 1906, p 225.
79 Primitive Methodist Minutes 1907, p 225.
80 Obelkevich, as 23 above, p. 235.
81 Stark, W., *The Sociology of Religion*, Routledge and Kegan Paul 1967, Vol. II, Ch. 3, p. 301.
82 Primitive Methodist Minutes 1866, p. 77.
83 Peake, as 66 above, Ch. 1, p. 26.
84 *Primitive Methodist Leader*, 28 July 1921, p. 495.
85 *Primitive Methodist Magazine*, 1891, p. 141.
86 *Primitive Methodist Leader*, 17 Jan 1924, p. 34.
87 Primitive Methodist Minutes 1913, p. 11.
88 Pope, as 2 above, Ch. 7, pp. 122–6.
89 Primitive Methodist Minutes 1896.
90 See Sims, G. R., *The Bitter Cry of Outcast London*, Congregational Union 1883.
91 See Booth, C., *Life and Labour in London*, Collected Edition, Macmillan 1904.
92 Munson, J., *The Nonconformists*, SPCK 1991, Ch. 2, p. 57.
93 See 92 above.
94 *Primitive Methodist Magazine*, 1892, pp. 252–3.
95 Primitive Methodist Minutes 1885, p. 106.
96 Barber, B. A., *A Methodist Pageant*, pp. 200–202.
97 Barber, as 96 above, p. 204.
98 Primitive Methodist Minutes 1890.
99 This line is taken from Bishop Heber's hymn, 'From Greenland's icy mountains', *Primitive Methodist Hymnal* (1889) No. 845. The verse from which this line is taken was expurgated from the *Methodist Hymnal* (1933) and the hymn completely omitted from *Hymns and Psalms* (1983).
100 Primitive Methodist Minutes 1857.
101 Primitive Methodist Minutes 1860.
102 Kendall, as 9 above, Vol. II, Ch. 7, p. 500.

103 For an account of Buckenham's journey see Stamp, E., 'When First the Work Began Its Widening Way', in Nightingale (ed.), *The Widening Way*, Cargate Press 1952, Ch. 1, pp. 8–13.
104 Davies, R. E., *Methodism*, Pelican (Penguin Books) 1963, Ch. 7, pp. 151–2.
105 Thompson, E. P., *The Making of English Working Class*, Pelican (Penguin Books) 1963, Ch. 11, p. 436.
106 Davies, as 104 above, Ch. 7, p. 153.
107 Wearmouth, R. F., See *Methodism and the Working Class Movements of England* and *The Social and Political Influence of Methodism in the Twentieth Century*, Epworth Press.
108 Webb, S., *The Story of the Durham Miners 1662–1921*, Fabian Society 1921, p. 28.
109 Scotland, N., *Methodism and the Revolt of the Field*, Alan Sutton, Ch. 2, p. 37.
110 Hempton, D., *Methodism and Politics in British Society*, Hutchinson 1984, p. 215.
111 Moore, R., *Pitmen, Preachers and Politics*, Cambridge 1974, p. 27.
112 As 111 above.
113 *Primitive Methodist Leader*, 14 December 1903.
114 Figures taken from Koss, S., *Nonconformity in Modern British Politics*, Batsford 1975, pp. 228–36.
115 Primitive Methodist Minutes 1907 p. 219.
116 Primitive Methodist Minutes 1904.
117 Kendall, H. B., *The Origin and History of the Primitive Methodist Church*, Vol. I, p. 159.
118 As 117 above.
119 Peake, as 66 above, Ch. 9, pp. 125–9.
120 Primitive Methodist Minutes 1898.
121 Primitive Methodist Deed Poll.
122 Minutes of Methodist New Connexion 1866, p. 57. See also Townsend, W. J., *The Story of Methodist Union*, Milner and Co., Undated, Ch. 6, p. 99.
123 Quoted in Townsend, as 122 above, Ch. 6, p. 102.

124 Townsend, as 122 above, Ch. 8, pp. 158–9.
125 No reference to this Committee appears in the Wesleyan Minutes for 1881.
126 Kent, J., *The Age of Disunity*, Epworth Press, 1966, Ch. 1, p. 1.
127 Primitive Methodist Minutes 1894.
128 Quoted in Townsend, as 122 above, Ch 9, p. 185.
129 Wesleyan Methodist Minutes 1904.
130 Minutes of Wesleyan Conference 1913, p. 97.
131 'Tentative Scheme for the union of the Wesleyan Methodist, Primitive Methodist and United Methodist Churches' prepared by the United Committee appointed by the three churches and submitted to the Conferences of 1923.
132 Bowmer, J. C., *Methodist Union Journal of the Wesleyan Historical Society*, Vol. XLIII, Part 5, Sept 1982, p. 105.
133 Kent, as 126 above, Ch. 1, p. 42.
134 Wilkinson, J. T., in *Arthur Samuel Peake 1865–1929*, Epworth Press 1958, p. 45.
135 Quoted in Wilkinson, as 134 above, p. 45.
136 See for example *Primitive Methodist Leader*, 12 March 1924, p. 167; 26 Aug 1924, p. 567; 4 Sept 1924, p. 583; 11 Sept 1924, p. 595; 2 Oct 1924, pp. 645 and 647; 13 Nov 1924, p. 747; 20 Nov 1924, pp. 755 and 761.
137 See especially Kent, J., *The Age of Disunity*, Epworth Press 1966, Ch. 1; Currie, R., *Methodism Divided*, Faber and Faber 1968; and Thomson Brake, G., *Policy and Politics in British Methodism 1932–1982*, Edsall of London 1984, Ch. 1.
138 Currie, R., *Methodism Divided*, Faber and Faber 1968, Ch. 9, p. 296.
139 Primitive Methodist Minutes 1932, p. 274.

Chapter 5: Churches, Ministers and People

1 Kendall, H. B., *History of the Primitive Methodist Church*, Dalton Vol. I, pp, 225–7.
2 *Centenary Celebrations 1881–1981*, Methodist Church, Lane Head, Lowton, p. 2.

3 Rowe, W., 'The Work of God at Lowton', *Primitive Methodist Magazine*, 1843, pp. 431–2.
4 Sheard, M., *The Origin and Early Development of Primitive Methodism in Cheshire and Lancashire 1800–1860*, Unpublished PhD thesis, Manchester 1976, Vol. I, p. 89.
5 Laqueur, T. W., *Religion and Respectability: Sunday Schools and Working Class Culture 1780–1850*, Yale University Press 1976, Epilogue, p. 247.
6 Martin, David, *A Sociology of English Religion*, Heinemann 1967, Ch. 2, p. 42.
7 Laqueur, as 5 above, Epilogue, p. 244.
8 Daniels, R., *Conversations with Cardus*, Gollancz 1976, Ch. 4, p. 63.
9 Potter, W., *Thomas Jackson of Whitechapel*, Working Lads' Institute, London 1929, pp. 8–9.
10 Boydell, M., *Morning and Spring Time*, 1933, p. 222.
11 Kent, J., *The Age of Disunity*, Epworth Press 1966, Ch. 1, p. 7.
12 Leary, W., *Directory of Primitive Methodist Ministers and Their Circuits*, Teamprint in Association with the Wesley Historical Society 1990.
13 Davies, H., *Worship of the English Puritans*, Dacre Press 1948, Ch. 6, pp. 59–61.
14 Minutes of Primitive Methodist Conference 1819, p. 5.
15 Letter from Alfred Taberner to the writer quoted in *Robert Wilfrid Callin, Parson, Padre, Poet*, Church in the Market Place Press, Buxton 1997, p. 28.
16 Kendall, H. B., *Handbook of Primitive Methodist Church Principles and Polity*, Holborn Publishing House 1928, p. 64.
17 Primitive Methodist Minutes 1896.
18 Brown, W. D., *A Social History of the Nonconformist Ministry in England*, Oxford 1988, Tables 1–7, pp. 40–41.
19 Much of the material for this section is taken from *Primitive Methodist Rules*, Revised 1922, paras. 352–94.
20 Primitive Methodist Minutes 1904, pp. 215–16.
21 Primitive Methodist Minutes 1932, p. 240.
22 *Primitive Methodist General Rules*, 1922, para. 370, p. 85.

23 *Statistics of Public Education for the Year 1922–23*, Table 71, pp. 82–8.
24 *Education in 1938, Annual Report of the Board of Education*, HMSO, Table 33, p. 130.
25 Compiled from the *Primitive Methodist Yearly Handbook and Almanac 1932*.
26 Wearmouth, R. F., *Pages from a Padre's Diary*, self-published (undated), Ch. 2, pp. 10–11.
27 Wearmouth, as 26 above, Ch. 4, p. 32.
28 See Kent, J., *The Age of Disunity*, Epworth Press 1966, Ch. 2.
29 Burdon, A., *An Exploration of the Relationship Between Doctrine Expression and Liturgical Action as reflected in John Wesley's Ordinations and the Subsequent Development of Ministry in the Methodist Church of Great Britain*, Unpublished PhD thesis, Manchester 1993, p. 172.
30 Much of the material for this section is taken from *Primitive Methodist Rules*, Revised 1922, paras. 414–15.
31 Taken from *The Tongue: The Worst and Best of Everything*, Primitive Methodist Bookroom, Undated. Ch. 3, pp. 32–3.
32 Crockford, *Clerical Directory*, 1932.
33 *The Value of a £1: Prices and Incomes in Britain 1900–1993*, HMSO, p. 50.
34 Leary, W., *Directory of Primitive Methodist Ministers and Their Circuits*, Teamprint in Association with the Wesley Historical Society 1990.
35 Brown, K. D., *A Social History of the Nonconformist Ministry in England and Wales 1806–1930*, Clarendon Press, Table 5.8, following p. 191.
36 Government Actuaries Department, *Health of Adults in Britain 1841–1994*, Ch. 3, Table 3.3, p. 20.
37 Despite an extensive search, no earlier plans or other sources showing memberships of all the seven chapels appear to have survived.
38 Dempsey, K., 'Conflict in Minister/Lay Relations' in Martin, D. (ed.), *A Sociological Year Book of Religion in Britain*, SCM Press 1939, p. 63.

39 Forman, Charles, *Industrial Town: St Helens in the 1920s*, Ch. 6, p. 175.
40 Brown, as 35 above, Ch. 6, p. 201.
41 Source not known.
42 Crump, Lieutenant, quoted in Weatherhead, L. D., *How Can I Find God?* Hodder and Stoughton 1937, p. 214.
43 *Primitive Methodist Hymnal Supplement*, 1912, No. 193, p. 244.

Chapter 6: Beliefs

1 Kendall, H. B., *Handbook of Primitive Methodist Church Principles, History and Polity*, Primitive Methodist Publishing House 1928, p. 60.
2 Mews, S. (ed.), *Modern Rebels*, Epworth Press 1993, Ch. 11, pp. 206–7.
3 Mews, S., 'Against the Simple Gospel: John Day Thompson and the New Evangelism in Primitive Methodism' in *Modern Rebels*, Epworth Press 1998, Ch. 11, pp. 206–25.
4 Kent, J., *The Age of Disunity*, Epworth Press 1966, Ch. 1, p. 3.
5 Wilson, B., *Religion in Secular Society*, Pelican 1966, Ch. 5, p. 97.
6 Hooker, Morna D., 'Ministerial Training: the Contribution of A. S. Peake', *Epworth Review*, Sept 1985, pp. 64–76.
7 Huxtable, J., *The Preachers' Integrity*, Epworth Press 1966, Ch. 1, p. 11.
8 Paley, W., *Natural Theology*, Ch. 1.
9 Dawkins, R., *The Blind Watchmaker*, Penguin Books 1988.
10 Watts, Isaac, 'We Give Immortal Praise', *Methodist Hymn Book*, No. 40; *Hymns and Psalms*, No. 18.
11 Phillips, J. B., *Your God is Too Small*, Wyvern Books 1956, p. 55.
12 Barton, Bruce, *The Man Nobody Knows*, Constable & Co. 1930, Ch. 1, pp. 1–2.
13 Macquarrie, J., *Principles of Christian Theology*, SCM Press Ltd 1977, Ch. 13, p. 314.
14 *Methodist Hymn Book* 1933, Verses No. 13.
15 Blake, W., *Auguries of Innocence*.
16 Glover, T. R., *The Jesus of History*, SCM Press 1918, Ch. 1, p. 17.

17 Weatherhead, L. D., *His Life and Ours*, Hodder and Stoughton 1932, Preface p. viii.
18 *Baptist Hymn Book* 1962, No. 578.
19 Küng, Hans, *On Being a Christian*, Collins Fount Paperbacks 1978, Ch. 7, p. 468.
20 *Methodist Hymn Book* 1933, No. 973.
21 Omar Khayyam, *The Rubaiyat Stanza.*
22 Complete Works of John Bunyan (1862), Vol. I. p. 8.
23 Tennyson, *In Memoriam*, Stanza 94.
24 Butterfield, Herbert, *Christianity and History*, G. Bell & Sons Ltd. 1950, Ch. 7, p. 146.

Chapter 7: Ethics and Moral Theology

1 Preston, R. H., *The Future of Christian Ethics*, SCM Press Ltd 1987, Ch. 3, p. 46.
2 Weber, M., trans Parsons, T., *The Protestant Ethic and the Spirit of Capitalism*, London 1930.
3 Tawney, R. H., *Religion and the Rise of Capitalism*, Pelican Books 1937, Ch. 4, p. 238.
4 Tawney, as 3 above, Ch. 4, p. 239.
5 Wesley, C., 'A charge to keep I have', *Hymns and Psalms*, No. 785, Verse 2.
6 Wesley, C., 'Forth in Thy name, O Lord, I go', *Hymns and Psalms*, No. 381, Verse 2.
7 Tawney, as 3 above, Ch. 4, p. 244.
8 Bebbington, D. W., *The Nonconformist Conscience*, George Allen & Unwin 1982, pp. 12–13.
9 Arnold, M., *Culture and Anarchy.*
10 Currie, R., *Methodism Divided*, Faber and Faber 1968, Ch. 4, p. 112.
11 *Primitive Methodist Magazine*, 1819, p. 218.
12 As 8 above.
13 Peake, A. S., *Life of Sir William Hartley*, Hodder and Stoughton 1926, pp. 37 and 77.
14 Peake, as 13 above, Ch. 17, p. 218.
15 Wigley, J., *The Rise and Fall of the Victorian Sunday*, Manchester University Press 1980, Ch. 1, p. 21.

16 Barclay, W., *The Plain Man's Guide to Ethics*, Collins 1973, Ch. 5, p. 27.
17 Harrison, B., *Drink and the Victorians*, Faber and Faber 1971, Ch. 4, p. 88.
18 Trevelyan, G. M., *English Social History*, Longmans 1942, Ch. 10, p. 296.
19 Pilkington, W., *Makers of Preston Methodism and the Relation of Methodism to the Temperance Movement*, Preston 1890, p. 224.
20 As 19 above.
21 Edwards, Maldwyn, *Methodism and England*, Epworth Press 1943, Ch. 6, p. 105.
22 Pilkington, as 19 above, pp. 228–31.
23 As 22 above.
24 As 19 above.
25 Kendall, *History of the Primitive Methodist Church*, Vol. II, p. 129.
26 Barber, B. A., *A Methodist Pageant*, Holborn Publishing House 1932, p. 237.
27 Harrison, as 17 above, Ch. 10, pp. 233–4.
28 Harrison, as 17 above, Ch. 17, p. 399.
29 Blatchford, R., *Britain for the British*, 1902, p. 107.
30 1 Timothy 5.23.
31 Quoted in Fryer, *Mrs Grundy: Studies in English Prudery*, Dobson 1963, Ch. 13, p. 142.
32 *Primitive Methodist Hymnal Supplement*, No. 239.
33 *Primitive Methodist Hymnal Supplement*, No. 237; *SS Hymn Book* No. 575.
34 *Primitive Methodist Sunday Schools Hymnal*, No. 585.
35 'Declaration of the Methodist Church on Total Abstinence and Temperance Reform', adopted by Conference 1951 in *Declarations of Conference on Social Questions*, Epworth Press 1959, p. 60.
36 Harrison, as 17 above, Ch. 17, p. 393.
37 As 35 above, p. 64.
38 'Declaration of the Methodist Church on the Gambling Problem 1936' in *Declarations of Conference on Social Questions*, Epworth Press 1959, p. 63. This has now been superceded

by the 'Statement on Gambling' issued by the Methodist Conference in 1992.

39 *Stevenson's Book of Quotations* p. 753 attributes it to *Poor Robin's Almanac*, 1676.

40 Royal Commission on Betting, Lotteries and Gambling 1949, 13 December 1949. Evidence of E. Benson Perkins. Paras. 2903, 2904.

41 Much of this information is taken from Jones, J. P., *Gambling Yesterday and Today*, David and Charles 1973, Ch. 7. The Methodist Church published a statement on the National Lottery in 1996.

42 The Methodist Church, *Statement on Gambling*, 1992.

43 Stead, W. T., quoted in Cunningham, V., *Everywhere Spoken Against*, Oxford University Press 1975, Ch. 2, p. 55.

44 *Primitive Methodist Magazine*, 1870. The Family Department.

45 Cunningham, V., *Everywhere Spoken Against*, Oxford University Press 1975, Ch. 2, p. 60.

46 Cunningham, as 45 above, Ch. 2.

47 Drummond, A. L., *The Churches in English Fiction*, Edward Backus, Leicester 1950, Ch. 7, p. 279.

48 Hocking, S. K., *Her Benny*, reprint by Gallery Press, Liverpool 1985, Original Preface, 1879.

49 Cunningham, as 45 above, Ch. 2, p. 52.

50 Dews, C., *Revd Hugh Gilmore: Christian Socialist and Primitive Methodist Catholic*, Unpublished lecture 1997.

51 Fryer, P., *Mrs Grundy*, Dennis Dobson, London 1963. Ch. 23, p. 221; Ch. 24, p. 226.

52 Quoted in Baleman, M. and Skenning, S., *The Wit of the Church*, Leslie Frewin, London 1967, p. 54.

53 The Methodist Church Standing Orders, 1964, p. 15.

54 Preston, R., 'Ethical Aspects of Gambling' in *Crucible*, October–December 1974, pp. 156–62.

55 *Methodist Statement on Gambling*, adopted by the Methodist Conference 1992, p. 50.

56 Preston, R., 'Ethical Aspects of Gambling: A New Look', *Crucible*, October–November 1974, p. 157.

57 Harrison, J., *Our Knowledge of Right and Wrong*, George Allen and Unwin 1971, Ch. 11, p. 247.

Chapter 8: Worship

1 *Hymns and Psalms*, No. 354.
2 *Methodist Hymn Book*, No. 972.
3 See the last two lines of *Hymns and Psalms*, No. 302, verse 2.
4 *Primitive Methodist Supplement*, No. 248.
5 Python, Monty, parody of 'All things bright and beautiful' in Baker, K. (ed.), *Unauthorised Versions*, Faber and Faber, 1990, p. 3.
6 Sellers, I., *The Hymnody of Primitive Methodism*, Lancashire and Cheshire Wesley Historical Society 1993, p. 14.
7 Martin, D., *The Sociology of English Religion*, Heinemann Educational 1967, Ch. 4, p. 86.
8 Kent, J., *Holding the Fort: Studies in Victorian Revivalism*, Ch. 6, pp. 232–3.
9 *Hymns and Psalms*, No. 529.
10 Moore, R., *Pit Men, Preachers and Politics*, Cambridge University Press 1974, Ch. 4, p. 116.
11 *Primitive Methodist Sunday School Hymnal*, No. 340.
12 *Book of Common Prayer*, Catechism.
13 Kendall, H. B., *The Origin and History of the Primitive Methodist Church*, Vol. I, pp. 335–6.
14 Quoted in Foury, C. L., *Further Thought on Wesley's 'And Can It Be'*, Hymn Society Bulletin 191, April 1992, p. 118.
15 Quoted in Foury, C. L., as 14 above, p. 119.
16 Davies, H., *The Worship of the English Puritans,* Dacre Press 1948, Ch. 8, p. 105.
17 Willey, B., *Spots of Time: A Retrospect of the Years 1897–1920* quoted in Burdon, A., *The Preachers' Service: the Glory of the Methodists*, Grove Books 1997, p. 35.
18 Taylor, J., *Two Discourses*, London 1682, quoted in Davies, as 16 above, Ch. 8, p. 104.
19 Henry, M., *A Method of Prayer Etc.*, London 1710, quoted in Davies, as 16 above, Ch. 8, p. 114.

20 *Hymns and Psalms*, No. 142.
21 Coffin, H. S., *The Public Worship of God*, Independent Press 1950, Ch. 9, p. 158.
22 Davies, as 16 above, Ch. 11, p. 182.
23 Bradshaw, W., *English Puritanisme, containing the maine opinions of the rigidest sort of those that are called Puritanes in the Realm of England*, 1605, quoted in Davies, as 16 above, Ch. 8, p. 103.
24 Davies, as 16 above, Ch 11, p. 187.
25 Baxter, *Five Disputations of Church Government and Worship*, 1659, quoted in Davies, as 16 above, Ch 11, p. 188.
26 MacLaren, Ian, *Beside the Bonnie Brier Bush*, Hodder and Stoughton 1895.
27 Sangster, W. E., *The Craft of Sermon Illustration*, Ch. 1, pp. 6–9.
28 Benson, Irving, 'Dr Frank Boreham: The Man and the Writer', in Boreham, F. W., *The Last Milestone*, Epworth Press 1961, p. 12.
29 Wilkinson, J. T., *Hugh Bourne 1772–1852*, Epworth Press 1952, pp. 21–32.
30 Davies, W. J., *The Minister at Work*, Charles H. Kelly 1910, Ch. 7, p. 93.
31 Graham, E. D., 'Women Local Preachers' in Milburn, G. and Batty, M., *Workaday Preachers*.
32 Methodist Publishing House 1995, Ch. 8, p. 182.
33 Wilkinson, A., *Dissent or Conform: War, Peace and the English Churches 1900–1945*, SCM Press 1986, Ch. 2, p. 30.
34 Bowran, J. G., *The Life of Arthur Thomas Guttery DD*, Holborn Publishing House *c.* 1921, Ch. 3, p. 46.
35 Wilkinson, A., as 33 above, Ch. 2, p. 28.
36 *Aldersgate Magazine*, 1929, p. 375.
37 *Aldersgate Magazine*, 1927, p. 151.
38 Smith, G. A., *The Book of Isaiah*, Hodder and Stoughton, Vol. II, Ch. 6, p. 105.
39 In Milner-White, E. and Briggs, G. W., *Daily Prayer*, Pelican 1959, p. 183.
40 Ritson, J., *The Romance of Primitive Methodism*, Edward Dalton Primitive Methodist Publishing House 1909, Ch. 9, pp. 176–7.

41 These anecdotes are taken from Ridyard, R., *Memories of Lowton*, PTM Brooks Ltd, Leigh, Undated, pp. 43–4.
42 As 41 above.
43 Milburn, G. (ed.), *Workaday Preachers*.
44 Field, C. D., 'The Social Structure of English Methodism: Eighteenth–Twentieth Centuries', *British Journal of Sociology* June 1977, Vol. XXVIII, No. 2, pp. 199–221.
45 Worsley, H., in *The Link – The Makerfield Circuit Magazine*, June 1996, Bi-centenary of Local Preachers issue, p. 11.
46 *Forms for the Administration of Baptism etc.*, George Lamb, London 1860, p. 28.
47 Quoted in Davies, as 16 above, Ch. 6, p. 73.
48 Bowmer, J. C., *The Lord's Supper in Methodism 1791–1960*, Epworth Press 1961, Ch. 4, p. 47.
49 As 48 above.
50 Quoted in Hodgkins, H., *The Congregational Way*, Congregational Federation 1982, Ch. 7, p. 71.
51 Minutes of the Methodist Conference 1946, p. 203.
52 Davies, as 16 above, Ch. 11, p. 182.
53 *Order of Administration of Baptism and Other Services*, Robert Bryant, Undated, p. 5.
54 *Hymns and Psalms*, No. 588.
55 Holland, B., *The Doctrine of Infant Baptism in Non-Wesleyan Methodism*, Wesley Historical Society Occasional Publication (New Series 1) 1970.
56 Davies, as 16 above, Ch. 12, p. 204.
57 Jones-Davies, W., *The Minister at Work*, Charles Kelly 1910, Ch. 17, pp. 269–70.
58 *Primitive Methodist Hymn Book*, 1889, No. 745.
59 *Hymns and Psalms*, No. 608.

Chapter 9: Church and Chapel

1 Sellar, W. C., and Yeatman, R. J., *1066 and All That*, Methuen 1997.
2 Christopher Wordsworth (1807–85) was Bishop of Lincoln and a noted hymn writer. Six of his hymns were in the

Methodist Hymn Book, two of which have survived in *Hymns and Psalms*.

3 Ridyard, R., *Memories of Lowton*, P. T. H. Brooks, Leigh, *c.* 1935. Much of what follows in this section has been adapted from Ridyard, pp. 48–51.

4 Quoted in Ridyard, as 3 above.

5 Quoted in Ridyard, as 3 above.

6 Selbie, W. B., *Nonconformity*, Thornton Butterworth 1912, pp. 214–15

7 *The Times*, 4 December 1890.

8 Bebington, D. W., *The Nonconformist Conscience*, George Allen & Unwin 1982, Ch. 1, p. 10.

9 Koss, S. E., *Nonconformity in Modern British Politics*, Batsford 1975, Ch. 1, p. 18.

10 Addison, W. G., *Religious Equality in Modern England 1714–1914*, SPCK 1944, Ch. 12, p. 1771.

11 The Origins of the National Society date back to 1808.

12 Taken from Cruickshank, *Church and State in English Education*, Macmillan 1964, Appendix C.

13 See Matthews, H. F., *Methodism and the Education of the People*, Epworth Press 1949, Ch. 4, p. 123–7.

14 Minutes of Primitive Methodist Conference 1860, Minute 546.

15 Russell, R., *History of Schools and Education in Lindsey, Lincolnshire 1800–1902*, Ch. 1.

16 Stamford University, 4 May 1877, quoted in Russell, R., as 15 above, Ch. 2, p. 461.

17 Russell, as 15 above, Ch. 1, p. 21.

18 McKeon, F. J., *Religion, Education and Leisure in Primitive Methodism 1812–1932*, Unpublished MA, Keele, 1973, p. 105.

19 These are referred to in the *Board of Education Report* for 1903.

20 Cruickshank, M., *Church and State in English Education*, Macmillan 1964, Ch. 2, p. 34.

21 NEA 73, *Voluntary Schools and Public Funds*, p. 13.

22 Quoted in Cruickshank, as 20 above, Ch. 3, p. 60.

23 McKeon, as 18 above, p. 141.

24 *Primitive Methodist Magazine*, 1867.
25 The activities of the League are described in Evans, W. and Claridge, W., *James Hirst Hollowell and the Movement for the Civic Control of Education 1911* from which the policy statement is taken.
26 Primitive Methodist Minutes 1907.
27 *Aldersgate Magazine*, 1900, pp. 237–41.
28 Quoted in Bebbington, D. W., *The Nonconformist Conscience*, George Allen and Unwin 1982, Ch. 7, p. 139.
29 *Aldersgate Magazine*, as 27 above.
30 Primitive Methodist Minutes 1901, p. 194.
31 Koss, S., *Nonconformity in Modern British Politics*, Batsford 1975, Ch. 2, p. 38.
32 Primitive Methodist Minutes 1902, p. 182.
33 Davies, R. E. (ed.), *John Scott Lidgett*, Epworth Press, Ch. 4, p. 135.
34 See Jordan, E. K. H., *Free Church Unity*, Lutterworth Press 1956, Ch. 5, pp. 84–7.
35 Primitive Methodist Minutes 1903, p. 201.
36 *Aldersgate Magazine*, 1904, p. 416.
37 As 36 above, p. 838.
38 As 36 above, p. 920.
39 *Aldersgate Magazine*, 1905, pp. 62–7.
40 As 36 above, p. 920.
41 Munson, J., *The Nonconformists*, SPCK 1991, Ch. 9, p. 270.
42 Jordon, as 34 above, Ch. 5, p. 93.
43 *Aldersgate Magazine*, 1906, p. 80.
44 Munson, as 41 above, Ch. 5, pp. 281–2.
45 Parliamentary Debates 1906, Ciii. 1024.
46 Parliamentary Debates 1906, Ciii 24.
47 Lidgett, J. S., *My Guided Life*, pp. 191–2.
48 *Aldersgate Magazine*, 1908, pp. 834–5.
49 *Aldersgate Magazine*, 1909, p. 80.
50 Spender, S., *The Life of Henry Campbell Bannerman*, Ch. 2, p. 312.
51 Primitive Methodist Minutes 1910, p. 210,

52 Primitive Methodist Minutes 1915, p. 235.
53 Primitive Methodist Minutes 1918, p. 187.
54 Primitive Methodist Minutes 1923, pp. 194–5.
55 Primitive Methodist Minutes 1929, p. 206.
56 Primitive Methodist Minutes 1932, p. 229.
57 Cruickshank, as 20 above, Ch. 4, p. 88.
58 Bowmer, J. C., *The Lord's Supper in Methodism 1791–1960*, Epworth Press 1961, p. 41.
59 Curtis, S. J., *History of Education in Great Britain*, University Tutorial Press 1948, Ch. 11, p. 320.
60 Rogers, S. A., 'Churches and Children: A Study in the Controversy over the 1902 Education Act', *Journal of Educational History*, 1959, p. 29.
61 Simon, B., *Education and the Labour Movement 1870–1920*, Lawrence and Wishart 1965, Ch. 7, p. 231.
62 TUC Report 1907, p. 188.
63 As 62 above.
64 Conveyance dated 1751 in the Leigh Archives of the Wigan Local History Library.
65 Conveyance dated 1855 in the Leigh Archives, as 64 above.
66 Bishop of Liverpool, 1923–44.
67 Wood, T., *Institutes of the Laws of England*, quoted in the *Everyman Encyclopaedia*, Dent 1967, Vol. XII, pp. 35–6.
68 Roper, G. H., General Secretary to the Free Church Federal Council, letter to the writer, 15 January 1998.
69 Best, G. F. A., *Temporal Pillars, Queen Anne's Bounty, the Ecclesiastical Commissioners and the Church of England*, Cambridge University Press 1964, Ch. 10, p. 479.
70 'Tithes' in *Everyman Encyclopaedia* 1967, Vol. XII, p. 36.